Religious Experience
and other Essays and Addresses

Religious Experience
and other Essays and Addresses

William Temple
96th Archbishop of Canterbury

collected and edited with an introduction
by A.E. Baker

The Lutterworth Press
Cambridge

Published by
The Lutterworth Press
P.O. Box 60
Cambridge
CB1 2NT
England

e-mail: **publishing@lutterworth.com**
website: **http://www.lutterworth.com**

ISBN 0 7188 9118 X hardback
ISBN 0 7188 9117 1 paperback

British Library Cataloguing in Publication Data:
A catalogue record is available from the British Library.

First published by James Clarke & Co., 1958,
reprinted 1959, 2002

Contents

1881   Born October 15.

1904   President of the Oxford Union.
Fellow and Lecturer in Philosophy,
    Queen's College, Oxford.

1908   Deacon.

1909   Priest.

1910   Headmaster of Repton.

1914   Rector of St. James's, Piccadilly.

1915   Editor of *The Challenge*.

1916   Marriage with Frances Anson.

1919   Canon of Westminster.

1921   Bishop of Manchester.

1929   Translated to York.

1932   Gifford Lecturer.

1942   Translated to Canterbury.

1944   Died October 26.

Introduction

I

HE HAS BEEN DEAD more than twelve years, and what he was and did and said may be not much more than a word to many who have grown up during that time. But he was an outstanding person, able, much loved, of unique achievements, the most " variously distinguished " of the Archbishops of Canterbury since Anselm. He had troops of friends (not mere acquaintances) of every nation and class and denomination. He spent himself for individuals, with a constant awareness of each person's difference, and many would have gladly given all that they had, their very lives, if they could do him service. Of his many and great achievements the central one, perhaps, was what journalists described in the words: " He put Christianity on the map "; or as Dr. Matthews has expressed it: " He spread a comprehension of the meaning of Christianity among persons who were bewildered by the conflicting voices of our time."

His own life and work were rooted in a profound sense of vocation. He wrote that God's will is not only the source of world order but also determines the special place within that order of every finite mind and its appropriate contribution to the life of the whole. It means, if I may put it in my own unsophisticated way, that I have a place in God's heart, and a place to occupy on God's throne (Rev. iii, 21) that no other can fill, and therefore a contribution that no one else can make to the working out of His purpose: it is part of what it means to call Him, " Father ". Temple pointed out that vocation is, of its very nature, individual, so that to each individual his own vocation is peculiar. God's will or purpose, which determines my vocation, determines also the world order in which all events take place, so that it must be possible in principle for a man to discover his vocation by considering with sufficient thoroughness his own nature and circumstances.

Sometimes, however, he discovers the direction of his vocation by a conscious communion with God, by the guidance of an Inner Light, as it is experienced and seriously practised, for example, by Christians in the Society of Friends. But, characteristically, the Archbishop added that vocation " may also be found by the ordinary exercise of a mind which has in prayer committed itself to the divine

I

guidance." Such confident living after careful prayer was characteristic of Temple's life and a fundamental factor in his faith. He
believed that when a decision had to be taken one should say one's
prayers, putting before God all the aspects of the matter so far as one
understood them, and then, with all the common sense and insight
at one's command, one should make up one's mind and act on it;
and never waste time afterwards in vain regrets, or wondering if one
had really chosen the right course, or murmuring "If only . . ."

He said that God has no need that we should tell Him of our
wants or desires. He knows what is good for us better than we do
ourselves, and it is always His will to give it. We must not in prayer
have any thought of suggesting to God what was already in His
mind—still less of changing His mind or purpose. But because the
worst of all diseases of the soul is detachment from God, the first
requirement in prayer is that we trust Him for all blessing, and the
next, because He wishes to detach our faith in Him from all trust in
our own judgment, is that we should persevere in prayer in spite of
disappointment; so that, as our wills become identified with the will
of God, we are praying for what He desires to give and waits to give
until we recognize Him as its source so that our reception of it will
strengthen our faith and not encourage our neglect of Him. The
essential act of prayer is not the bending of God's will to ours—of
course not—but the bending of our will to His.

At various times and in different ways and connections, he was
often saying that the great aim of all true religion is to transfer the
centre of interest and concern from self to God. It is right to say
that man's chief end is to glorify God and—as an incidental by-
product of that—to enjoy Him for ever. It would be entirely wrong
and irreligious to make a man's religion the centre of his concern:
the enjoyment he gets from going to church (or even the spiritual
profit) or singing hymns or listening to anthems or even from
contemplating Christ's Passion or meditating before the Blessed
Sacrament, while committing to the circumference of his attention
that reasonable service which is the offering of himself and his life
to the doing of God's will and the setting forward of His Kingdom.
The Lord's dictum was that whoever wants to save his soul will
lose it, but whoever is willing to lose his soul "*for My sake*" shall
save it. Many of us, Catholics and Protestants alike, need this warning of Temple's: "It is the old paradox. You cannot have salvation
so long as you want it. Only when God has so drawn you into the
embrace of His love and into obedience to His will that in devotion
to Him you cease to care about yourself, can your self be saved."

It has been said that Temple was by temperament conservative and traditionalist, but I have found no reason to agree with that judgment except, perhaps, in his naïve acceptance of the view that the author of St. John's Gospel was an "eye-witness," and his identification of the words of the Johannine Christ with the actual teaching of Jesus of Nazareth. Generally, there was in his thinking a notable balance between traditionalism and independence, the former stemming from his sensitive awareness of the value of fellowship, the latter expressing his profound conviction of Christ's careful respect for each individual soul and its value and freedom. Consider, first, what he believed about fellowship. Rightly or wrongly, perhaps with a certain use of rose-tinted spectacles, he saw in the Church of England a comprehensiveness (what her critics sometimes call compromise), and he valued it. He is, indeed, the outstanding illustration of what the Anglican temper and tradition produce when they are fully understood and trusted and practised. And he never fell into the besetting sin of the parson, which is dogmatism. And one fruit of all this was a profound belief in and an unfailing practice of toleration. He once wrote an Introduction to a pacifist pamphlet *because* the author had said that he disagreed with the Archbishop. And he began an official charge to the clergy and laity of the diocese of York by saying that some of them would disagree with what he was going to say—but what is the use of pooling our thoughts if we all agree to begin with? Not too many bishops begin their charges in that way.

This tolerant spirit appears in many and various relations. He had contacts with people of all sorts of Christian societies; he was grateful for his own heritage in Anglicanism, but he recognized also God's gifts to His people through other traditions. He encouraged the comparative study of religions, less because of the information it might bring than for the genuine respect it gives for the beliefs of other men. And he emphasized the value of the sort of education which makes men eager to think for themselves and to appreciate the truth in any opinion from which they dissent. Indeed, he once said that we should not feel independently and think in the mass, but think independently and feel in the mass. Toleration is, indeed, a difficult but quite basic Christian virtue. So far is it from implying —as Catholics and Communists believe—that we are indifferent to truth or error, that it means that we shall strive for the truth we have seen, but shall never suppose that there is no truth but what we have seen (this means that there are no infallibilities); we shall believe that fellowship and goodwill are worth more than any triumph of our own opinions, because only in such fellowship can be found the fuller truth than that which the various disputants possess. It came partly from being a Hegelian and believing in that mysterious method, the Dialectic. He once wrote that he had learned from Edward Caird (the Hegelian Master of Balliol) his habitual tendency to believe that everybody is quite right. Part of his gift as a chairman—it amounted to genius—was that he could listen to two speakers propounding diametrically opposite views, and could make a statement which included what each of them meant. His unself-conscious tolerance was part of his being a Liberal. I use that word advisedly, not forgetting the great disservice that Newman did to the English language—and still more, perhaps, to Christian theology —when he poisoned that grand word for all whom he influenced, and remembering also that, partly as a result of what Newman wrote, in many circles today—theological, philosophical and even political—the word " liberal " is used merely as a term of abuse. But Temple was a Liberal all his life, from the days when Francis Paget, Bishop of Oxford, declined to ordain him because of his *undogmatic* statements on the Virgin Birth and the Empty Tomb, until the last period when, as Archbishop of Canterbury, he wrote of the neo-Scholastics (they were then the " young " neo-Scholastics) at Oxford and elsewhere that " in their eagerness to re-assert the truth and authority of the Bible [they] are ignoring the lesson of the nine-teenth century and becoming involved in a position which is either obscurantist or humbug." It is, indeed, a sorry, topsy-turvy state of things when the older men are Liberal and the younger men are Conservative.[1]

It was once said of Temple that the philosophers thought he was a theologian but the theologians thought he was a philosopher. That may have been intended for smart japery, but it can well be accepted as a considered estimate of his approach and method and attitude to the major problems of life and religion. Although few people could have any right to pass judgment on the extent and thorough-ness of his scholarship, he was always more a thinker than a scholar; although he had the sort of memory that becomes a legend, he knew that the heart of a man's faith must be his own value-judgments,[2] rather than any traditional definitions—insight rather than memory. From the first of his books to the last he was careful to base his

[1] Plato, at the opening of the tenth book of the Laws, takes for granted the opposite condition.

[2] " He (Christ) asserts the whole principle that religious ordinances are to be used according to the benefit to be derived from them, according to the movement of the free spirit, and not according to the rigid enforcement of regulations." Temple, *The Kingdom of God*. " Let us suppose that we have accepted the Christian view of life on the ground that it commends itself to our hearts and minds and consciences, or, if not to all of these, then to one of them sufficiently for us to take it as the guide and basis of life." (Ibid., p. 6.)

presentation of the Christian case not on the presuppositions of conventional orthodoxy (although he was never one of those who use the word "orthodox" as a term of abuse) but, after the example of Socrates's questions and Plato's dialectic, he used to assume what the non-Christian will accept and then help him to recognize that this involves what Jesus manifests of God. His theology grows in a philosophical soil, although the germ of it is a religious experience which most men have, although many do not recognize that name for it.[3]

William Temple, then, was a Liberal Christian; he inherited his lifelong Liberalism from his great father, for whose intellectual and spiritual achievement and integrity he had a reverence which only stopped short this side of idolatry. Frederick Temple was one of the writers in that notorious composite book, *Essays and Reviews*, which had appeared in the year after *The Origin of Species*. The authors, concerned at "the great amount of reticence in every class of society in regard to religious views," put the Liberal, critical position in a way which outraged many, although most of it seems pretty harmless now. But although no departure from the most scrupulous orthodoxy could ever be proved against Frederick Temple, to the end he was pursued with a McCarthy-like fury by the forces of reaction. Nine years later, when he was nominated Bishop of Exeter, an unholy alliance of angry Catholics and complacent Evangelicals, under the leadership of Dr. Pusey and Lord Shaftesbury (bigotry makes strange bedfellows), used every device, indecent as well as decent, to prevent his consecration. He was charged with being disloyal to Christ; he was invited to try to allay the misgivings of the cowardly and the thoughtless by making statements over and above those which the Law requires. In the interests of *toleration*—and he insisted that toleration must be active as well as passive—he declined to do anything of the sort. The Church of England, Frederick Temple declared, has a more Catholic character than any other body of Christians possesses, just because it allows liberty to its members and officers. But the opposition was not to be put off. Temple's elder sister had to appear in Bow Church, when his election was confirmed, to prove that he had been born in wedlock. The *Odium Theologicum* is "a horrid thing, a very horrid thing."

[3] "There are many men who pay little attention to their religious experience, and in whom (often for that reason) it is rudimentary. . . . But it is doubtful if any man can go through life without ever feeling reverence for something which is morally so high above him as to be out of his reach, or awe before the great Reality on which he is utterly dependent. And it may safely be said that no one escapes, although he may to his own satisfaction explain away the sense of absolute obligation. All of these are in their true nature religious experiences—the recognition of the Absolute." (*Christus Veritas*, p. 39.)

It is no wonder, then, that the story of the treatment meted out
to his father made a deep impression on William's imagination.
Certainly, consciously or unconsciously, it moulded his life. Bishop
Francis Paget's refusal to ordain him reminds one that although the
Lux Mundi men had been irked by the readiness of others to draw
lines, they themselves retaliated by drawing lines to keep others out:
a temerarious habit, if only because the heresies which shock one
generation become the platitudes which make their successors yawn.
And—*laus Deo*—there is no authority in Anglicanism which dare
define what is or what is not heresy.

But to return to Temple's Liberalism: he wrote to his brother in
India, at the time of the Paget incident, that the notion of being
pained at disagreeing with the Church seemed so remote as to be
ridiculous, and that he did not know anyone of their generation
who would feel pain on such grounds. That shakes me a bit, I must
say; but he went on to say: "I am sure that this is a gain, for it
means that we shall come nearer to co-operating for Christian work
while leaving opinions quite free—which is no doubt the way to
make them true."[4] That was an abiding principle with him all his
life—the conviction that toleration and charity are the soil in which
true belief grows.

Six years after the trouble with Paget—having been ordained by
Davidson and established, though only for a short time, as Headmaster of Repton—Temple wrote three essays in a volume called
*Foundations, a statement of Christian Belief in Terms of Modern
Thought, by Seven Oxford Men.* A *Church Times* reviewer said of
it: "The greatest honour is due to the men who have produced the
essays. They have been inspired not only by an enthusiasm for
learning, but also by a real enthusiasm for the Christian and Catholic
faith. This attempt has certainly been justified." But that was not
everybody's verdict. The distinguished author now called Monsignor
Ronald Knox produced a skit called *Some Loose Stones*, which title
showed what some thought of the *Foundations* (for it was rumoured
that much of Knox's material had not come from his own quarry).
There was a sketch of a bank manager named Jones, educated
beyond his intelligence, who scarcely ever went to church and could
not say what he thought of religion, but was "such a good man,
anima naturaliter Christiana, and all that." Jones, Knox declared, is

---

[4] Iremonger, *William Temple, Archbishop of Canterbury: His Life and Letters*,
p. 113. And during the next summer he wrote again to his brother: "More and
more I come to regard 'churchiness' as a survival of the useless; it was necessary
once; without the dogmatism and ecclesiasticism of the early mediaeval Church the
whole of Christianity would have gone into smoke. But the walls built to protect
now only confine and cramp, and should be pulled down." (Ibid., p. 114.)

the hero of *Foundations*, which is an attempt to reach not a fixed
deposit of truth, but an irreducible minimum of truth which will
just be inclusive of Jones.

In 1913, when Temple was in the full vigour of his early thirties,
Knox could scarcely expect to get away with that. Iremonger printed
a letter in which Temple asserts a large measure of agreement with
Knox's positive doctrine but an emphatic difference from him on
method. And it is the method of arriving at his convictions which
mark a man a liberal: not what he believes, but why. Temple went
on to say—and I think this immensely important coming from a
priest of the Church—that he is not a spiritual doctor trying to see
how much Jones can swallow and keep down. " I am more respectable than that: *I am Jones himself asking what there is to eat.*"

It needs to be reiterated that when he wrote that, Temple was an
ordained priest, authorized, commissioned to teach the Gospel of
Christ. *I am Jones himself asking what there is to eat.* That is what
I mean when I say he was a Liberal. He believed that every Christian
should be a Liberal in that sense. Quoting an early letter of his
father's he said that we must strive for a theology which will escape
both petrification and putrefaction (a dogmatic theology never yet
practised by the Church); much of it, William says, will consist of
distinct refusals to define, coupled with a repeated effort to restate
and understand as far as may be—not because definition is an evil
thing, nor because the fact is in its nature unintelligible, but because
all our language and mental apparatus is constructed to deal with a
different class of data.

I am Jones himself asking what there is to eat: I want to make the
point that for a man of Temple's intellectual power to say that is an
illustration of that meek humility which John Oman desiderated as
the necessary quality in the Church's teachers. William Temple was
genuinely, startlingly humble—no one who enjoyed his friendship
or even acquaintance doubts that. But there is evidence that it was
not always so; it was more than temperament. It was a supernatural
grace, in some sense an achievement. When he was an undergraduate, we are told that some thought him a little too *certain*, his
manner was almost obviously *confident*. Like Matthew Arnold he
went to Balliol " wide welcomed for a father's fame," and some
thought that like Arnold, again, he

... entered with free bold step that seemed to claim Fame for himself.

And Balliol in 1900 was not particularly patient of such an attitude.
What tinge of justification there was for such an impression I cannot
say. But there was nothing remotely like it in the last twenty years

of his too short life. He did not talk or write much of humility—nothing like so much as John Oman did. But seeking always to have his imagination filled full of that Divine Love which was incarnate in Christ's sacrifice he was never unaware of the chasm between what we *can* be and—that. It is utter self-delusion (he had every variety of strong language for it—" Pharisee," " prig," " self-righteous," " Pelagian ") to set standards for others or for ourselves which assume the Christian standard of values in its purity. " No one accepts the Christian standard for himself," Temple said; " that Jesus of Nazareth did so is precisely what constitutes the gulf between Him and all other men." And an imperfect Christian must not force himself to a line of conduct which his own character does not support. " To be consciously in the presence of Christ is to grow to be nothing." Temple denied all human freedom over against God, as he affirmed complete freedom in submission to God. That, as we grow into it, is Christian humility—which reminds us how perverse was Bernard Shaw's misunderstanding when he said that cowards make their cowardice into a virtue and call it humility. And the fruit of humility, of course, is achievement. For the highest achievement, Temple said, the humility must be perfect.

"Freedom in doctrine is the life-breath of the Church of England"; it lifts one's heart to remember that the man who believed that, who said it, who acted on it, was chosen to sit on the throne of St. Augustine—chosen by a Conservative Prime Minister because he knew that it was the will of the Church and people of England. He never ceased to believe that it is through complete freedom of thought within the Christian community that men will grow into *orthodoxy*. Temple saw that it is a natural weakness among Christians to crave for a final and unquestionable authority, which is what drives men on from an infallible Book, first to an infallible Church to interpret the infallible Book, and so to an infallible Spokesman of the infallible Church. He said that the traditional doctrine of revelation implies that God has overridden and superseded the normal human faculties of the Biblical writers so as to save their utterances from error. But over against that view must be set the common experience of life, which is that God empowers men to do His will by the enlightening of their natural faculties and the kindling of their natural affections, and not by the supersession of them. God does not *dictate to men*, in or through Scripture or elsewhere. But Temple also asserted that Christ is in nothing more remarkable than in His unfailing respect for the spiritual liberty of those with whom He has dealings. He appears to desire none but willing disciples, and to them He gave teaching designed rather to stimulate and direct their thought than to provide formulated doctrines claiming acceptance on His authority. Faith is not the holding of correct doctrines, the Archbishop said, but personal fellowship with the living God. What is needed, however, is a right balance between tradition and reason. What we inherit and enter into of what our fathers have told us constitutes our common life in Church and nation. It not only strengthens our faith but provides the driving power to live by the pattern of faith; but it will by itself do little to purify or enlarge faith. For this we must look to the criticism of conscience and reason; it will save religion from super-stition and maintain its dignity. But the philosophy of religion could hardly have stopped infanticide and homicidal public spectacles or slavery, studded Europe with hospitals, or inspired crusades against prostitution.

His was, indeed, ever a fighting faith; victory over the world, being confident in what is hoped for, the putting to proof of what cannot be seen. He went so far as to assert the paradox that the despair with which some sensitive men have watched the processes of history is, in fact, faith's fiercest protest. And somewhere he suggests that Thomas Hardy's atheism is essentially that kind of protest, to be compared, indeed, with the cry, " My God, My God, why hast Thou forsaken me? " Always Temple saw the problem of evil as the only serious argument against faith, and the Cross as God's contribution to the solution of that problem. "For kings of the earth men have been called upon to die, but this King first died for His subjects." He had, indeed, a habit of taking what have become homiletic platitudes and by a flash of insight, or one of those sentences which startle us because they are so meaningful, he restores them to vitality. For example: " It was not only a lost Friend that they mourned [on Good Friday], but a defeated cause. And they learned that what they took for defeat was itself the means to the victory they desired. It was not the purpose of one will which asserted itself successfully against others and prevailed. Judged from that standpoint the Cross remains a defeat, and the Resurrection is at best a mere reversal of it. The triumph that we witness is a triumph in which no one is conscious of defeat at all; for to be defeated by Christ can only mean the loss of self-will and the acceptance of His love, so that in His triumph the conquered rejoice as truly as the conqueror." And if we are to apply all this to ourselves we must keep alive by prayer and Communion our own intercourse with God. " Do not be frightened," he says, " by the times when all your prayers seem cold and dead. Go on fixing your mind on what we know of God as He has shown Himself to us in Christ; and at least once every day say the Lord's Prayer slowly, trying hard to mean some one petition in it with all your soul—and a different one each day. Then come regularly to receive the Body that was broken for the Kingdom of God and the Blood that was shed for the Kingdom of God." That was his faith—prayer as conversation with God, and the Holy Communion as the climax of it. "The proper relation in thought between prayer and conduct is not that conduct is supremely important and prayer may help it, but that prayer is supremely important and conduct tests it."

II

Towards the end of 1942, Temple, accompanied by the Archbishop of York, addressed a series of meetings in London, Birmingham, Edinburgh, and elsewhere, arranged "to widen the sense of citizenship and to Christianize it." Dr. Garbett urged, with authority, the urgent need for better working-class housing, but Temple, in his first speech, said that our banking system is greatly in need of reform. The "City" took umbrage. There were letters to *The Times* suggesting that the cobbler should stick to his last. And although at Birmingham he explained that what he said on the methods and tactics of economic or social reform was not to be taken as committing the Christian Church, but as his own private illustrations of how he thought Christian principles might be applied, the demand persisted that the Archbishop should mind his own business. Indeed, that was far from being the first time that objection had been made. During the inter-war years, for example, when Neville Chamberlain was Chancellor of the Exchequer and there were millions of unemployed, he urged people to write to the Chancellor, explain that they were income tax payers, and ask that if there was not enough money both to increase the "dole" and to reduce the income tax, he would increase the "dole." Chamberlain commented, rather tartly, "I wish the Archbishop of York would mind his own business." But Temple was not to be put off so easily: "Here are two men with buckets," he said, "and I suggest to the man who is better off that he should say: 'If there is not enough for both of us to get something, please give it to him.' And I think it very much the business of a Christian minister to give that sort of advice."

His interest in and knowledge of the working classes had its effective beginning when he joined the W.E.A. in 1903, although that involvement in working-class education had been inherited from his father. But more than once in his speeches and writings he makes the point that a person's mind and spirit are formed not merely by classes or schools but by his political and social environment:

> The social order at once expresses the sense of values active in the
> minds of citizens and tends to reproduce the same sense of values in
> each new generation. If the State is so ordered as to give great promi-
> nence to military leaders as Sparta was, as Prussia was, as Nazi
> Germany is, this must represent the fact that the effective body of
> citizens, which may be a compact minority, regards the military
> qualities as specially honourable or specially important; and the system
> expressing that estimate impresses it by perpetual suggestion upon
> every growing generation. We throw most young Englishmen out into
> a world of fierce competition where each has to stand on his own
> feet (which is good) and fight for his own interest (which is bad), if
> he is not to be submerged. Our system is not deliberately planned, but
> it produces effects just the same. It offers a perpetual suggestion in the
> direction of combative self-assertiveness. It is recognized on all hands
> that the economic system is an educative influence, for good or ill,
> of immense potency. . . . If so, then assuredly the Church must be
> concerned with it. For a primary concern of the Church is to develop
> in men a Christian character. . . . It is enough to say that the Church
> cannot, without betraying its own trust, omit criticism of the economic
> system or fail to urge such action as may be prompted by that criticism.

He held that it is a fundamental principle of far-reaching importance that Governments affect the conduct of their subjects far more
by the principles implicit in their acts than by the requirements of
legislation, or by the severity of the penalties attached to the neglect
of those requirements. Thus the earlier attempts to put down crimes
of violence and various kinds of theft by means of savage punishment
were a total failure. The callousness in inflicting pain, or the readiness to take life displayed by the Government, encouraged these bad
qualities in its subjects more than the penalties restrained them. To
bring this home to the legislators of his generation was one of the
great achievements of Jeremy Bentham. So Temple taught that the
main argument for democracy is its *educational* value—its effect in
developing the personality of the citizen. He expounded this, of all
places, in an article he wrote for the Girls' Friendly Society.
Vox populi, Vox Dei, he said, is nonsense, and on any new issue the
majority is sure to be a little wrong. But because there is no way of
discovering which of the minorities is right, it is safer to let the
majority rule than the minority. But the real defence of democracy
is that by calling upon people to exercise responsibility on the matters
before the country at any time, you develop their personal qualities.
You make them feel that they belong to one another, and so you
tend to deepen and intensify personal fellowship. You are leading
people forward from the relationship of the herd to that of real

B

fellowship by the mere process of calling upon them to take their share in the government of the groups to which they belong. You are educating a more alert and disciplined intelligence among the citizens, less likely to be swayed by mass-hysteria or to become victims of propaganda (a subtle peril of democracy).

He was, indeed, far from uncritical of democracy, working, as it must, through methods which call the herd-instinct into play, and make independent feeling and judgment difficult. It needs courage to be *contra mundum*, and there is great need for toleration and charity in the majority, which are far from easy. But if that courage and charity are not forthcoming, the Archbishop wrote, democracy will have destroyed itself, for it will have crushed out the individuality, respect for which is its very life-blood. Mob rule, he held, is the worst of all tyrannies. And in all his teaching on political discussion he insisted that rights and duties are correlative: where men have no duties they have no rights and, conversely, where they have no rights, no duties can be expected from them. But Christians must aim at putting their own duties before their rights.

The Christian, *as such*, may not be an expert on economics or foreign affairs. Must he not remain silent, then, when these matters are urgent, decisions have to be taken, and political parties are divided—when there is a railway strike, for example, or a difference between Egypt and Britain? There has been much crude interfering by Christians: politics in the pulpit—whether that of the Primrose League or of some Leftish clique—is not edifying; and economics in the pulpit is usually out of place. Temple used to say that Christians are responsible for trying to apply the principles of their faith to the actual problems of life, to show the goal to be aimed at, to proclaim a standard by which policies should be judged. On February 4, 1943, for example, he lectured to members of the Bank Officers' Guild, on "The Christian View of the Right Relationship between Finance, Production and Consumption." What right had an Archbishop to speak on Finance? Why didn't he mind his own business? But always, from the beginning, Temple took for granted that Christianity is concerned, not only with the salvation of individuals but also with the transformation of the social order. Charles Gore had an abiding influence on his thinking. He had a large part in COPEC (an interdenominational Conference on Politics Economics and Citizenship) and he was the chairman and moving spirit in the Malvern Conference, which was an Anglican meeting with a similar concern. Men looked to him for leadership in securing that the "brave new world" which was to replace Hitlerism should be Christian, and in helping them to be Christians in it. For he himself believed that the nearer we come to making a Christian order the more essential it will be that we shall be converted Christians if the order is not to break down. He told the Bank Officers that he had no special qualifications for speaking on Banking but his concern was to see where men's various occupations fit into the general picture of life as it must be drawn on Christian principles, " so that those who are engaged in them, if they have the desire—as I hope they have—to conform their practice to the Christian standard, will see where it still needs modification, where it may need even revolutionary change; or even—very dull but sometimes salutary—where it is already perfectly sound and has only to be kept going as it is." He had written on Finance in the *Fortnightly Review* that we have reached a stage when an article cannot be produced unless it *pays* someone to produce it. Supply of need is not now a sufficient motive, there must also be payment for ownership. That is intolerable, and the profit motive in industry and finance, *when given such freedom and prominence as it now has* (italics mine), becomes a profoundly and pervasively disturbing factor. Finance exists for the sake of production, and production exists for the sake of consumption. The hungry and needy public ought to be the controlling group. Finance may rightly exercise a check, calling a halt to avoid bankruptcy; but for positive control it is functionally unfitted.

Similarly, of Industry: its function in the community is indispensable, he said, but it is clearly subordinate. A nation does not exist to produce material wealth. The only true interests of industry are those which serve the interests of the community. The Archbishop saw that as one of the roots of theoretical Socialism, and he said that *in itself it is incontrovertible*. For a few months he had been a member of the Labour Party, but he stated quite clearly the real objection to Socialism in any fully developed form, which is that no person or body of persons is likely to be available wise enough to conduct, without grave mistakes, so immensely complicated a business as would by such a system be entrusted to the State. If the right spirit were forthcoming, free industry would have more prosperity in itself, and serve the public better, than industry under public control. But the right spirit is at present not forthcoming in anything like adequate volume, and it is hard to see how the joint stock company, left to itself, can show it. Quite evidently, " we are all Socialists now." But we differ on the conception of the general well-being to which industry should be subservient. The capitalist's view tends to be too narrowly economic, because his human life is less immediately dependent on economic policy from day to day. In a strike, for example the amenities of life are seriously diminished for the miners, but the employers' lives are not much affected. So the working man always sees an economic issue as fundamentally a human issue; sometimes his consciousness of the human values at stake may so stir his sentiments as to make him blind to economic facts, yet at the root his view is right, even if it is blurred and confused.

All this economic theory and practice must be taken into Church, of course. Worship is not apart from work—if it is Christian worship it includes work.[5] It is no accident or merely trivial irrelevance that, as Temple used to say, Christianity is the most materialistic of all religions. The Word of God, by which the whole Creation is maintained, became Man that He might redeem *the world*, not redeem men out of the world, win the whole of life for God. It is this which is represented in the Eucharist. " In the Holy Communion service we take the bread and wine—man's industrial and commercial life in symbol—and offer it to God; and because we have offered it to Him, He gives it back to us as the means of nurturing us, not in our animal nature alone, but as agents of His purpose, limbs of a body responsive to His will; and as we receive it back from Him, we share it with one another in true fellowship. If we think of the service in this way, it is a perfect picture of what secular society ought to be; and a Christian civilization is one where the citizens seek to make their ordered life something of which that service is the symbol."

Temple's personality was at once uniquely unified and richly comprehensive. He was interested in the arts, always a great reader of poetry, with a prodigious verbal memory, very knowledgeable on painting, a provocative writer on the method and meaning of tragedy, and he had a competent appreciation of music: he was one of the few ecclesiastical dignitaries who could sing the priest's part in the Eucharist with confidence. All this implied, of course, that he had a mind and eye for the concrete and particular, the individual aspects of experience, and this was reflected also in his voracious reading of history and biography. But it was balanced by his mastery of metaphysics, from Plato and his predecessors to Whitehead and his interpreters. And he understood the principles and aims of

---

[5] Of the many memorable things the Archbishop wrote, perhaps none deserve to be recorded more than his repeated descriptions of worship: " What worship means is the submission of the whole being to the object of worship. It is the opening of the heart to receive the love of God; it is the subjection of conscience to be directed by Him; it is the declaration of need to be fulfilled by Him; it is the subjection of desire to be controlled by Him; and as the result of all these together it is the surrender of will to be used by Him. It is the total giving of self. . . . But it is evident that if this is what worship means, only the perfection alike of reality and goodness can claim it; and to offer worship, in the true sense of worship, to anything other than the true God must be at least the most disastrous, if it is not—as it probably is—the most wicked of all human activities." See also p. 163 below.

natural science, even though his ignorance of its methods was, as he
once remarked, so complete as to be distinguished. He had very little
parochial experience but he was a successful diocesan bishop, a first-
class chairman, and a very good listener with a ready laugh which
put most people at their ease. He was an energetic Church reformer,
in the sense that he wanted every member to have a responsible share
in guiding its policy, and he had a sensitive interest in and understanding of the needs and thought of ordinary people.

But all this richness of thought and experience was focused and
held together and its meaning was deepened by his devotion to Christ
and His Kingdom. He had given his heart to the Lord Jesus, and
every interest and purpose of his life was dominated by that affection.
I remember once hearing von Hügel, whose " foreign " English was
sometimes more expressive than idiomatic, say that the author of
the Fourth Gospel " loved the Lord like blazes ": well, that is how
Temple thought of the Lord Jesus. And he said once that Christ is,
of course, all humanity; he took for granted that every human concern is part of Christianity. He taught us that God is interested in
many other things beside religion, and he saw that it is not difficult
to be too religious, as von Hügel said the early leaders of the Oxford
Movement were. Temple's final message is summed up, Iremonger
said, in a passage in the Introduction to his last book, *The Church
Looks Forward:*

> Our need is a new integration of life: Religion, Art, Science,
> Politics, Education, Industry, Commerce, Finance—all these need to
> be brought into a unity as agents of a single purpose. That purpose
> can hardly be found in human aspirations, it must be the divine pur-
> pose. That divine purpose is presented to us in the Bible under the
> name of the Kingdom (Sovereignty) of God, or as the summing up
> of all things in Christ, or as the coming down out of heaven of the
> holy city, the New Jerusalem. In all those descriptions two thoughts
> are prominent: the priority of God and the universality of scope.
> Nothing is to be omitted: " all things " are to be summed up in
> Christ, but it is in Christ that they are thus gathered into one. All
> nations are to walk in the light of the holy city, but it comes down out
> of heaven from God. The Kingdom of God is the goal of human
> history, but it is His Kingdom, not man's.

III

At his enthronement in York he made a powerful plea for toleration:
" We shall strive for the truth as we see it, but shall never suppose
that there is no truth but what we have seen. . . . In all controversy
our aim will be to appreciate and incorporate in our own theory or

action all that we can find good or wise in the views of our opponents. . . . Can we find a phrase to sum up what is required of us in the circumstances of our time? May we not say that our obligation is to lay aside all other partisanship and become partisans of good will? " It is an illustration of this to point out that he went out of his way to say that the toleration of Biblical criticism in and by members of the Church means, of course, a greater gentleness on the part of the critics. And we must never forget that the letter killeth but the spirit maketh alive. (*It is a good thing*, he said, that of no recorded word or act of Jesus can we be quite certain that He said or did precisely that.) And he insisted that if one has to choose between the sole authority of the Bible and the sole authority of the Church, in Heaven's name let us have the Church, which is alive and because *plainly* subject to error, is also capable of truth.

On most subjects the Archbishop believed what most Anglicans believe, but nearly always he had his own reasons for what he believed, e.g., the Anglican, like the majority of Christian communions, accepts wholeheartedly the two great creeds. Temple did. But he insisted that although doctrine is of an importance too great to be exaggerated, its place is secondary, not primary. " I do not believe in any creed," he wrote, " but I use certain creeds to express, conserve and to deepen my faith in God."

Similarly, of the Anglican system as a whole: the system by which the guiding word on matters of faith and practice is committed, not to the sheep but to the shepherds—not to the scholar, however real our readiness to consider with respect what he has to say, but to the bishops. He accepted that. He spoke with reverent gratitude of the ministry of bishops, priests and deacons, which through the centuries has been preserved for the Church. " The Apostles," he wrote, " were in no sense ministers of the laity; they were ministers of Christ to the Laity, and to the world waiting to be won." But he interpreted " the impressive, age-long insistence of the East and West that the Eucharist must always be celebrated by a priest " as meaning that it *should* always be so celebrated, not that it *can only be* so celebrated. In a Charge to the Diocese of York he said:

> If it be held that episcopal ordination confers a *power* of making sacraments, so that when an episcopally ordained priest celebrates the Eucharist something happens in the world of fact which does not happen on any other conditions, then these bodies [the Protestant Free Churches] have no real sacraments. But that is a theory to which I find it impossible to attach any intelligible meaning. It is admitted that the peril to which strongly sacramental doctrine is most liable is that of falling into conceptions properly described as magical; and this

theory seems to lie on the wrong side of the dividing line. What is conferred in ordination is not the *power* to make sacramental a rite which otherwise would not be such, but *authority* (*potestas*) to administer sacraments which belong to the Church, and which, therefore, can only be administered by those who hold the Church's commission to do so.

With the majority of Christians, he believed in the two sacraments of the Gospel, Baptism and Holy Communion. And he was an unashamed advocate of infant baptism. The point in the discussion of this which seemed to him of special importance is that it is an expression of the Divine initiative in making a man a Christian, a member of Christ's Church. "Those who were Christians before me, my parents and godparents, brought me, without my knowledge or consent, that I might be made ' a member of Christ, the child of God, and the present possessor of the Kingdom of Heaven.' So I take no credit for being a Christian; I am humbly grateful for what the Holy Spirit did for me." William Temple was always profoundly disturbed at anything which seemed to base faith in Christ or the life in Him on the responsibility or initiative of the human individual. Pelagianism, he often said, is the only essentially damnable heresy.

He was a regular, but not a daily communicant. But, again, this is no place to elaborate his theories of Holy Communion. Over against the Roman theory of the consecrated elements, that the *substance* of bread and wine has ceased to be, that the substance is now the Body and Blood of Christ, Temple used to say that the Church of England makes no statement on what is *not* there, but says that Christ *is* there. A basic element in all his philosophical thinking was *value*, and he thought it important to consider that what takes place at the consecration is the transvaluation of the bread and wine to become the Body and Blood of Christ. And the centre and crown and climax of his understanding of that service is that it is a sacrifice. It is the sacrifice of Christ, but Christ is all humanity, and what was set forth on Calvary is in truth the inner reality of the perpetual sacrifice which is the coming of mankind into perfect obedience to God. The sacrament is the medium of His Presence, given to be received; it incorporates us into His Body, that we may take our allotted share in His offering to God. "So there is one Sacrifice," Temple said, " achieved in fact and power on Calvary, represented in the breaking of the bread whereby He taught us the meaning of Calvary, reproduced in our self-dedication and in our life of practical service in the world resulting therefrom, consummated in the final coming of the Kingdom." And the religious value of this sacramental theology is

obvious. " It is not the movement of our bodies up the chancel," he
said to his boys in the chapel of Repton school, " it is the movement
of our attention from selfish or worldly aims to the Purpose of God
and Christ, it is our ascension in heart and mind to the heaven which
is ever about us, which gives that service its significance."

And so we come to what he thought and did for Christian unity,
and in the hope of the final reunion of the Christian Church. For he
could never tolerate the thought that it would be a good thing if the
denominations remained distinct, merely putting a friendly co-operation in place of jealous and suspicious rivalry.

> The unity of the Church, (he wrote) is precious not only for its
> utility in strengthening the Church as an evangelistic agent. It is itself
> in principle the consummation to which all history moves. The pur-
> pose of God in creation was and is to fashion a fellowship of free
> spirits knit together by a love in all its members which answers to the
> manifested love of God—or, as St. Paul expressed it, " to sum up all
> things in Christ " (Eph. i, 10) . . . It is the love of God in Christ
> possessing the hearts of men, so as to unite them in itself—as the
> Father and the Son are united in that love of Each for Each which
> is the Holy Spirit. The unity which the Lord prays that His disciples
> may enjoy is that which is eternally characteristic of the Triune God.
> It is, therefore, something more than a means to any end—even though
> that end be the evangelization of the world; it is itself the one worthy
> end of all human aspiration; it is the life of heaven. For His prayer
> is not only *that they may be one*; it is *that they may be one as we.*[6]

In hoping and planning and praying for *reunion*, everything
depends on how we set about it: in particular, on the spirit in which
we approach each other. It is possible, as men have discovered, to
wield an olive-branch as though it were a shillelagh. There were
three thoughts in front of his mind:

First, the great divisions among those who believe in Christ
and seek to live as His disciples, are divisions within the Church,
the Body of Christ, and do not effect separation from it. When
I pray for " the whole state of Christ's Church militant here on
earth " I am praying for Lutherans and Presbyterians, Baptists and
Methodists, Anglicans and Congregationalists, Romans and Greek
Orthodox and Friends—and for all others who claim the Christian
name, however far from Headquarters they may seem to me to be.
In quite early days he wrote, " I don't believe in the ideal of a
Church with sharply defined boundaries; its unity (as I have heard
Waggett express it) is like that of a ray of light—bright in the centre
(Rome?) but ending none knows exactly where."[7] Those who hold

[6] *Readings in St. John's Gospel*, p. 320.
[7] Iremonger, op. cit., 162.

the three-branch theory of Catholicism (according to which the only Christians we recognize are Romans and Greeks, who will not recognize us), or who develop a permanent crick in their spiritual neck by trying not to see Baptists or Methodists, while straining to catch the eye of some Jesuit or Archimandrite, will find little comfort in Temple. We are all in schism—Roman and Anglican, Quaker and Congregationalist—and schism is a sinful state. But they are not *guilty* who are loyal to the spirit of what they have received. And each of the great Christian societies is a genuine part of Christ's Holy Catholic Church.

Secondly, faith and order are not equally essential. There must be agreement on the vital points of the Christian faith: God the Father, Creator, who in Jesus Christ has visited and redeemed His People, whose Spirit is the response in men's hearts to this revelation. There must be agreement on this, Temple held, before union and communion are possible. But that we should agree about any necessary order in the Church for maintaining that faith seemed to him less important and, he was inclined to think, not necessary at all.

> That we must agree what order is in fact to be adopted is plain, for Reunion means the adoption of a common order, but we know quite well that it makes all the difference in our approach to our Free Church brethren whether we say that the Church order which we recommend—and which many of them are after all ready to accept— is the best for achieving the purpose which the Church has in view and therefore is to be adopted; or that it is the only one which constitutes the Church as a Church at all and that, therefore, as long as they do not adopt it they forfeit all right to that name.

The third guiding principle in Temple's approach to reunion— and this was particularly important as marking his behaviour in actual conference with non-Anglicans—was that he thought that those who take part in such meetings should be more concerned to appropriate what is true and valuable in other traditions than to explain to others, whether Protestants, Catholics or Eastern Orthodox, where they have gone astray or come short.[8] This, of course, is exactly opposite to what we do. Whenever there is talk of reunion

---

[8] " In our dealings with one another let us be more eager to understand those who differ from us than either to refute them or to press upon them our own tradition. Our whole manner of speech and conduct, and of course our mode of worship, will inevitably give expression to our own tradition. Wherever there are divisions there is sure to be something of value on both sides. We ought always to be eager to learn the truth which others possess in fuller degree than ourselves, and to learn why some give to various elements in our common belief greater emphasis than we are accustomed to give. Our temper in conference must be rather that of learners than of champions." (*The Church Looks Forward*, p. 29.)

we begin at once to look for arguments to support our own heritage. Learned books appear or, often, symposia by learned men, to make the most of what little evidence there is for the first links in the Apostolic succession, as well as ponderous monographs by verbose monks reporting the questionable gleanings that they dare to call the doctrine and practice of confirmation: powder and shot for our men in reunion conferences.

IV

For Temple, the Incarnation rather than the Atonement, and Bethlehem more than Calvary are the centre of Christianity. It is difficult to write of this without exaggeration but, partly because of the powerful Hegelian factor in his thinking, his sense of guilt was not the formative influence in his thinking or teaching at any time. As early as 1907 when, as a young lay don at Queen's, he went to one of his first Student Movement conferences, he wrote to his mother: " There was a lot of talk about forgiveness and so on to which I was unable to attach a particle of meaning." And I think that until the very end of his life he was quite unable to believe that any person whom he *knew* personally, with whom he had any actual personal relations, was *wicked*. Some of the people whom he read about, in books or newspapers, *might be* wicked, but not the people whose faces he looked at.

This must not be taken to mean that the Atonement had a small or unimportant place in his thinking; but the Incarnation was central. We have all heard or read his most moving expositions of the truth that if we want to realize what our sin means to God we see it in the Cross. And I am constrained to remind you of what he once wrote for those, inside the Church as well as outside it, who deprecate what Percy Dearmer once called " this sin obsession ":

> If anyone feels that the language which the Church asks him to use is exaggerated—" We do earnestly repent and are heartily sorry for these our misdoings; the remembrance of them is grievous unto us, the burden of them is intolerable "—then let him think of slums and sweating and prostitution and war, and ask if the remembrance of these is not grievous, and if the burden of them ought not to be intolerable.

And then he strikes a note which sounds over and over again in his books and sermons:

> Let him remember that these horrible things are there, not because some men are outrageously wicked, but because millions of men are as good as we are, and no better. (*Personal Religion and the Life of Fellowship*, p. 44.)

For him, nevertheless, the central fundamental affirmation of the
Christian religion is that Jesus of Nazareth is the unique, final manifestation of God. We have it on his own authority that the centre
and circumference of his theology was the Incarnation. In a letter to
Ronald Knox (October 1913), he wrote: "The whole of my
theology is an attempt to understand and verify the words: 'He
that hath seen Me hath seen the Father.'"[9] This is the theme of an
essay in *Foundations* (1912), of a chapter called "The Word
Incarnate" in *Mens Creatrix* (1917), of a long sermon, "The
Philosophy of the Incarnation," before the University of Cambridge
(1918), and of the masterly volume which appeared after another
six years entitled *Christus Veritas*. Naturally, and rightly, he had
not much on the subject in his Gifford lectures, but he refers on
page 314 to the "Incarnation in a human life of that self-utterance
of God which is the ground of the created universe," and a few
pages further on to "a life which was lived by God Himself." I, at
least, find that very obscure. It must, of course, be beyond our understanding, but Temple used to insist that it is no more than our duty
to secure that our words and thoughts on the Incarnation shall not
be more inadequate than is necessary.

> What we see in Him is what we should see in the history of the
> universe if we could apprehend that history in its completeness. And
> even then it is to be remembered that we have not the World-History
> without the Incarnation as one expression of the Divine Will and the
> Life of the Incarnate as another; for that Life is a part of History,
> though it reveals the principle of the whole, and it is through its
> occurrence in the midst of History that History is fashioned into an
> expression of the principle there revealed. We have here a series which
> is part of another series and is yet perfectly representative of it. (Cf.
> the Supplementary Essay in Royce's *The World and the Individual*.)
> But here the series which is contained (the Life, Death and Resurrec-
> tion of Christ) only becomes representative of the series which contains
> it (the entire history of the world) in view of the influence which by
> occurring within the latter it is able to exercise upon it. Therefore,
> though Transcendence and Immanence are fused into one, the Trans-
> cendent aspect is always dominant. (*Mens Creatrix*, p. 318.)

Because Temple was the acknowledged master of a unique con-
ciseness of utterance, it is like nothing more than gilding refined
gold to summarize what he said on this subject, but I cannot bu·
attempt it.

[9] I dare not omit from this Introduction a priceless footnote from *Foundations*,
p. 228: "The spiritual value of Semi-Arianism, with its Christ who is not God but
is like God, has been epigrammatically expressed in the following fable:
    CHILD. I want Mother.
    NURSE. I don't know where your Mother is, but here's Auntie."

I begin with a passage from a University Sermon on the philosophy of the Incarnation which he preached in Cambridge in 1918:

> The revelation of absolute Godhead in sheer Humanity is possible and intelligible because the whole creation, with man who is, so far as this planet is concerned, its crown, is itself the self-revelation of God. Its order is the impress of His Reason; its beauty is the reflection of His; and man with his aspirations and endeavours is the uprising in the creation of the only perfect response to His intention, because the only one with freedom to choose love instead of hostility and neglect. In all the world we see God; in man, though only fitfully, his light shines brightest. But in the one perfection of manhood the light streams forth unflickering and in plenitude of strength, " the effulgence of His glory and the express image of his person."

The dogma, he reiterates, is not primarily concerned with a historical individual who lived about nineteen centuries ago; it is a statement about God:

> The fact is that most of us are not able to attribute any such meaning to the word " *divine* " as will enable us to use the word of Christ, unless we have first seen God in Christ Himself. To ask whether Christ is Divine is to suggest that Christ is an enigma while Deity is a simple and familiar conception. But the truth is the exact opposite of this. We know, if we will open our eyes and look, the life and character of Christ; but of God we have no clear vision. " No man hath seen God at any time." (*Foundations*, p. 214.)
>
> If we are to form a right conception of God we must look at Christ. The wise question is not, " Is Christ Divine? " but, " What is God like? " And the answer to that is " Christ." So, too, we must not form a conception of Humanity and either ask if Christ is human or insist on reducing Him to the limits of our conception; we must ask, " What is Humanity? " and look at Christ to find the answer (op. cit., p. 259).

This comes over and over again. The advance of science, Temple said, has made the unity of the world a dominant idea. " Apart from Him hath not one thing happened," as St. John declares; and Temple goes on to declare that the character of this Unknown Almighty Power is revealed in a historical figure—Jesus of Nazareth. St. Paul sometimes seems to speak of His life as a period of humiliation between two eternities of glory. But this view is not the deepest; it suggests that the heavenly glory is something quite different from the earthly life of Christ—a splendour which He left and to which He returned. But if we are to believe that in Christ we see the Father, we must go further and say with St. John that the self-humbling and self-emptying and the self-forgetting sacrifice are themselves part of the eternal glory of God. There was no leaving of heaven when He came to earth. " The Word was made Flesh . . . and we beheld His glory." God has revealed Himself in Jesus Christ: that is the central truth. But if so, we are driven to ask who or what is Jesus Christ. Is He a man like other men? Or is He a Divine Being breaking in upon our world, a God in a human body? Neither suggestion can explain what He has done. Somehow or other He must be " Perfect God and Perfect Man " (op. cit., p. 223).

There follows, in the *Foundations* essay, a re-examination of the classic attempts to solve the problem, first in the Greek Fathers—among whom St. Athanasius is supreme—and then in the West by St. Augustine, Anselm, Abelard and so on. The Athanasian formula is well known: " He became human that we might be made divine." But because the Greeks thought in terms of *substance*, and not of will or personality, that formula did not mean anything like as much as we are inclined to read into it. Christ is God and Man; in Him two perfect substances are united. But Temple insisted that the *spiritual cannot be* expressed in terms of substance, the higher and more personal in terms of the more abstract and impersonal; the whole set-up is materialistic.[10]

The Latins had a simpler way: they thought in terms of function. The same man may be both consul and augur—as we might say, a rural district councillor and the parson of a parish; so the same Christ may be both God and Man.

The Greek Fathers tried to say that God became " Man " in some inclusive sense, He took the human nature which all men share. There have been enigmas about an " impersonal " humanity; Christ was not " a Man " but " Man." In a debate on Reservation in the Bishops' meeting, Temple said, quite casually and " by the way ": " Christ is, of course, all humanity." And in *Foundations* he had stated, with lucid simplicity, his characteristically personal and ethical interpretation of this. As Christ is drawing all men to Himself, so winning the victory over evil in them, His claim to reveal the Father is vindicated and He shows what mankind is destined to become. That is how God and Man are one Christ.[11]

Christ's " inclusiveness " is not " substantial," not quantitative

[10] But if He (God) is truly described as Love, then once it is clear that no distinction can be drawn between His will and His substance and that the motive for drawing such a distinction is gone. Love itself is a disposition and energy of the will, and if this is what God is, then His very substance is will. (*Fellowship with God*, p. 221.)

[11] The fact to be explained or articulated has been tersely summarized in the words of the late Dr. Moberly " Christ is God—not generically but identically. Christ is Man—not generically but inclusively "; or, as we may paraphrase the words, Christ is not A God (or A Divine Being) but God; Christ is not only A Man, but Man. (*Foundations*, p. 247.)

but qualitative, accomplished through personal influence. We are in
Christ as Christ is in God (we shall see what that means in a little).
His Spirit has come upon us and we have (a little) yielded ourselves
to it. If we loved Him wholly and took His Purpose for our own,
with all the pains that must involve, we should find in that the true
consummation of our being. " This is life eternal, that they might
know Thee the only true God, and Jesus Christ whom Thou has
sent." Gradually we are drawn to return His Love and accept
His purpose as our own; gradually He becomes all-inclusive, because
we become like Him when we see Him as He is. Christ " includes "
us in this sense; we freely will His purpose, because it is His, and
whatever is true of Him is therefore true of us, if and so far as we
are as yet devoted to Him.

In a personal being—in a man, for example—there can be no
distinction between Will and Substance. " Will is the only substance
there is in a man; it is not a part of him, it is just himself as a moral
(or, indeed, " active ") being.[12] The Will of Christ is His entire
active Personality. And He wills what the Father wills. Their purpose is the same. " Christ is not the Father, but Christ and the
Father are One. What we see Christ doing and desiring, that we
thereby know the Father does and desires." Jesus said: " Amen,
Amen I say to you, the Son cannot do anything of himself, except
he seeth the Father doing something. For what things soever HE
doeth, these also in like manner the Son doeth. For the Father loveth
the Son, and showeth him all things that he himself doeth." On
which passage Temple's comment is:

> *The Son can do nothing of himself.* That is why the ancient Greek
> and Hebrew ideas of the Logos could be used to interpret His being
> and function. A " word " does not utter itself; it must be somebody's
> word; and its importance depends on the person whose word it is.
> The *glory* that we see in Christ is not His own, but *from a Father*
> (i, 1). The Son is in all ways derivative and dependent—" begotten."
> But though in this way He is " subordinate," the range of His derived
> activity is co-extensive with the Father's. He can do nothing of Him-
> self, but He does all that the Father does. He is agent, not principal;
> but He is universal agent. *All things came to be through him* (i, 3).
> Therefore the revelation given in Him, though mediated, is complete
> and final. (*Readings in St. John's Gospel,* pp. 111, 112.)

[12] " And a man's will is most ' free,' not when he can do anything and no one
can count on him, but just when he is most dependable and *must* do this or *can't* do
that. Consequently, in putting all the emphasis on will, we are not, as Apollinaris
supposed, driven to accept a ' changeable ' Christ. Christ cannot be other than what
He is—could not, for example, yield to the three Messianic temptations at the
opening of His ministry—because He *is* Himself, that is, One in Character and
Purpose with God." (*Foundations,* p. 248.)

He is the Man whose will is united to God's. He is thus the first-fruits of the Creation—the first response from the Creation to the love of the Creator. But because He is this, He is the perfect expression of the Divine in terms of human life. There are not two Gods, but in Christ we see God. Christ is identically God; the whole content of His being—His thought, feeling and purpose—is also that of God. This is the only substance of a spiritual being, for it is all that there is of him at all.[13] The Human affections of Christ are God's affections; His suffering is God's, His glory is God's. So Temple quotes the closing passage from Browning's *An Epistle*:

> The very God! Think, Abib; dost thou think?
> So, the All-great were the All-loving too—
> So, through the thunder comes a human voice
> Saying, " O heart I made, a heart beats here!
> Face my hands fashioned, see it in Myself!
> Thou hast no power nor mayest conceive of mine,
> But love I gave thee, with Myself to love,
> And thou must love Me who have died for thee!"

And he refers to the 28th stanza of *Saul*:

> As thy Love is discovered almighty, almighty be proved
> Thy power, that exists with it, of being Beloved!
> He who did most shall bear most; the strongest shall stand the most weak.
> 'Tis the weakness in strength that I cry for! My flesh that I seek
> In the Godhead! I seek and I find it. O Saul, it shall be
> A Face like my face that receives thee; a Man like to me,
> Thou shalt love and be loved by, for ever: a Hand like this hand
> Shall throw open the gates of new life to thee! See the Christ stand!

We say " two minds with but a single thought," but they are not merely merged in one another. Neither do God and Christ lose their personal distinctness, even though the identity extends to the whole of consciousness.[14] While the limitations of our Lord's human knowledge remind us that He is not the Absolute God in all His fullness of Being (" The Father is greater than I "), yet in all which directly concerns the spiritual relation of God to Man, Christ is identically

---

[13] " In the language of logicians, formally (as pure subjects) God and Christ are distinct; materially (that is, in the content of the two consciousnesses) God and Christ are One and the Same (cf. Bosanquet, *Individuality and Value*, p. 272). Clearly, it is the Logos—the Divine Humanity—that pre-exists. The ' finite centre of consciousness ' (Jesus) had a beginning." (*Foundations*, p. 249.)

[14] " To be with the Father is the fulfilment of His being, and that He should go to the Father is the ground of their help and strength." (*Readings in St. John's Gospel*, p. 249.)

one with the Father in the content of His Being ("I and the Father are one ").[15] In content of heart and will, Christ is identically one with God.

When you say that the *Infinite* God is manifest in the individual person, Jesus of Nazareth, the word "infinite" is qualitative, not quantitative. And because the discussion is in the realm of personality, it is meaningless to ask whether the whole of God or only a part was in Christ. There the holy love of God was finally shown. What is revealed in Jesus is *all the love of God*. There can be no further, more adequate revelation of God's love than this. There it was seen that there can be no circumstances in which love cannot be shown, and no person whom it is not willing to serve and save. It is already an infinite. You have reached a limit beyond which it is self-contradictory that you could ask to go; there cannot be more love than absolute, unconditional self-giving to all, and to each one. That is the Incarnation. But Temple noted that it is important to realize that the Divinity of the Man Christ Jesus means the eternal Humanity of God. "We are dealing with a Particular (Jesus of Nazareth) which perfectly embodies its own universal (Humanity)." But the discussion of the Person of Christ through the Christian centuries has not really been concerned, when all is said, with the problem of who or what He was who lived 2,000 years ago. What we all want to know is, *what is God like?* In his criticism of *Foundations*, Ronald Knox said that on Temple's basis, "To say that Jesus was Divine will be merely to say that Jesus was Jesus-like," but Temple replied that it will not be merely that; it will be to say "God is Jesus-like." And that is to me, and I believe always has been for the Church, the ultimately important Christian intuition.

The Incarnation must be unique; the repeated appearances of Vishnu on earth which are part of Hinduism, for example, tend to become trivial, if not to demonstrate themselves as unhistorical. Not long ago, Emil Brunner, in a talk on the Third programme, said that the climax of God's revelation is an event which is, at once, the perfection of His revelation as absolute person and the perfection of the characteristic element of history, namely, oneness—that is, the event which, taking place, has taken place once and for all. Here in this event, Jesus Christ, it becomes evident that the absolutely personal and the absolute historical belong together, in correlation. It is only the absolutely personal God who can give an historical

---

[15] "It is a stupendous affirmation of union with the Deity. As at the national feast He asserted His priority to the founder of the nation so at this Church feast He asserts His union with the God to whom the worship of the Church is offered. . . . The famous saying is not wholly illegitimate ' Per *sumus* refutatur Sabellius, per *unum* Arius '." (*Readings*, p. 172.)

event the content of absolute meaning, making it an event which cannot happen more than once. Once and for all. It is the event in which eternity becomes time, when Godhead becomes Manhood, when the absolute God is revealed in Historical person.

And von Hügel, a theologian whose standpoint was widely different from that of Brunner, used to lay stress on this same thing, the once-for-allness of Jesus Christ. It is clear, indeed, that whether one approaches the Incarnation from the practical point of view—of salvation achieved by His full, perfect and sufficient sacrifice—or from the philosophical problem of the eternal significance of a particular thing or event, in each case it is of the essence of what happened that it could not be repeated. At the end of the argument, I suppose, it involves the individuality, the uniqueness of love.

But, because the Incarnation must be essentially unique, it cannot be defined, if only because a definition is a statement of something else. The Incarnation is a mystery, not in the sense of some guess which cannot be proved, but in the sense of a Divine certainty, a revelation too large or an intuition too deep to be put into words. Nothing better can be hoped for than that from various points of view we should throw out at the Incarnation hints which are a little less inadequate than silence. It is a primitive Christian intuition, for example, that the Christian Society is the Body of Christ. That is more than a metaphor, and the richness of the organic reality is more adequately expressed by saying that we are " members " of Christ than " limbs " of His body. In his Lent book, *Personal Religion and the Life of Fellowship*, Temple interpreted that phrase, the " Body of Christ," to mean that the Church is " the organism which moves spontaneously in obedience to His will; . . . all the old divisions had become negligible. There was one man, and that man was Christ Jesus. If the will of Christ prevails throughout a society, for all practical purposes Christ is the only person there. *So Christ is the Person of the Church as God is the Person of Jesus Christ.*" That last sentence seems challengingly illuminating, for it points the way to a vision of what is meant by the term " Incarnation." He said very much the same in his great book, *Christus Veritas* (1924). The will in Jesus, he said, always expresses the will of God, is one with God's will. Ideally, *will* and *personality* are interchangeable terms—i.e. when personality is perfectly developed and unified. So to say that the will of Jesus is *one with* the Father's will is to say that there is *one person*, one living and energizing Being. The human personality does not exist side by side with the divine personality; it is subsumed in it.

c

" There are two wills in the Incarnate in the sense that His human nature comes through struggle and effort to an ever deeper union with the Divine in completeness of self-sacrifice. And it is only because there is this real human will or personality that there is any revelation to humanity of the Divine Will. Thus I do not speak of His humanity as impersonal. If we imagine the divine Word withdrawn from Jesus of Nazareth, as the Gnostics believed to have occurred before the Passion, I think that there would be left, not nothing at all, but a man. The question is so unreal that even to ask it is to make false suggestions; but I leave the illustration as an expression of my meaning, which is deliberately crude for the sake of pointedness." (*Christus Veritas*, p. 150.)

When this book appeared more than thirty years ago, the *Church Times* reviewer expressed grave concern at this statement which we have just considered, and said that it needed more explanation than Temple had given it. He went on to point out that this way of stating the doctrine of Christ's Person as though *a man* had been taken up into God was certainly deliberate because in a later chapter Temple wrote:

There is no general humanity in which the Divine Word could be clothed, apart from all particular centres of experience; but the Divine Word took to himself human experience in one such centre, so completely subsuming the human personality that God and Man in Jesus Christ are one Person.

An interesting piece of " secret history " is that two or three weeks after the review appeared a letter was received from a Professor of Theology in the Roman Catholic University at Louvain, giving quotations from St. Thomas which demonstrated that Temple's Christology is in the middle of Catholic tradition.

At the risk of seeming to underline the obvious, here are three passages which explain the devotional content of the Archbishop's Christology:

All else is to be valued because, and only because it leads men to the feet of Jesus Christ, and aids their loyalty to His allegiance. Our first concern is to nothing on earth at all, whether Church or Creed or Sacrament or Order, it is to uphold before men's hearts and minds and consciences and wills the claim of Jesus Christ as Lord upon their obedience, their trust, their love. (Enthronement Address at York, 1929.)

Our characters are shaped by our companions and by the objects to which we give most of our thought and with which we fill our imaginations. We cannot always be thinking even about Christ, but we can refuse to dwell on any thoughts which are out of tune with Him. We can, above all, quite deliberately turn our minds towards Him at any time when those thoughts come in. You will find it impossible for a vivid memory of Jesus Christ and an unclean thought or a mean and treacherous desire to be in your mind at the same time. It cannot happen. (*Christian Faith and Life*, pp. 35, 36.)

For all the anguish of the world there are three consolations. The Epicurean says, " It is but for a time; ere long we shall fall asleep in the unending slumber "; which is comfort of a sort. The Stoic says, " Rise above it all; to the wise these things are nugatory "; which is no comfort at all if we are not wise. Christianity says, " Christ also suffered "; and that, with the Christian interpretation of " Christ," is real consolation, a human answer to our humanity." (*Mens Creatrix*, pp. 279, 280.)

V

After he had gone to Canterbury the Archbishop once said, in a very private conversation, that he would resign at seventy and write a book on the Holy Spirit. The Church has to do without that book, but we can discover some of his thoughts on the subject (although not so easily as we might hope, for of all his many books there is only one that has an index).

He used to say that so far from this being a peculiarly difficult and remote part of Christian belief, the Holy Spirit is the Person in the Trinity with whom we are most constantly in conscious contact. The advance from chaos to order disclosed by science in the evolutionary series of development, culminating up to date in life as a vehicle of intelligent purpose and spiritual devotion, is the work of the Spirit of God in the universe, as is the creation of ever more perfect order in human history—in the unification of individual personality and its enrichment through the deepening and extension of social intercourse. " All the great theologians have always said that the love wherewith a man loves God or his neighbour is the Holy Ghost. It is not the *work* of the Holy Ghost only, it *is* the Holy Ghost " (*Christian Faith and Life*, p. 90). And not only so, but wherever a man is mastered by any absolute claim—of beauty or truth or goodness—the Holy Ghost is the response to that transcendent claim.

The new power which God obtained over the hearts of men through the manifestation of His love in the life and person of Jesus Christ, and the new relationship so established, not of slaves but of sons, is the Holy Spirit.[16] As he set it forth in a profound passage in *Christus Veritas*:

> The Holy Spirit, as made known to us in our experience, is the power whereby the created universe—which the Father creates by the agency of the Son, His self-revealing Word—is brought into harmonious response to the love which originated it. The divine self-utterance is creative; within the thing so created the divine self-utterance speaks in Jesus Christ; the divine impetus which is in the created thing by virtue of its origin is thus released in full power to make the created thing correspond to the Creator's purpose. Love creates; Love by self-sacrifice reveals itself to the created thing; Love thereby calls out from the created thing the Love which belongs to it as Love's creature, thus making it what Love created it to be." (Op. cit., pp. 278, 279.)

This doctrine of the Holy Trinity, creative Love in every way expressing itself without restriction or discrimination or any sort of limitation, so that the goal of time is that every individual human being shall become a person, an atom of the Holy Trinity, was the inspiration and sanction and power of the Christian social teaching and action which made William Temple " the people's Archbishop." But it made the problem of evil acute for his theology and philosophy. Of that he used to say that it was the one element in men's thought which really drove them into unbelief, and that it would make any theism untenable unless men, in practice, found that sin and suffering can be overcome by sympathy and sacrifice. He described how, in a discussion, a working man told the story of his wife's appalling sufferings from cancer, and ended by saying, " If Jesus were God, that would not happen." The Archbishop's immediate comment on that may seem somewhat coldly theoretical: " Our consciences claim the right and exercise the right of criticizing God as we know Him." But what did he actually believe, in face of the heart-breaking human world in which we live?

> " There cannot be a God of love," men say, " because if there were, and He looked upon this world, His heart would break."
> The Church points to the Cross and says, " His heart does break."
> " It is God who has made the world," men say; " it is He who is responsible, and it is He who should bear the load."
> The Church points to the Cross, and says, " He does bear it." (*The Preacher's Theme Today*, p. 62.)

[16] " By ' Holy Spirit ' St. Paul and St. John, at least for the most part, understand the fullness of response called out from men by the fullness of divine self-manifestation in Christ; cf. Romans, viii, 9–27, specially 14–17 and 23; St. John, vii, 39; 16, 7." (*Nature, Man and God*, p. 319n.)

The power of Temple as a popular teacher, great beyond my ability to assess, was due not chiefly to his notable capacity for lucid because exact and closely articulated statement, but primarily to the wide and comprehensive quality of what he had to communicate: a richly varied and " all-round " body of knowledge and thought, fused into a unity by his understanding of the mental need and his sympathy with the human longings of the comman man. He had the interest in and understanding of the concrete and particular which come from the inner identification characteristic of the artistic temperament; this is seen in his lectures on Plato, his essay on Browning, his informed enjoyment of music, but more systematically in his first large book, *Mens Creatrix*. But this was combined, to a quite unusual degree, with the philosopher's impulse to find a truth which should be generally valid. It is this combination for which his name stands in modern theology: the consistent and persuasive exposition of the view that religion binds together vision and thought, spiritual vitality wedded to intellectual integrity.

Robert Browning

THERE IS SOMETHING absurd in the attempt to deal with so vast a subject as I have proposed for myself in a single short paper; but what constitutes the absurdity is also what impels me to make the attempt, for, extravagant as it may sound, I certainly regard Robert Browning as the greatest product of the nineteenth century, and with Shakespeare the greatest figure in our literature. He is, of course, far below Shakespeare in many respects, but in some he is above him: with Shakespeare life is either irresistibly and nobly comic, or an insoluble and appalling mystery; he had boundless sympathy, but was utterly without faith or hope; his great tragedies are in themselves beyond criticism, but in none of them is there depicted a great man moulding his destiny. The impulse to action, except in the case of villains, is invariably external. In Browning all this is reversed. Shakespeare is magnificent, but with a pagan magnificence; Browning's genius is less stupendous, but it is fundamentally and thoroughly Christian. In both there is the joy of comedy, but in Browning only is there also the joy of work and worship. I do not at present claim this place for him as a poet, because in many ways he does not answer to the ordinary conception of a poet: his subjects are rather reflective than emotional; his aim is literal truth rather than imaginative beauty; his language is often rough and grotesque, and, occasionally to those unfamiliar with his methods, almost unintelligible.

It is sometimes asked, Why, if he was not going to write poetry, did he write in metre? There are several very satisfactory answers, indeed an unmetrical Browning is unthinkable (as a mere matter of fact Browning is one of the very few poets who scarcely wrote a line that was not pure poetry; but we shall come back to that). Then the advantages of metre are obvious; by his rough rhythm and uncouth rhymes, he is able to increase very greatly the humour of his work, and humour is one of Browning's greatest gifts. Not infrequently people say the incongruity and roughness found in so many of his poems is a sign of deficiency; but it is not so; we have sufficient proof that Browning could write with the highest elegance when he so desired, but often he feels that he can achieve his purpose better by other means. Above all, the metrical form enables him to introduce in the most commonplace connexion passages of brilliant

33

poetry; and nothing delights him more than to raise everyday topics as it were from earth to highest empyrean by this means, or in a similar way to bring us back with a most salutary jar from visionary excursions in the realm of fancy to the everyday world and solid fact. He hates idle dreamers, perhaps more than men who never dream at all: " Dream by all means," he seems to say, " and then try to realize your dreams." Further, I protest altogether against the division of literature into prose and poetry for the purposes of criticism. No two people will agree as to where the dividing line should be drawn. To discuss whether Browning or any one else is a poet or not, in this sense, is pure waste of time: what we have to consider is simply whether the works in question, regarded as literature—that is, the expression of thought in words—deserve praise or blame. The opposition of prose and poetry is, indeed, really untenable, for the two are not *in pari materia*; as Coleridge pointed out, the opposite of prose is not poetry but metre, and the opposite of poetry is not prose but science.

A more serious charge than the unsuitability of metre for such composition is the charge of obscurity. Now let us observe at once that if we regard Browning as a teacher, which is a risky thing to do, he is not the only one who thought fit to convey his message to the world by means of dark sayings. Browning is not always quite clear, and he has no desire to be so; but the charge of obscurity is greatly exaggerated. No doubt there are some tricks of style that are confusing, until we are used to them: such are the almost invariable omission of the relative pronoun, and the frequent insertion of parenthetical, and sometimes apparently irrelevant, passages between the subject of the sentence and its verb. But, on the other hand, Browning is a very grammatical writer, and his sentences always have a construction, which cannot be said of all poets. It is after all not Browning's tricks of style, but the sturdy Briton's tricks of reading that produce obscurity: many of Browning's writings are pure bubbling fun, and many are colloquial. We can hardly be surprised that a person who reads the delightful poem *Of Pacchiarotto and how he worked in distemper* in the same tone and accents as Wordsworth's *Excursion,* or Blougram's highly conversational *Apology,* as if it were Milton trying again to justify the ways of God to men, finds very little sense in either of these works.

The real cause, however, of the apparent obscurity of Browning's works, so far as it extends beyond the language, lies in his philosophic and dramatic instinct; the two go very much together, for while his philosophy forces him to see many sides to every question, his dramatic power enables him to express each in turn: now it is the satirical Bishop Blougram refuting the clever but shallow Gigadibs, who was pleased to assert that no one but a fool could really believe in a God; now it is Browning himself complaining " how very hard it is to be a Christian! " and showing that none but fools can swallow the Bible's narrative and precepts without a hesitation or a qualm. It is in such contradictions as this that people find his obscurity: " you call him a teacher," they say, " but he has no teaching to give us: first he says one thing, then another, and we never know what he wants us to think." No, for on that point he has no desires at all: he does not want to give us opinions, but, so far as he is a teacher at all, to make us form our own: his gift to us is not thoughts, but thought.

Let us take as an example what he says about the relative value of ideas and actions, or, as theologians would say, of faith and works. Browning may be claimed in support of either view that may be held on this subject. Often and often he tells us that what we achieve is of no importance. For, as his Pope says in *The Ring and the Book*,

> For I am 'ware it is the seed of the act
> God holds appraising in His hollow palm,
> Not act grown great thence on the world below,
> Leafage and branchage, vulgar eyes admire.

So again Rabbi Ben Ezra says:

> Thoughts hardly to be packed
> Into a narrow act,
> Fancies that broke through language and escaped:
> All I could never be,
> All men ignored in me,
> This I was worth to God whose wheel the pitcher shaped.

Yet again there is a striking passage of contrasts in *The Grammarian's Funeral* :

> That low man seeks a little thing to do,
> Sees it and does it :
> This high man, with a great thing to pursue,
> Dies ere he knows it :
> That low man goes on adding one to one,
> His hundred's soon hit;
> This high man, aiming at a million,
> Misses a unit.
> That has the world here—should he need the next,
> Let the world mind him !
> This throws himself on God, and unperplexed
> Seeking shall find Him.

The same will be expressed in some of the quotations introduced later on to illustrate other points. But now let us contrast with this the first answer of Bishop Blougram to the idealist, who wanted a great ideal to follow, not a dogmatic and at least half-incredible belief :

> So, drawing comfortable breath again,
> You weigh and find, whatever more or less
> I boast of my ideal realized,
> Is nothing in the balance when opposed
> To your ideal, your grand simple life,
> Of which you will not realize one jot.
> I am much, you are nothing; you would be all,
> I would be merely much : you beat me there.
> No, friend, you do not beat me : Hearken why !
> The common problem, yours, mine, every one's
> Is—not to fancy what were fair in life,
> Provided it could be—but, finding first
> What may be, then find how to make it fair
> Up to our means, a very different thing !
> No abstract intellectual plan of life
> Quite irrespective of life's plainest laws,
> But one a man, who is man and nothing more,
> May lead within a world which (by your leave)
> Is Rome or London—not fool's paradise !

The same view finds a more beautiful expression in *Paracelsus*, where Aprile—who perhaps represents Shelley, the idol of Browning's youth, and who, if so, would naturally be given the task of stating Browning's most valued thoughts—is made to say :

> Knowing ourselves, our world, our task so great,
> Our time so brief, 'tis clear if we refuse
> The means so limited, the tools so rude
> To execute our purpose, life will fleet
> And we shall fade and leave our task undone.

" But I thought that did not matter," urges the reader in perplexity; the prophet does not solve the problem; indeed it is not the problem that he is interested in, but its dramatic setting; Browning does not mean to tell us *his* opinions, but Blougram's opinions and Aprile's opinions, and these chiefly because they are an essential part of Blougram and Aprile.

Of course the ardent hero-worshipper wants to know what Browning really thought just for the interest of the thing, and to compare his view with that of other writers. Browning is quite aware of their indignation :

" Hoity toity! a street to explore,
    Your house the exception? with this same key
Shakespeare unlocked his heart, once more!"
    Did Shakespeare? if so the less Shakespeare he!

In the stanza next before this, in the strange poem entitled *House*,
he tells us how we may and how we may not find his own thoughts.
He will not open his house to the public :

Outside should suffice for evidence;
    And whoso desires to penetrate
Deeper, must dive by the spirit-sense;
    No optics like yours at any rate.

This of faith and works is one of the subjects which Browning
treats; but let us remember here and always that the subject of a
poem, so far as it is a thing that can be expressed in any analysis, is,
strictly speaking, not in the poem but outside it. It is not the poem;
it is what the poem is about. It is the material of the poet as the
marble block is the material of the sculptor. And for the purposes
of poetic criticism we must take care not to be biased by our personal
interest in the subject. I am inclined to think that Browning's
greatest poem is *A Death in the Desert*, but that is not because the
subject is sublime—though that is true—but because the treatment
of it is adequate. Much harm has been done by exaggerated attention
to Browning's philosophy in the narrower sense of that term. As his
greatest critic, John Nettleship, has said : " It should never be forgotten (as, alas, it sometimes is) that he is a poet in all senses; that
to huddle up winsome grace, humour, fancy, and pathos under one
grey cloak of philosophic idea would be as unpardonable as to robe
the Apollo Belvedere in a cassock." And yet the choice of subject
is important; for it shows what are the motive powers in a poet's
soul. The poet writes of what he feels and knows. And Browning's
greatness is partly this, that, first of poets, he took thought as well
as emotion and action for his material. As Wordsworth or Shelley
takes " the earth and every common sight," and throws upon them
the magic light of imagination, which transforms what it illuminates
—so does Browning deal with the greatest fact in nature, the thought
of man, and above all with thought as it exists and energizes in the
artist.
    The philosophic and dramatic instinct which, as we have seen,
is the cause of much apparent obscurity, is nowhere plainer than in
his poems on art. One does not need to be a connoisseur to appreciate
Fra Lippo Lippi or *Andrea del Sarto*; both poems are masterpieces
of dramatic situation. It is said that the former is a libel on the monk

painter. But that is no matter to us, nor probably to him; we have a delightful picture of a frolicsome young painter who loved the world dearly (though he renounced it at the age of eight), and who painted what he saw, not trying to import a spirituality that was not there : the monks objected, but he defended himself by saying that this is the purpose of art, to make us see in the world what we should not see without it.

> For, don't you mark? we are made so that we love
> First, when we see them painted, things we passed
> Perhaps a hundred times, nor cared to see.
> And so they're better painted—better to us,
> Which is the same thing. Art was given for that;
> God uses us to help each other so,
> Lending our minds out. . . . This world's no blot for us,
> Nor blank : it means intensely and means good :
> To find its meaning is my meat and drink.

There you have as satisfactory a statement of the mimetic function of art as is to be found in all the third book of Plato's *Republic*, and all the literature which that treatise has produced; Browning's power of condensation is nothing short of miraculous.

Andrea del Sarto is a far less dramatic work, but is on the whole more poetical; upon examination it is found to contain as clear a statement of the relation of form to spirit in painting as *Fra Lippo Lippi* contains of the relation of art to nature. The painter quotes a saying of Michael Angelo that Raphael himself would have blushed to see Andrea's work, and then turning to one of Raphael's pictures he goes on—

> And indeed the arm is wrong.
> I hardly dare,—yet, only you to see,
> Give the chalk here—quick, thus the line should go.
> Ay! but the soul! he's Raphael! rub it out!

Andrea may be the faultless painter; but he is the soulless painter too.

Far more remarkable is Browning's treatment of music; on this subject he is certainly supreme. There are three poems which stand out conspicuously—*Master Hugues of Saxe-Gotha, A Toccata of Galuppi's,* and *Abt Vogler.* The first of these is the soliloquy of an organist trying to master a Fugue by the imaginary composer who gives his name to the poem. It is a very dramatic work, and contains a wonderful description of a Fugue. A Fugue, it may be well to observe, is a musical composition based upon a short melody which is taken up by one part after another : in this case the various parts are represented as arguing; they are called 1, 2, 3, 4, 5, according to the order in which they enter the discussion.

First you deliver your phrase,
    Nothing propound, that I see,
Fit in itself for much blame or much praise—
    Answered no less, where no answer needs be:
Off start the Two on their ways.

Straight must a Third interpose,
    Volunteer needlessly help,
In strikes a Fourth, a Fifth thrusts in his nose;
    So the cry's open, the kennel's a yelp,
Argument's hot to the close.

One dissertates, he is candid;
    Two must discept, has distinguished;
Three helps the couple, if ever yet man did;
    Four protests; Five makes a dart at the thing wished;
Back to One goes the case bandied.

Est fuga, volvitur rota.
    On we drift; where looms the dim port?
One, Two, Three, Four, Five, contribute their quota;
    Something is gained if one caught but the import—
Show it us, Hugues of Saxe-Gotha!

Is it your moral of life?
    Such a web, simple and subtle,
Weave we on earth here in impotent strife,
    Backward and forward each throwing his shuttle,
Death ending all with a knife?

Over our heads truth and nature—
    Still our life's zigzags and dodges,
Ins and outs weaving a new legislature—
    God's gold just shining its last where that lodges,
Palled beneath man's usurpature.

So we o'ershroud stars and roses,
    Cherub and trophy and garland;
Nothings grow something which quietly closes
    Heaven's earnest eye: not a glimpse of the far land
Gets through our comments and glozes.

This is very good instance of Browning's method in dealing with music—and surely it is the true method. He does not treat the composition as a mere piece of programme-music, whose sounds are actual imitations of what they represent; but from the general impression of the whole he draws a moral. So it is, too, in the far finer

poem, *A Toccata of Galuppi's*. Galuppi was an Italian composer of
the eighteenth century, and Browning finds in his work with its cold
reserve a condemnation of Italian frivolity :

Oh, Galuppi, Baldassaro, this is very sad to find!
I can hardly misconceive you; it would prove me deaf and blind;
But, although I take your meaning, 'tis with such a heavy mind!

Here you come with your old music, and here's all the good it brings.
What, they lived once thus at Venice, where the merchants were the
    kings,
Where St. Mark's is, where the Doges used to wed the sea with rings?

Did young people take their pleasure when the sea was warm in May?
Balls and masques begun at midnight, burning ever to mid-day,
When they made up fresh adventures for the morrow, do you say?

Well, and it was graceful of them—they'd break talk off and afford—
She, to bite her mask's black velvet, he to finger on his sword,
While you sat and played toccatas stately at the clavichord.

What? those lesser thirds so plaintive, sixths diminished, sigh on sigh,
Told them something? those suspensions, those solutions,—" Must we
    die? "
Those commiserating sevenths—" Life might last, we can but try!"

" Were you happy? " " Yes." " And are you still as happy? " " Yes—
    and you? "
—" Then, more kisses!"—" Did I stop them when a million seemed so
    few? "
Hark, the dominant's persistence till it must be answered to!

So, an octave struck the answer. Oh, they praised you, I dare say?
" Brave Galuppi! That was music! good alike at grave and gay!
I can always leave off talking when I hear a master play!"

Then they left you for their pleasure : till in due time, one by one,
Some with lives that came to nothing, some with deeds as well undone,
Death stepped tacitly and took them where they never see the sun.

As for Venice and her people, merely born to bloom and drop,
Here on earth they bore their fruitage—mirth and folly were the crop :
What of soul was left, I wonder, when the kissing had to stop?

" Dust and ashes "—so you creak it, and I want the heart to scold.
Dear dead women, with such hair, too—what's become of all the gold
Used to hang and brush their bosoms? I feel chilly and grown old.

Grander still is *Abt Vogler*, which takes its name from a musician who has just been extemporizing, and falls to wondering how it is that anything so beautiful as the sounds that he had produced should perish so utterly; and then, taking his music as a type of all beautiful and lovely things, he breaks into a confession of faith—

There shall never be one lost good! what was shall live as before!
    The evil is null, is naught, is silence implying sound;
What was good shall be good, with, for evil, so much good more:
    On the earth the broken arcs; in the heaven a perfect round.

All we have willed or hoped or dreamed of good shall exist—
    Not its semblance, but itself; no beauty, nor good, nor power,
Whose voice has gone forth, but each survives for the melodist
    When eternity affirms the conception of an hour.
The high that proved *too* high, the heroic for earth *too* hard,
    The passion that left the ground to *lose* itself in the sky,
Are music sent up to God by the lover and the bard:
    Enough that He heard it once: we shall hear it by and by.

But before this he describes the effect which his music had upon him—lifting him above the conditions of time and space—"for earth had attained to heaven; there was no more near nor far."

Nay more; for there wanted not who walked in the glare and glow,
    Presences plain in the place; or, fresh from the Protoplast,
Furnished for ages to come, when a kindlier wind should blow,
    Lured now to begin and live, in a house to their liking at last;
Or else the wonderful Dead who have passed through the body and gone,
    But were back once more to breathe in an old world worth their new:
What never had been, was now; what was, as it shall be anon;
    And what is,—shall I say, matched both? for I was made perfect too.

Music had changed the world; those destined to live when centuries should have softened its hardships, and removed its evils, were lured to come before their appointed time, and the wonderful Dead were constrained to leave Paradise for a better life still on earth. The musician was made perfect and had become "The spectator of all time and of all existence."

This is immediately followed by an exquisite passage in praise of music, setting it far above the arts of painting and poetry, for in these the musician asserts—

Ye know why the forms are fair; ye hear how the tale is told.
It is all triumphant art, but art in obedience to laws,
    Painter and poet are proud in the artist list enrolled.

But here is the finger of God, a flash of the will that can,
  Existent behind all laws that made them, and lo, they are!
And I know not if, save in this, such gift be allowed to man,
  That out of three sounds he frame not a fourth sound but a star.
Consider it well: each tone of our scale in itself is nought;
  It is everywhere in the world, loud, soft, and all is said:
Give it to me to use! I mix it with two in my thought;
And there! ye have heard and seen: consider and bow the head!

Perhaps nothing is more striking about this passage, when once one
has recovered from its magnificence, than its splendid mendacity :
it is a dramatic triumph, for even a musician, when not carried away
by his own art, would be forced to admit that in painting and poetry,
just as in music, we do not "know why the forms are fair " or
"hear how the tale is told." The secret of beauty is in as safe keeping
with poets and painters as with musicians. Sometimes this passage is
quoted as Browning's opinion of the relative merits of the arts; but
such a use of it is quite unjustifiable, for it is Abt Vogler's view, not
Browning's: and in *Paracelsus*, Browning puts into the mouth of the
dying Aprile a eulogy of poetry which exalts it even higher above all
other arts than music is here exalted above poetry and painting.
Aprile is lying on Paracelsus' breast, dying as he grasps the truth
that would have changed his life had he known it before—the truth
of his art's dignity.

To speak but once, and die! yet by his side!
Hush! Hush! Ha! go you ever girt about
With phantoms, powers? I have created such,
But these seem real as I. . . . Stay; I know,
I know them: who should know them as well as I?
White brows lit up with glory; Poets all!
Yes; I see now: God is the perfect poet
Who in His Person acts His own creations.
Had you but told me this at first. Hush! Hush!

Such is Browning's treatment of the arts, philosophical and
dramatic, each poem giving expression to one view of the question,
so that the whole is discussed, but the view accepted by Browning
himself is not disclosed. But it must not be thought that Browning
simply chose subjects for this kind of discussion; the dramatic instinct
in him is far stronger even than the philosophic, and as long as we
do not take what he says *in persona* as his own opinion, we are by
no means bound to split up his work into subjects as I have done,
though some interest is gained by such a method. Browning is no
mere dissector; he does not cut men piecemeal, and then examine

the lifeless fragments : but he knows that on the whole every man adopts permanently one point of view, and so he creates his characters as the living expression of various mental attitudes; but they are by no means rigid or fixed. What is permanent is rather a bias or disposition than any logical conclusion. If his work sometimes seems piecemeal it is because he chiefly depicts single men in given circumstances, and no doubt he is more successful in his dramatic monologues than in his plays : yet the dramatic monologues reveal each a whole character; Browning's men and women come to us singly, but they are none the less real and living.

People have a strange habit of asking, But what is his view of life as a whole? and if the question can be answered the writer concerned is unworthy of great admiration, for it means that he can be compassed by a formula. To a man of open mind, life presents a different appearance every day, which is affected by countless accidents from the state of his liver to the activity of his conscience. Who can tell us what was Shakespeare's view of life? who can tell us how he approached it except that it was as a terrible reality? We carry away from him a new insight, and perhaps a new grasp of the excellence of laughter and the sanctity of sorrow, but there is no theory of Shakespeare. So too it is with Browning : from him we carry away a cheerful vigour and perhaps a new sense of duty. We can only say of him that his hope never fails. With him, as with every great writer, there is present an almost indefinite abundance of insight and illustration, and every reader must take what inspiration he can. To expatiate on his merits or demerits in general is a useless task.

Probably the most characteristic single poem is the Epilogue to *Ferishtah's Fancies* with its note of strong conviction—strong enough to face the last worst question, " what if all be error? "— and its assertion of love as the one sure reality of life.

We are, however, bound to remember that while we study the poems as supplementary of each other, they were not necessarily so written. As the whole of Browning has its single indescribable effect, so must each poem have its peculiar effect : for each is complete in itself. Browning's poems will stand by themselves, without reference to their neighbours, and many of them very high. One could make a long list of poems by him which are unsurpassed in our literature, partly perhaps because there is nothing that can fairly be compared with them, so original is the choice of subject and the mode of treatment, but also because of their pure literary pre-eminence. Nettleship speaks of his " winsome grace, humour and pathos." And they are all there. As a teller of stories he is unequalled; I need only mention that supreme masterpiece *The Flight of the Duchess*, and *Clive*, his

D

most powerful narrative. There is no love poetry in the language
within even a measurable distance of Browning's love poetry. There
is much of it—most of the Dramatic Lyrics are love poems. It is of
no use to quote their names; rather let me quote a few stanzas from
the greatest—*By the Fireside.*

XXVI

My own, see where the years conduct!
  At first, 'twas something our two souls
Should mix as mists do; each is sucked
  In each now; on, the new stream rolls,
Whatever rocks obstruct.

XXVII

Think, when our one soul understands
  The great Word which makes all things new,
When earth breaks up and heaven expands,
  How will the change strike me and you
In the House not made with hands?

XXX

Come back with me to the first of all,
  Let us lean and love it over again,
Let us now forget and now recall,
  Break the rosary in a pearly rain,
And gather what we let fall!

XXXIII

Hither we walked then, side by side,
  Arm in arm and cheek to cheek,
And still I questioned or replied,
  While my heart, convulsed to really speak,
Lay choking in its pride.

XXXIV

Silent the crumbling bridge we cross,
  And pity and praise the chapel sweet,
And care about the fresco's loss,
  And wish for our souls a like retreat,
And wonder at the moss.

XXXV

Stoop and kneel on the settle under,
  Look through the window's grated square:
Nothing to see! for fear of plunder,
  The cross is down and the altar bare,
As if thieves don't fear thunder.

XXXVI

We stoop and look in through the grate,
  See the little porch and rustic door,
Read duly the dead builder's date;
  Then cross the bridge that we crossed before,
Take the path again—but wait!

XXXVII

Oh moment, one and infinite!
  The water slips o'er stock and stone;
The west is tender, hardly bright:
  How grey at once is the evening grown—
One star, its chrysolite!

XXXVIII

We two stood there with never a third,
  But each by each, as each knew well;
The sights we saw and the sounds we heard,
  The lights and the shades made up a spell
Till the trouble grew and stirred.

XXXIX

Oh, the little more, and how much it is!
  And the little less, and what worlds away!
How a sound shall quicken content to bliss,
  Or a breath suspend the blood's best play,
And life be a proof of this!

XL

Had she willed it, still had stood the screen
  So slight, so sure, 'twixt my love and her:
I could fix her face with a guard between,
  And find her soul as when friends confer,
Friends—lovers that might have been.

XLVII

A moment after, and hands unseen
  Were hanging the night around us fast;
But we knew that a bar was broken between
  Life and life; we were mixed at last
In spite of the mortal screen.

XLVIII

The forests had done it; there they stood—
  We caught for a moment the powers at play:
They had mingled us so, for once and good,
  Their work was done—we might go or stay,
They relapsed to their ancient mood.

LIII

So earth has gained by one man the more,
    And the gain of earth must be Heaven's gain too,
And the whole is well worth thinking o'er
    When autumn comes: which I mean to do
One day, as I said before.

I must also mention the exquisite and mystical *Last Ride Together*, which has, not absurdly, been called his greatest poem. Then above all there are the two poems to his own wife—the peerless *One Word More*—too long, and I trust too well known to quote—and the dedication of *The Ring and the Book*, not to her memory, but to herself alive in another world.

A Ring without a posy, and that ring mine?

O lyric Love, half angel and half bird
And all a wonder and a wild desire—
Boldest of hearts that ever braved the sun—
Took sanctuary within the holier blue,
And sang a kindred soul out to his face,—
Yet human at the red ripe of the heart—
When the first summons from the darkling earth,
Reached thee among thy chambers, blanched their blue,
And bared them of their glory—to drop down,
To toil for man, to suffer or to die,—
This is the same voice; can thy soul know change?
Hail then, and hearken from the realms of help!
Never may I commence my song, my due
To God who best taught song by gift of thee,
Except with bent head and beseeching hand—
That still, despite the distance and the dark,
What was, again may be; some interchange
Of grace, some splendour once thy very thought,
Some benediction anciently thy smile:
Never conclude, but raising hand and head
Thither where eyes, that cannot reach, yet yearn
For all hope, all sustainment, all reward,
Their utmost up and on,—so blessing back
In those thy realms of help, that heaven thy home,
Some whiteness which, I judge, thy face makes proud,
Some wanness where, I think, thy foot may fall!

One of Browning's most unique gifts, if not one of his greatest, is his power of bringing one face to face with the sublime when one least expects it. I will quote one instance from *Aristophanes' Apology*:

So, swift to supper, Poet! No mistake,
This play; nor, like the unflavoured " Grasshoppers,"
Salt without thyme! Right merrily we supped,
Till—something happened.
             Out it shall at last!
Mirth drew to ending, for the cup was crowned
To the Triumphant! " Kleonclapper erst,
Now, plier of a scourge Euripides
Fairly turns tail from, flying Attike
For Makedonia's rocks and frosts and bears,
Where, furry grown, he growls to match the squeak
Of girl-voiced, crocus-vested Agathon!
Ha ha, he he!" When, suddenly a knock—
Sharp, solitary, cold, authoritative.

" Babaiax! Sokrates a-passing by,
A-peering in for Aristullos' sake,
To put a question touching comic law? "
No! Enters an old pale-swathed majesty,
Makes slow mute passage through two ranks as mute
(Strattis stood up with all the rest, the sneak!)
Grey brow still bent on ground, upraised at length
When, our priest reached, full front the vision paused.

" Priest!"—the deep tone succeeded the fixed gaze—
" Thou carest that thy god have spectacle
Decent and seemly; wherefore I announce
That, since Euripides is dead to-day,
My Choros, at the Greater Feast next month,
Shall, clothed in black, appear ungarlanded!"

Then the grey brow sank low, and Sophokles
Re-swathed him, sweeping doorward: mutely passed
'Twixt rows as mute, to mingle possibly
With certain gods who convoy age to port;
And night resumed him.

But greatest of all his gifts is the creation of character. He never
depicts development of character; so far as there is any in his plays
it goes on between the acts : Strafford, for instance, is a different man
in every act—but we never see the change take place. Browning does
not shed the steady light of day on his characters, but the intenser
flash of lightning. For a moment they are revealed, naked and surprised : the conventional veils are stripped away : there are no villains
so black as Browning's villains; yet just because the villainy is completely depicted, the purpose of it is shown too. The subject is not

elaborated logically, but revealed imaginatively; but the resultant creed is the same. Evil is necessary to the existence of good, says the logician, by the law of contradictories : evil exists indeed to be over-come, but if there had never been any the world would not have been better, but worse. Evil is necessary to the existence of good, says the poet : "but for Guido, Pompilia might have remained a soulless beauty, and Caponsacchi would probably have become a dilettante cardinal."

The patience of the Society—to say nothing of my stock of lauda-tory epithets—must be coming to an end. There is, however, one subject which Browning has treated in so remarkable a manner that I must say a little about it. On the subject of old age we can have no doubt of Browning's own opinions. Browning shows wonderful sympathy with this subject, especially with the labours of an old man for a coming generation which will enjoy the fruit of them when he is gone : perhaps I have a special personal sympathy with this, but I am tempted to quote the Pope's pathetic description of himself and his toil :

> Again there is another man, weighed now
> By twice eight years beyond the seven times ten
> Appointed over-weight to break our branch;
> And this man's loaded branch lifts, more than snow,
> All the world's cark and care, though a bird's nest
> Were a superfluous burthen : notably
> Hath he been pressed, as if his age were youth,
> From to-day's dawn till now that day departs,
> Trying one question with true sweat of soul.

The same sympathy appears in the exquisite close of *A Death in the Desert*, to which we shall come in a moment. There are three very great poems which, as I believe, deal with this subject—*Childe Roland to the Dark Tower came, Rabbi Ben Ezra*, and *A Death in the Desert*. About the first there has been some dispute : indeed it has been the cause of vast quantities of literature, and every writer has a notion of his own as to the meaning. I shall assume, however, for the present that what it *does* mean is the experience of old age, where many fail, but only perseverance is needed for success and attainment. Man is represented as a traveller, who has come to a dreary and desolate tract, which becomes as he proceeds more and more full of horrors : he half doubts his instructor of the way, but still holds on. The description of the desolation is really blood-curd-ling; the only variety in the unending plain is a stream he has to ford; but this is only a source of new terrors: for

> While I forded—Good Saints, how I feared
> To set my foot upon a dead man's cheek,
> Each step, or feel the spear I thrust to seek
> For hollows, tangled in his hair or beard!
> It may have been a water-rat I speared,
> But ugh! It sounded like a baby's shriek.

But still he holds on, till at last he comes to a valley shut in by rugged hills, and in the middle of it the Dark Tower. Here it is that most relics are found of previous adventurers who gave up hope at the last moment, and so perished; and these are now ranged on the hillsides to witness one more failure; but that was not to be. The traveller will not give up now. The ideal of his life, that had seemed so glorious in youth, turns out to be prosaic enough now that he has reached it. But it is what he has lived for.

> There they stood, ranged along the hillsides, met
> To view the last of me, a living frame
> For one more picture! in a sheet of flame
> I saw them, and I knew them all. And yet
> Dauntless the slug-horn to my lips I set,
> And blew. *Childe Roland to the Dark Tower came.*

In *Rabbi Ben Ezra* whose last line,

> Let age approve of youth, and death complete the same,

might be called the text of the whole, we have the ethics of old age; it is too well known to need any explanation or praise from me; the first stanza really contains the germ of all that afterwards appears in the poem :

> Grow old along with me!
> The best is yet to be,
> The last of life for which the first was made;
> Our times are in His hand
> Who saith " A whole I planned;
> Youth shows but half; trust God : see all, nor be afraid."

If in these two poems we have the experience and ethics of old age, both of them optimistic in their conclusion, and one of them throughout, then in *A Death in the Desert* we have the religion of old age. It is an elaboration of the same thought which the Pope expresses in *The Ring and the Book*, when he speaks of himself as

> This grey ultimate decrepitude,
> Yet sensible of fires that more and more
> Visit a soul in passage to the sky,
> Left nakeder than when flesh-robe was new.

Now, just for the sake of contrast, let us look at two exquisite passages in Blougram's *Apology*; Blougram is clearly in middle life, or at any rate is not yet a really old man : and for him faith means a victorious struggle with unbelief; once he says that unbelief might be all very well if it were possible : but it is not.

> Just when we are safest, there's a sunset-touch,
> A fancy from a flower-bell, some one's death,
> A chorus-ending from Euripides,—
> And that's enough for fifty hopes and fears
> As new and old at once as Nature's self,
> To rap and knock and enter in our soul,
> Take hands and dance there, a fantastic ring,
> Round the ancient idol, on his base again,
> The grand Perhaps! We look on helplessly.

So again later on the Bishop states the other side of the case :—

> Pure faith indeed! You know not what you ask;
> Naked belief in God the Omnipotent,
> Omniscient, Omnipresent, sears too much
> The sense of conscious creatures to be borne.
> It were the seeing Him no flesh shall dare.
>
> .   .   .   .
>
> With me, faith means perpetual unbelief
> Kept quiet like the snake 'neath Michael's foot,
> Who stands calm just because he feels it writhe.

If we now contrast with this the words of Browning's St. John, as he dies in the desert, we may realize how genuinely Browning has caught the spirit of the author of that stupendous First Epistle : " I write unto you, fathers, because ye have known Him that is from the beginning. I write unto you, young men, because ye are strong! " In Blougram at his best there is a sense of conscious effort : but with St. John, in *A Death in the Desert*, the effort is passed; he knows; and his only thought is how to give to others some glimpse of the truth that is breaking with so much glory on himself.

> And how shall I assure them? can they share—
> They who have flesh, a veil of youth and strength
> About each spirit, that needs must bide its time,
> Living and learning still as years assist,
> Which wear the thickness thin and let men see—
> With me who hardly am withheld at all,
> But shudderingly, scarce a shred between,
> Lie bare to the universal prick of light?
> Is it for nothing we grow old and weak,

We whom God loves? When pain ends gains ends too.
To me that Story, ay that Life and Death,
Of which I wrote—" It was "—to me it is—
Is, here and now : I apprehend naught else.

I cannot refrain from reading the close of this poem : there is nothing like it; criticism is useless :

" Such is the burthen of the latest time.
I have survived to hear it with my ears,
Answer it with my lips : does this suffice?
For if there be a further woe than such,
Wherein my brothers struggling need a hand,
So long as any pulse is left in mine,
May I be absent even longer yet,
Plucking the blind ones back from the abyss,
Though I should tarry a new hundred years !"

But he was dead; 'twas about noon, the day
Somewhat declining : we five buried him
That eve, and then, dividing went five ways,
And I, disguised, returned to Ephesus.
By this, the cave's mouth must be filled with sand.
Valens is lost, I know not of his trace;
The Bactrian was but a wild childish man,
And could not write nor speak, but only loved.
So, lest the memory of this go quite,
Seeing that I to-morrow fight the beasts,
I tell the same to Phoebas, whom believe !
For many look again to find that face,
Beloved John's, to whom I ministered,
Somewhere in life about the world; they err,
Either mistaking what was darkly spoke
At ending of his book, as he relates,
Or misconceiving somewhat of this speech
Scattered from mouth to mouth, as I suppose.
Believe ye will not see him any more
About the world with his divine regard !
For all was as I say, and now the man
Lies as he lay once, breast to breast with God.

This naturally leads to a subject of which I have said nothing and shall say very little; but it must be mentioned. For to Browning the climax of history, the crown of philosophy, and the consummation of poetry is unquestionably the Incarnation; belief in which inspires much of *Saul*, most of *Karshish*, almost all of *A Death in the Desert*, and the whole of *Christmas Eve* and *Easter Day*. The fullest expression of it is put into David's mouth as the climax of his song before Saul :

As Thy love is discovered almighty, almighty be proved
Thy power, that exists with and for it, of being beloved!
He who did most shall bear most; the strongest shall stand the most weak.
'Tis the weakness in strength that I cry for! my flesh that I seek
In the Godhead! I seek and I find it. Oh, Saul, it shall be
A Face like my face that receives thee : a Man like to me
Thou shalt love and be loved by for ever : a Hand like this hand
Shall throw open the gates of new life to thee! See the Christ stand!

It is in some such way as this that the great doctrine is always handled by Browning, and he is never tired of bringing us back to it : for so, and, as he, perhaps rightly, held, so only—" so the All-great is the All-loving too "; and this is no solitary truth struggling for supremacy with other truths—it is itself the sum total of all truths, and if once realized will take the place of experience, of thought, nay of worship itself.

Why, where's the need of temple, when the walls
O' the world are that? what use of swells and falls
From Levites' choir, Priests' cries, and trumpet calls?
That One Face, far from vanish rather grows,
Or decomposes but to recompose,
Become my universe that feels and knows.

This is our great prophet's highest message to men.

I fear I have spent too long in discussing Browning's treatment of various subjects, but it is necessary that something be said of a more general nature. And first, there is a heresy to be crushed—a heresy of deep subtlety and of the blackest venom. For the right faith is that Browning is primarily a great artist; by which I mean that so far as form and matter can be separated, his greatness is due to his form and not to his matter. Or—as form and matter are in the last resort identical, and nothing that has been said in one way can ever be said again, without alteration, in another way—let us rather say that Browning's greatness lies not in his thought but in his imagination. He is not a logician, but a poet. Sometimes people try to excuse Browning for writing what they consider bad verse because he was a great thinker; he himself satirizes this in *The Inn Album*:

That oblong book's the Album; hand it here!
Exactly! page on page of gratitude
For breakfast, dinner, supper, and the view!
I praise these poets : they leave margin space;
Each stanza seems to gather skirts around,

And primly, trimly, keep the foot's confine,
Modest and maid-like; lubber prose o'ersprawls
And straggling stops the path from left to right.
Since I want space to do my cypher work,
Which poem spares a corner? What comes first?
" Hail, calm acclivity, salubrious spot! "
(Open the window, we burn day-light, boy!)
Or see—succincter beauty, brief and bold—
" If a fellow can dine On rump steaks and port wine,
He need not despair Of dining well here—"
" Here! " I myself could find a better rhyme!
That bard's a Browning; he neglects the form;
But ah! the sense, ye gods, the weighty sense!

To excuse a poet's form in consideration of his matter is an
absurdity to which the British mind is prone. The Greeks knew that
reality and significance lie in the form, the ἰδέα, and not in the
matter, so far as the two are separable. But English goes so far the
other way that it speaks of " mere form," and has even invented a
verb " to matter," meaning " to signify." The phrase, " that does
not matter," is the *ne plus ultra* of philistinism. Now, of course,
Browning had some logical capacity—but not much; for instance,
the logic of *La Saisiaz, qua* logic, is ludicrous in its crudity; he deliberately asserts that he knows the existence of a thing, of whose
essence he is totally ignorant. And he had no logical originality at all;
I expect that from one end of Browning to the other there is not a
single conception which, so far as its logical content goes, has any
claim to originality. Nearly all his power, and quite all his originality, is imaginative and not logical. One of his greatest poems is
Cleon; the logical content of that is simply that intellectual pride
may lead a man to reject Christian doctrine even though it contains
the solution of his doubts and difficulties—not a very original or
abstruse thesis : the greatness of the poem lies in the dramatic presentation of the keen artistic temperament of Cleon, of his genuine
horror of old age and death.

The horror quickening still from year to year,
The consummation coming past escape
When I shall know most and yet least enjoy;—

all this followed by his contemptuous rejection of St. Paul's teaching—

Certain slaves
Who touched on this same isle preached him and Christ,
And, as I gathered from a bystander,
Their doctrine could be held by no sane man.

Then the reader says, " How splendidly original; I never thought of that before." But many other people had both thought of it before and said it before; the point is that they did not say it well enough; their art was at fault; and the old truth had to wait till the consummate artist gave it an effective form, and then for the first time it was realized by the public. Or we may say truly that no one ever said before what Browning says in *Cleon*; but that is not because the logical content is new—it is as old as the Church : but this is, strictly speaking, not part of the poem at all—it is only what the poem is about.

The poet's function is to take what we call brute facts, " The earth and every common sight," and fling upon them " The light that never was on sea or land, The consecration and the poet's dream." But that light transfigures and transforms, and the subject in the poem is different from what it was outside the poem, in consequence of the imaginative treatment; so it is here and not in the thought that the originality of Robert Browning should be sought. But the poetic originality of Browning goes further than this; he not only gave effective expression to truths not effectively expressed before, but to do this, as was indeed necessary, he actually invented several poetic forms. The forms of *Paracelsus*, of *Pippa Passes*, of *Ferishtah's Fancies*, of *The Ring and the Book* are absolutely original, and no one has yet been found to regret their invention.

What about roughness and lack of polish? Browning wrote many bad lines; but it is a mistake to suppose that he shares that distinction with Wordsworth alone. Every poet, except possibly Spenser, has many bad lines. Browning could not indeed have written Keats' *Ode to a Nightingale*, or such a stanza as this—

> Peace; come away : the song of woe
> Is after all an earthly song :
> Peace; come away : we do him wrong
> To sing so wildly; let us go.

Browning could not have written that. But what other poet could have written *Karshish, Cleon, Saul*, or *Ferishtah's Fancies?* Or, to take works of a lower order, but perfect in their kind, *Master Hugues of Saxe-Gotha*, and *The Heretic's Tragedy?* Sometimes I think it is forgotten what a very great amount of smoothly flowing verse Browning wrote: the rougher style was new, and so struck people as more characteristic. It is very often regarded as a lordly carelessness, but that is a thoroughly false view. Browning's roughness is, as a rule, both deliberate and artistic. Let me again refer to that miracle of beauty, *The Flight of the Duchess*. We do not call

a mountain " grand in spite of its ruggedness," or a thunderstorm
" magnificent in spite of its irregularity."

Browning's art is of the Turneresque order. Or rather, to state
plainly what I believe to be the truth, it is the first application to
poetry of the principles of Gothic art. That is why I said at first that
" in many ways he does not answer to the ordinary conception of
a poet." All poetry hitherto had been Greek; Browning's is Gothic.
In an old Norman Church or Early English Cathedral you will find
a rich effect produced from the decoration of the capitals and other
suitable spaces: if you inspect this decoration closely, you will find
that it consists largely of grotesques hideous in themselves, and at
first sight irrelevant to the building. Poetry had hitherto followed
the severe lines and accurate proportions of a Greek Temple; in
Browning, and simultaneously in Walt Whitman, it emancipated
itself as architecture had done long before, and broke into the " laby-
rinthine lawlessness of a Gothic Cathedral." The reason for the
comparative delay was, of course, that the Gothic nations needed
houses and temples before they learnt Greek; but, by comparison,
they did not need poetry, and so poetry felt the Greek influence
more strongly. Now, no one accuses a Gothic gargoyle of irrelevance;
and when once Browning's method has ceased to surprise, no one
will object to the corresponding excrescence in poetry. On the contrary, it will be welcomed, for it is more lifelike. The universe, so
far as we understand it, is not a symmetrical orderly thing at all;
and it cannot be finally expressed in the Greek categories. For every
work of art is nothing more nor less than a complex predicate—the
predicate whose subject and copula are the two words " Life is ";
only so has it any meaning. And the Gothic method supplies a truer
predicate than the Greek, just because it can harmonize incongruity
without abolishing it.

This leads to another point: Browning is the greatest of all realists.
He has no belief that some things are significant and others insignifi-
cant: everything is brimming with significance. And so he writes
his great epic, not about a Titanic war between east and west, nor
about a war in heaven and the consequent origin of evil, but about
a peculiarly sordid police case, in which he finds the whole horror
of sin and the whole truth of God. And not only so, but he has
ceased to believe that his own is the one and only point of view.
Bishop Blougram and Mr. Sludge have each a point of view from
which their conduct is reasonable if not justifiable; even Guido
Franceschini has a point of view from which his villainies look
venial: and each must be allowed to state his own case before any
verdict is given. But this involves a terrible unveiling; Chesterton

says truly that there is nothing weakly sentimental in Browning's universal sympathy—" it is as merciless as the mercy of God." But every detail is allowed its full significance; every point of view deserves its own expression. Browning does not, in the manner of some realists, crowd his canvas with masses of details that mean nothing; he extracts full measure of meaning from every one, and this because he is a fearless optimist. There are indeed pessimistic sayings, as where he tells us in *La Saisiaz* that " Sorrow did, and joy did nowise—life well weighed—preponderate." There are poems like *Halbert and Hob* where he seems to have found an evil that is really incurable. But on the whole he is an optimist. All that exists has good in it; and not only so, all that exists—even the worldling and the liar—stand in direct relation to God and trust confidently to Him. This is Browning's greatest paradox, and it is his greatest truth.

But poetry so unconventional and aspiring can never be popular: however far short of the standard one may fall oneself, one can yet see that before a man can fully appreciate Browning he must be artist enough to be free from artistic prejudice, moralist enough to transcend all moral canons, Christian enough to believe the hard saying that God's perfection is shown precisely in His making His sun to rise alike on the evil and on the good, and in His sending rain alike on the just and on the unjust. Even the British public might one day learn the secrets of Gothic art; but it will always regard Browning's idealism as dangerous, even when it understands it, which is still a far-off consummation. Perhaps the public will never understand him; for it has got abroad too soon that Browning is a great man, and the public looks for its own views in great men, and consequently finds them. So the public will read his poems, but it will never read him; and with that pathetic testimony to his supreme greatness we must do by him as he did by his own " Grammarian," and

" Leave him, still loftier than the world suspects
Living and dying."

(An essay read at Balliol, 1904)

Religious Experience

THE FOLLOWING is the full text of the sermon preached at Manchester Cathedral on Sunday morning [July 6, 1914] by the Rev. William Temple, Headmaster of Repton School, Rector-designate of St. James's, Piccadilly:

" Nicodemus answered and said unto Him. How can these things be? Jesus answered and said unto him, Art thou the teacher of Israel and understandest not these things? " St. John iii, 9, 10.

Nicodemus had come secretly to our Lord and introduced himself with compliments. " We know that Thou art a teacher come from God; for no man can do these signs that thou doest, except God be with him." He occupied an important position in the Jewish Church; his influence with the authorities would be of the greatest possible help to the new movement; and he could help more if he did not declare himself, for if once he did that he would have taken sides, and so lost his influence with opponents and authorities alike. Surely the Leader of the new movement will welcome him and urge him to continue his timely interest.

THE POWER OF THE SPIRIT

No, not a bit of it; Nicodemus is told that unless he is ready to break with all his traditions he will never have a glimpse of what the new movement is aiming at. " Except a man be born anew, he cannot see the Kingdom of God." Nicodemus says that such a fresh start in the middle of an established career is as utterly impossible as a literal physical rebirth; " How can a man be born when he is old? Can he enter a second time into his mother's womb and be born? " But the answer is that the new birth is perfectly open to him. John the Baptist had made public baptism in the Jordan the outward sign of sin confessed, of repentance, and of expectation of the Kingdom of God; and our Lord's disciples, several of whom had formerly been disciples of the Baptist, were administering the same rite. Nicodemus could make public profession of his belief that the new teaching was from God by submitting to baptism; he could be " born of water." That, however, would not be enough; the change which he thought impossible would be wrought in him by the Spirit of God if he would submit to its influence. That Spirit moves as it will; its origin and

57

goal are unknown; it cannot be led along the channels of organized religious observances; it is like the wind which blows none knows whence or whither, but whose sound we hear and whose breath we may feel if we will but go out of doors. " Except a man be born of water and of the Spirit, he cannot enter into the Kingdom of God. That which is born of the flesh is flesh; that which is born of the Spirit is spirit. Marvel not that I said unto thee, Ye must be born anew. The wind bloweth where it listeth and thou hearest the voice thereof, but knoweth not whence it cometh and whither it goeth; so is everyone that is born of the Spirit." But for Nicodemus that makes matters worse; he knew the means of Grace; the Law of Moses was Divinely instituted; what is meant by this uncontrollable force which moves at its own direction in the world? " Nicodemus answered and said unto Him, How can these things be? " And our Lord turns to him in amazement. "Art thou the teacher of Israel and understandest not these things? Verily, verily I say unto thee, We speak that we do know and bear witness of that we have seen." For the Lord and His disciples this power of the Spirit was a fact of familiar experience, and He asks in wonder how any man who professes to teach religion can be ignorant of it. For the Lord and His disciples religion was first and foremost not doctrine, whether traditional or rationalist, and not ceremonial; it was first and foremost a personal experience.

Discipline and Service

The great mark of most of the religious thought of our own day is its constant appeal to religious experience. But that term is itself very largely misunderstood, because in the great mystical Saints, who are the clearest examples of that experience, it reaches a pitch of development and of detachment from other concerns which makes it seem something with which the ordinary man—even the ordinary devout man—has no personal acquaintance. As with the Holy Grail, the vision is granted to a Galahad and one or two beside, but the quest is only for the few. Now, of course, it is true that the great mystic has a particular joy which no other has in like degree; but so has the great philosopher and the great artist and the great musician and the great poet. And each of these has a contribution to make which no one else can make to the whole welfare of mankind, to the building of the Body of the Christ. But we all enter into their peculiar joy in our own degree. And while we admire these men for their great gifts and powers, we do not regard the gifts themselves as meritorious; moral merit is to be found in the study which develops the gift or in the use that is made of it, but not in the gift itself. Just so it is with religious experience in that vivid form which is rightly called mystical. Some people are blessed with the faculty for such experience; and while we admire the gift, we find no moral excellence in it. That is to be found in the discipline that cultivates it and the service of God and man that springs from it.

GIFTS AND THEIR VALUE

In the Church at Corinth to which St. Paul wrote his letters there were people who prided themselves on their religious experience; they had spiritual gifts; they could prophesy, and work miracles of healing: they could fall into ecstasy in which they uttered unintelligible sounds which others, under the influence of the same emotion, could interpret. It appears that they had asked St. Paul which of these were the more excellent gifts, and they were themselves inclined to rank highest those that seemed most unusual. And St. Paul answers their question by asking what gifts are of most service to the community; these are the most desirable. But in the middle of the argument he impatiently breaks off and changes his whole style as he insists that all such gifts are mere instruments, good or bad according to the use made of them, and having nothing specifically Christian about them. " Desire earnestly the greater gifts: and a still more excellent way show I unto you. Though I speak with the tongues of men and angels and have not charity, I am become sounding brass or a clanging cymbal." The brass and the cymbal are not mere instruments of noise, they are the accompaniment of the revels of Dionysus. You may have all the spiritual gifts there are, says St. Paul, but if you have not love or charity, you are no more a worshipper of Christ than of Dionysus. St. John deals with any self-centred religious experience with even greater trenchancy: " If a man say, I love God, and hateth his brother, he is a liar." There is then no merit and no peculiar Christianity in mystical experience as such; that experience is a gift, like a capacity for poetry or music, and its moral value depends on the use that is made of it.

THE USES OF EXPERIENCE

And yet the poet and the musician keep alive in us something that we value greatly and should lose without them. They reveal to us a beauty in the world which is really there, but which, apart from them, we should have passed by: their keener faculties catch the fleeting glory, and fix it so that our duller powers may apprehend it and appreciate it. And so we enter into their experience. So, too, the mystic and the saint keep alive a side of human nature which in ordinary men is often near to perishing. They hear the voice of the wind of the Spirit as it blows none knows whence or whither, and they interpret what they hear into the language of our duller faculties, so that through them our spiritual instincts, sluggish, perhaps, by nature, and almost paralysed by the duties or the pleasures of life, are kept alive and nurtured, and in our degree we make their experience our own. We may never have had visions or trances, nor any thrill of conversion or assurance of acceptance, but we have said prayers when we knew that we were heard; we have asked for guidance and received it; we have made surrenders of our wills to find that in that act we most fulfilled them. But such a catalogue of isolated events can never exhaust or explain what we mean by our religious experience. These are merely the outstanding moments in a life which tries to see the world and act in it as though with the eyes and will of God. This attempt, half-hearted as it usually is, yet brings with it not only in moments of exaltation, but in the gradual crystallization of conviction, an assurance of its own essential rightness, which is hard to communicate or to justify, precisely because it is built up of numberless occurrences, some unnoticed, almost all of them unremembered:

> He who has felt the Spirit of the Highest
> Cannot confound nor doubt Him nor deny;
> Yea, with one voice, O world, though thou deniest,
> Stand thou on that side, for on this am I.

To ask a religious man why he believes in God is like asking a happy man why he enjoys life. No verbal answer can be given. But if we live in that man's fellowship, or in the fellowship of a society of such men, which is what the Church ought to be, we may catch the secret by sympathy. Yet this trust, whose foundation is vague just because it is so widely laid, is of the same stuff as the vivid intuition of the Saints, and from them we shall learn its nature more clearly than from ourselves.

THE NEED FOR GOD

Every branch of man's activity leads him towards God; and yet not all of these together make up religion, without something more besides. The intellect at its furthest flight is found pronouncing that the whole universe is one, and one by virtue of the intellectual coherence of the whole; but it can only guess at the Omniscient Mind which alone could grasp that coherence. Art, concentrating contemplation upon its creation, claims therein to offer satisfaction to the soul; but it can only meet its own claim in so far as it presents what is adorable, when the contemplation passes into worship. Duty ends in the command that we should love our neighbours as ourselves, a command that we cannot even set out to obey unless the voice of duty is for us the voice of the Father of all men Who loves all His children, and our neighbour is seen in the light of our Father's purpose for him. Knowledge, art, duty—all are waiting for something which shall perfect each and bind them each to other. But they only show the need for God; they do not show that God exists to meet the need.

THE SEARCH FOR GOD

Men seek God by the way of knowledge; but at the end of the road they have only formed a conception of Him; they have not met with Him. Men seek God by the way of beauty, but at the end they have not found Him; they have only formed a yearning which no beauty on earth can satisfy. Men seek God by the way of conduct; but they only find a law from which they infer a Law-giver; God is still hidden. If we begin without God and try to find our way to Him, we shall at best reach a vague Pantheism, which will only satisfy if we read into it a personal intercourse for which in strict logic it has no room. That is, indeed, what many do; having some real religious experience but not recognizing it for what it is. They suppose that they have begun without God and have also ended to their full satisfaction without God, when, as a matter of fact, they have been with Him all along.

STARTING WITH GOD

But when the religious experience is recognized for what it is, whether it come in the form of visions or intuitions, or in the form of a gradually crystallized conviction or habit of mind towards life, it is recognized as something overmastering. Art sometimes appears so to the artist; but to the religious man invariably his religion becomes, not something which he uses, but something that uses him. And therein it becomes terrifying. We find ourselves confronted with a God, or it may be fleeing from a God, Who demands every moment of our time, every tittle of our energy. We do not yet trust Him to give us all we need, and fear to make our submission absolute:

> For though I knew His Love who follows,
> Yet was I sore adread
> Lest, having Him, I must have nought beside.

We know His Love; we recognize His claim. Yet we fear He would break us in the using, and we still flee on " from those strong Feet that follow, follow after ":

Ah! must—
Designer infinite!—
Ah! must thou char the wood ere thou canst limn with it?

But at last we find—so all the Saints assure us, though for ourselves
we have not found it yet—that all, whose loss we feared, is not lost
but found when we find Him, and can only be found there. Knowledge and beauty and goodness will all at last be his who starts with
God:

All which thy child's mistake
Fancies as lost, I have stored for thee at home;
Rise, clasp My hand and come.

The Wind of the Spirit

Now no man is entirely without such intercourse with God; for no
man is utterly without love. " God is Love; he that loveth his brother
abideth in God "—and that, whether he knows it or not. This is
the centre of the Christian revelation. " He that hath seen Me hath
seen the Father "; " God is Love." And herein for the first time
Heaven, which is the presence or fellowship of God, becomes
accessible to all men. Not only spiritual athletes, not only heroes of
moral rectitude, but weak and futile men who have any love in their
hearts and therein already experiencing in some measure the intercourse with God, whose full measure is the goal of man's existence.
How, then, can we foster this germ of the life Divine which is in all
of us until we recognize and yield to its imperious claims so that it
shall become the dominating force of our existence? There is no one
way. " The wind bloweth where it listeth." But we know from its
sound where its breath may be felt. Let us place ourselves there and
open the lungs of our souls to receive it. We hear the passing of the
wind of the Spirit in all those aspirations which are the source of
the unrest of our day; in the claim for a recognition of real personality in those who have often been regarded as only "hands"
of their employers; in the demand for more widely diffused education, so that all the sons of civilization may enter upon their rightful
inheritance in the realms of literature, history, science, and art; in
the drawing together of religious bodies under the desire for that
unity among His disciples for which Christ prayed before the
Passion. In these and many other movements of our time we hear
the movement of the Spirit. Let us be careful not to stand aside while
it passes by, but to be in the full rush and tumult of its onward
sweep. But if we submit to the Spirit's impetus only in active work
we shall forget that He is the Spirit of God and become deaf to much

that He would teach us; just as if we listen only in prayer and meditation we shall forget that He is the Spirit of Love going forth to all men, and so, too, become deaf to much that He would teach us. But we must pray for the spirit of devotion in our work, and work for the realization of the petitions in our prayers. That alone is the way of saintliness. One man can only realize a little of the whole truth of God, and only the whole and completed Church Catholic can grasp it in its entirety, but it is the life so lived which has in it that religious experience by which in the end all doctrines must be tested, and from which in the end the solution of every problem comes.

(The *Guardian*, July 9, 1914)

The Godhead of Jesus

MY APPROACH to the momentous subject which has been allotted to me in this series of lectures must be determined with reference to the subjects allotted to other lecturers. It is inevitable that I should to some extent trench upon their several provinces; and, in particular, I must occupy some of the ground allotted to Canon Storr, who is to lecture on the Incarnation. But each of us has a subject which it is hard to handle within the limits of one lecture, and it would therefore be a waste of precious time if I were to discuss fully points which are to form the main theme of subsequent lecturers. I am bound to fix the limits of my subject so as to observe this principle. Consequently I must omit all reference to, or at least all serious discussion of, many matters which would naturally find a place in a lecture on the Deity of our Lord if there were no other lectures to follow in the same series. But I shall endeavour to deal with three main topics: first, our confession of the Deity of Jesus Christ and the grounds for it; secondly, the resultant modification in our conception of God, or, in other words, the doctrine of the Trinity; thirdly, the mode of the union of God and Man in Jesus Christ. In this third section I am plainly dealing with the Incarnation but I cannot handle my own subject without touching the question, "How is Jesus Christ God?" I shall not at all deal with the question, "How is Jesus Christ Man?" In other words, I am attempting to deal with the matter which was in dispute in the Arian controversy, not at all with those in dispute in the Apollinarian, Nestorian, or Eutychian controversies.

I

We turn first to the record given in the New Testament of the growth of the disciples' understanding of our Lord. The main point which will emerge is that spiritual appreciation always preceded dogmatic formulation. At no point is the doctrine imposed by authority upon merely acquiescent minds.

The first disciples inevitably began by thinking of their Master as a man; yet from the first there was in Him something mysterious which was the starting point for a fuller apprehension. There were strange sayings uttered by John the Baptist which had attributed to Him such powers as a man could hardly exercise. His teaching had

64

both a graciousness and an authority that seemed hard to reconcile with His supposed origin. His wonderful works exceeded what was known of contemporaries or recorded of any in past times except the greatest. After a period of specially close intercourse with Him they were ready to follow St. Peter in acknowledging Him as the promised Messiah. But this is still far short of a confession of His Deity. In our day many people identify the terms superhuman and divine. They think that if in our Lord besides humanity there was something more than humanity, that something must be Divinity. But this is quite a baseless assumption, and the Jews did not make it. What, from the scene at Caesarea Philippi onwards, the Apostles certainly believed is that their Master was more than human in the sense in which we are human. The Messiah was at that date conceived as a superhuman and celestial Being, who might properly be spoken of as in a peculiar sense the Son of God; but He was not conceived as Divine in such a fashion as would lead to his being spoken of as God the Son. St. John, whom I believe to be the author of the Fourth Gospel and an eye-witness of what he narrated, records an exclamation of devotion by St. Thomas after the Resurrection which contains the whole Christian doctrine, but this remains an isolated utterance, and the theology implied by it was not yet intellectually grasped. If the Apostles reflected at the time on the saying, " I and the Father are one," they would remember that He justified that saying by a reference to the Psalm where those to whom the word of the Lord came are dignified with the Divine title. He claimed to be the revelation of God, but the disciples who heard Him say, " He that hath seen Me hath seen the Father," only reached, before the Passion, at any rate, the confession that He was one sent by God (St. John xvi, 30). Our Lord's language did not necessarily imply that He claimed to be Himself Jehovah. And if it had, we can see that it could only have baffled and perplexed their minds. They were Jews with all the Old Testament behind them; it needed more than a verbal claim to persuade them to ascribe to a man Divine honours.

This is still the doctrinal situation in the first days after Pentecost. In the speeches of St. Peter in Acts ii–v, there is still no suggestion that Jesus, the prophet of Nazareth, is identified in the speaker's mind with the God of Israel. He is the Anointed—the Christ—of God; He is exalted to be a Prince and a Saviour; but He is not presented as Himself God.

This is still true of St. Stephen; but here we see a change beginning. St. Stephen is not only the first martyr, but the first Christian of whose death we have any record. The vision of Jesus at the right

hand of God does not necessarily carry us beyond the celestial
Messiah of contemporary apocalyptic literature. But the words which
follow imply something more than that : " Lord Jesus, receive my
spirit." Every Jew knew the words of Psalm xxxi, which our Lord
Himself had uttered on the Cross, though by adding the word
" Father " He had given them a new note of intimacy : " Father,
into Thy hands I commend my spirit." But here the first Christian
to die commends his spirit to Jesus. It is a devotional, not a dogmatic
utterance; but its implications will need a whole theology to state
them. It is a devotional equation of Jesus with the God of the spirits
of all flesh. It is characteristic of the growth of Christian theology
that religious experience should precede dogmatic formula. Indeed,
it is just because of this that Christian theology is a veritable science.

It was St. Stephen, and the movement with which he was associated, who freed Christianity from the limitations of Judaism. It is
scarcely possible to doubt that St. Stephen was the chief human
agent in the conversion of St. Paul. Certainly the form of Christianity
to which St. Paul was converted was that for preaching which St.
Stephen had been stoned. But at first his doctrinal position is not
distinguishable from that of St. Peter's early sermons. We must
remember, however, the spiritual antecedents are different. St. Peter
had been with the Lord in His earthly ministry; he had walked with
Him in the cornfields; he had sat with Him in the boat upon the
lake; he had supped with Him among His friends. For him the risen
and ascended Christ is chiefly the Man whom God exalted to be a
Prince and a Saviour. St. Paul had probably never seen the Lord
till on the Damascus road his eyes were blinded by the dazzling
light, and he heard the voice which said, " I am Jesus whom thou
persecutest." For him the Christ who died upon the Cross is first
and foremost the celestial Messiah, who even in the earliest epistles is
associated with God in the opening greetings as a source of grace
and peace.

Here, too, experience comes first. There is the experience of the
conversion itself; following on that comes the realization of reconciliation to God by fellowship with Christ; resultant from that comes
the apprehension that in Christ is found the explanation of history
because He is the revelation of the Father's will and the agent of its
fulfilment. It would be impossible to construct a theological system
which should do justice to all the elements in St. Paul's religious
experience without affirming the Deity of Christ. But St. Paul,
though a man of supreme intellectual penetration and grasp, was
not in his Epistles writing systematic theology. It was never his
primary concern to give an intellectually satisfying account of his

whole religious experience and conviction; and it is not quite certain that he ever used the word " God " as a title of Jesus Christ. But he often comes so near to it that it is only for purposes of almost pedantic accuracy that we can distinguish between what he does say and such an explicit confession. He says that " in Christ dwelt all the fullness of the Godhead bodily "; he says that Christ existed before the Incarnation " in the form of God "; he says that Christ is " the image of the invisible God "; he says that " God was in Christ reconciling the world unto Himself." Only the Trinitarian position can theologically do justice to such expressions. But it is true that he seldom, and perhaps never, said in so many words that Jesus Christ is God. The punctuation of Romans ix, 5, is doubtful; the reading (as well as the authorship) is doubtful in I Timothy iii, 16; and the doubts affect the very question at issue. Personally, I am quite convinced that on some occasions at least the word " Lord " (Κύριος) as applied by him to Jesus Christ is to be interpreted as meaning an identification with Jehovah. It is only possible to escape from this and from the Trinitarian implications of the phrases already quoted by a series of unnatural interpretations. But those interpretations are not absolutely impossible, and if we are being scrupulously exact we cannot say that beyond all doubt St. Paul identified Jesus of Nazareth with the God of Israel, though we are entitled to say that the alternative view which involves a frequent straining of language can hardly be correct. After all, the familiar words with which II Corinthians closes ("The grace of our Lord," etc.), especially when we pay attention to the order of the phrases, cannot be interpreted on any theory which does not attribute to Jesus Christ the dignity of God Himself. In short, I am entirely convinced that St. Paul fully believed in the Deity of our Lord; it is certain that, even if he had not formulated this belief to himself, his faith can only be articulated by Trinitarian theology; but this faith is usually expressed in the language of spiritual function and experience, not usually, and just possibly never, in a specific theological declaration.

The Epistle to the Hebrews exalts Christ above the angels, and attributes His pre-eminence to His inheritance as Son of God. Possibly the quotation from Psalm xlv in Chapter i, verse 8, is intended as an attribution of Deity to the Son, but here, too, there is a doubt about the interpretation. St. Paul and this author hold a religious position which absolutely necessitates the doctrine of the Deity of Jesus Christ, and far the most natural interpretation of their language maintains that they themselves accepted and affirmed this doctrine. But it is not possible to say with absolute certainty that they did so. And, indeed, if the doctrine of our Lord's Godhead had been specifically affirmed in very many of the New Testament Scriptures, the Arian controversy could never have arisen within the Church. The phrase " Athanasius contra mundum " reminds us that the great upholder of what we now rightly regard as the central and funda- mental article of the Christian Faith was for a time in a minority even among his brother bishops; and this would not have been possible at all if many of the Apostolic writings had been fully explicit.

And yet some of them are surely explicit. It is impossible to doubt the doctrine of the Johannine books. In the Apocalypse the associa- tion of the heavenly Christ with the Eternal and Almighty Father is so close that no doctrine short of the affirmation of His Deity can be said to express it; and in xxii, 13, the Christ is represented as claiming in His own Person the most supremely distinctive title of Almighty God, which the Almighty had used of Himself in i, 8. But the whole book intervenes. Christ is revealed as God through the seer's experience of His exercise of Divine functions, and only then is He presented as Himself the Almighty God.

In the Johannine Gospel and General Epistle the position is at last explicit, and is stated from the outset. He Who tabernacled among men under the name of Jesus is the eternal Word of God, Himself God, the Agent of creation. To be " in Him that is true " is the same thing as to be " in His Son, Jesus Christ " (I John v, 20). And of this God, who is one with Jesus Christ, it is said : " This is the true God and eternal life." Every supposed god except this God is an idol.

What is the upshot of this rapid survey of the New Testament Scriptures? It is that our faith in the Godhead of Jesus Christ does not rest chiefly on any single text or group of texts; it is a faith to which men found themselves irresistibly impelled by their growing spiritual experience as in the fellowship of the Holy Ghost they more and more deeply apprehended the grace of our Lord Jesus Christ and the love of God. We have not here a perplexing dogma imposed by authority upon men's reluctant minds; what we have is a trium- phant discovery based on experience as all scientific truth must be based. They use religious and devotional language which completely implies the doctrine of the Godhead of Jesus Christ before they state that doctrine in set terms. The experience comes first; the formula- tion comes later. That is a spiritual law, and our Lord always observed it. If He had made a claim of Deity in absolutely unmis- takable terms, He would have fallen under His own saying, " If I honour Myself, My honour is nothing," and He would have put mere intellectual apprehension before spiritual realization. And even so He would have hindered, not helped, intellectual apprehension. If, standing before them in the flesh, He had said to those devout Jews, " I am God," He would have reduced them to mere bewilderment. Therefore, though the claim is there, as we shall see later, its verbal expression is always so interwoven with the spiritual activity that it did not at first challenge the critical or merely intellectual understanding of the disciples. To this topic we must return. For the moment it is enough to say that an unquestionable declaration by our Lord would have largely robbed faith of its spiritual value. If St. Peter had proclaimed his Master as God directly after Pentecost, his authority would no doubt have weighed greatly with later disciples of the same Master. But far more weighty and cogent than any such impulsive declaration is the process that we actually see going on in the experience of the Apostles and of the infant Church At every stage the same principle is at work. Men trust and find themselves "justified " (to use St. Paul's favourite word) in trusting; as they trust more deeply the vindication becomes more complete. They become aware that Jesus Christ does what only God can do. The functions which He discharges are functions of God.

No man ever yet knew the substance of any actual thing. What we know is never substance, but always activity. It may be only the activity of reflecting light into our eyes or of stimulating our sense of touch; but actions and reactions are all we know. If Jesus Christ performs the acts of God, then Jesus Christ is God in the only sense in which any name can justifiably be attributed to any object. The method by which in the New Testament the supreme affirmation is reached is the only method by which any such affirmation could be scientifically justified.

There are some who feel that if it was by such a process, lasting through half a century or more, that the full and conscious belief in our Lord's Deity was reached, it may have been the product of a sort of self-hypnotism. The early believers would tend to exalt their Lord, and the process continued until they had set Him on the throne of the universe. But this objection ignores the actual conditions. Greeks might deify Heracles; Romans might deify the Caesars; because for them deification only meant admission to a Pantheon which contained a large number of other deities, each of them quite finite, with certain known interests and even with certain known defects. But the Apostles were Jews. For them to acclaim their Master as God was to recognize in their Friend the One Eternal and Almighty God. They did not say that He was one among other gods, as each of us is one among other men. They learnt to see in their Friend and Master the One Almighty, the One Eternal, the One

Uncreated, the One Incomprehensible. There was not, and there could not be, the smallest natural tendency to such a result. The recognition of Him as Messiah would make the result itself not easier, but more difficult, for Jehovah and the Messiah were in Jewish thought two beings and not one. Therefore, long before the doctrine is actually affirmed, we find the experience on which it rests. Before the last journey to Jerusalem the Apostles already regarded their Lord as superhuman. From St. Stephen's martyrdom onwards we find a realization of His relation to men's souls, which involves His Deity. St. Paul uses phrases which are only just short of the formal assertion of His Deity, and probably did formally assert it on one occasion at least (Romans ix, 5), while on others he identifies Jesus Christ with Jehovah by his use of the title " Lord." When St. John proclaims the doctrine in explicit language, he has added nothing of substance to what was already there; he has only formulated it. The doctrine is truly a formulation of experience.

But it is also inevitably more than that. The belief in the Godhead of Jesus Christ is not the mere identification of Jesus with Jehovah as known to the writers of the Old Testament. Rather it is the enlargement and enrichment of the thought of God by the necessity of making room within it for what men had learnt concerning God through the teaching, and still more through the Life, Death, and Resurrection of Jesus Christ. To this modification of the thought of God we must now turn.

II

The fundamental note in the Jewish conception of God was Unity. The dogma, " The Lord our God, the Lord is one," does not mean merely that, as a matter of fact, there is no other being who may fitly be called God. It rests on the fact that the Divine attributes are such as to exclude plurality. There cannot be two All-rulers. Poly-theism has always to allocate different spheres or departments to its various deities. When once God has been conceived as the Almighty or All-ruler, the bare notion of a multiplicity of Gods becomes impos-sible. It was natural and even necessary that this unity should at first be apprehended in its pure simplicity, free from any thought of distinction within it. But as soon as men had learnt to see God in Jesus Christ, problems arose to which the doctrine of the Trinity offers, not indeed a solution, but a formula of elucidation.

God is known as All-ruler; Jesus was limited in His action by the response that He could evoke. God is known as the All-knowing; Jesus experienced disappointment. If Jesus is God, then there are in the very Being of God elements which could not be combined in the experience of any one person conceived by the analogy of our personality. The men who were confronted with this problem had also the experience which led to the doctrine of the Holy Spirit as a Third Person in a Divine Trinity; but with this we are not now concerned except so far as it explains why the distinctions within the Unity are three and not only two.

The Being and Life of God surpass our powers of comprehension. Christian theology is, in this sense, emphatically agnostic. It constantly declares that God is above and beyond our knowledge. But it does not on that account admit that any one proposition is as true about Him as any other. The world as we see it exists in grades; and it is the destiny of each to be controlled by what is higher than itself; indeed, only as this happens does each grade reveal its own latent capacities. Thus matter is controlled by life, and reveals hitherto unsuspected qualities; life is controlled by mind, and reveals hitherto unsuspected qualities; mind is controlled by spirit, and reveals hitherto unsuspected qualities. Highest of all these grades is Personality. As known to us this may not be the last term. But it affords the best analogy we have for the Most High. We shall think of Him more accurately when we think of Him in terms of Personality than in any other way.

Now this Divine Personality cannot (as we saw) be the Personality of one Person only if it is true that God is seen in Jesus Christ. Yet there is assuredly one God and no more. The simple Christian need not go beyond this affirmation : " The Father is God, the Son is God, and the Holy Ghost is God. And yet there are not three Gods, but one God." But our task today is to understand this so far as we may.

What is it that constitutes the distinction of one person from another? And how far is this distinctness compatible with real unity of Being, or (to use the technical term) of Substance? It seems to me that we are distinguished from one another by two principles. One of these is essential; it is the mere numerical difference in the centres of consciousness themselves. I, in being myself, am not you; you, in being yourself, are not I. We are distinct selves. We may hold the same opinions, share the same experience, aim at the same goal; but we do it together and remain distinct. The other principle is accidental. I am the child of my parents, a native of my country, a member of my school and university; these things are not mere external appendages to my personality, but actually make it what it is. And any two finite persons, living under the conditions of space and time, will be distinguished for ever by the variety in the circumstances of their history. Even two twins can never have quite the same experience. They may stand side by side as they look at a mountain; yet they see it from slightly different angles. Even if they change places, the order in which they see it from the two angles of vision will be different.

Clearly these differences, which I have called accidental, are due to the conditions of our finitude. If we conceive centres of consciousness capable of envisaging the totality of things and themselves immune from the conditions of time and space, differences of this kind would vanish. But the other differences would remain. What we should then have would be three centres of one consciousness.

It is not possible to introduce as a parenthesis a complete disquisition on the doctrine of the Trinity. For our present purpose it is enough to say that this doctrine, like that of our Lord's Deity, rests on experience, and is an attempt to present in the most intelligible form that our minds can reach the various elements in the Being of God which are disclosed by Christian experience. There are problems concerning the relation between the Eternal Life of God and the temporal occurrences of the Birth, Death, Resurrection, and Ascension of God Incarnate, which time requires that I should either omit or handle only in the merest outline. In any case, such matters must be dealt with if at all when we have returned to the consideration of the Gospel record of Jesus Christ, as that is illuminated by the enriched conception of God which the Gospel itself has enabled and impelled Christians to form.

III

When we attempted a survey of the Gospels before it was to gauge the understanding of Jesus Christ which His disciples had reached at various stages. Now we turn back to the historic figure portrayed in the Gospels and ask how far we find there a basis for the faith which sprang up in the infant Church, and what light the record throws on the problem which that faith creates, the problem how Jesus Christ is God.

The first point to which I would call attention is the fact that the Synoptic evangelists are obviously concerned with history, and not with theology. No doubt they tell the story with a religious aim in view; no doubt they tell it, each according to the spiritual needs of those readers whom he has chiefly in view. But their concern is with history. So, to take the most signal instance for illustration, the facts of our Lord's Passion are minutely told, but there is no attempt to indicate a doctrine of the Atonement. The Synoptists are concerned to tell a story; what light does the story throw on our inquiry?

The earliest of the Gospels—St. Mark's—is plainly designed to suggest that with John the Baptist, and still more with our Lord, Divine power came into the world. His first words are : " The beginning of the Gospel of Jesus Christ, the Son of God." The words " Son of God " do not, as we have seen, necessarily imply Deity, though, of course, they are compatible with it. But they certainly imply something more than mere humanity. Our Lord never relies on His miracles as evidence for men's faith in Him to rest upon, but this only makes the more impressive the picture of power proceeding from Him in works of love as He moves about among men.

Again, there is that perfection of intercourse with the Father which every careful reader of the story notices. A man in the midst of the sinful world who is never separated from perfect communion with God is a miracle quite as great as any of the recorded wondrous works.

Further we note that explicit claim to be the Judge of all men and of all nations—surely a divine function. And we recall the untroubled confidence with which He substitutes for the Mosaic Law His own legislation as its fulfilment, though He not only admits but even insists upon the divine authority of the Mosaic Law. He calls the law divine, and alters it. In this He does not state a doctrinal theory of His own Person, nor even indicate that such a theory is in His mind. But He does, without either arrogance or incongruity, what only God can fitly do.

But besides this there are words of direct claim to be the Mediator between God and men. " All things have been delivered unto Me of My Father; and no one knoweth the Son save the Father; neither doth any know the Father save the Son, and he to whomsoever the Son willeth to reveal Him " (St. Matthew xi, 27; St. Luke x, 22). Those words, with their markedly Johannine ring, belong to what the critics tell us is the very oldest and safest strand of evidence— the non-Markan matter which is common to St. Matthew and St. Luke. But they are associated as such utterances always are, with spiritual experience. Both evangelists associated them with the words about revelation unto babes, and St. Matthew further associates them with the invitation, " Come unto Me," which is virtually their translation from the language of theology into the language of practical religion. Anyhow, the claim is not made as a claim, but rather in exposition of a spiritual experience, and it is so phrased as to be intelligible to those who recall it in the light of a fuller insight, but hardly intelligible to the Apostles as they first heard the words. We note this feature again in St. John's Gospel.

Did He ever make use of powers that are altogether outside the reach of ordinary man? The question is hard to answer, because we

simply do not know what power would be possessed by a man who
was, and always had been, in perfect fellowship with God. It is
narrated that St. Peter was able to walk on the water until his faith
gave way to fear. But perhaps at the stilling of the storm, and perhaps
at the Transfiguration, and certainly (as I should say) at the feeding
of the multitude, He displayed powers beyond those of men, however inspired. It is noticeable that when He stilled the storm He did
not pray to His Father, or invoke the Divine Name; He spoke as
the Lord of the elements, and we recall the bewilderment of the disciples at His doing so.

We turn to St. John's Gospel. It has long been my conviction that
the supposed contrast between the teaching of the Synoptists and of
St. John does not really exist. The two pictures are to some extent
supplementary, but they represent a Figure recognizably identical.
In St. John there are more frequent references to the unbroken
fellowship with the Father, but nothing that in principle goes further
than the passage already quoted, " All things have been delivered
unto Me of My Father," unless it be the words, " I and the Father
are one." And even these words are uttered, not primarily for their
theological significance, but in justification of an equation in spiritual
religion already implied : " No one shall snatch them out of My
hand," " No one is able to snatch them out of the Father's hand."
The claim, moreover, is itself justified by the reference to Psalm
lxxxii, which, as we saw, prevents it from being a dogmatic assertion
of absolute Deity.

The total impression, strong in the Synoptists and permanently
vivid in St. John, is that which St. John expresses in his Prologue :
" We beheld His glory, glory as of an only begotten from a Father."
Through the human life there worked a power which was felt as
coming from beyond, from God Himself, Who here had found His
uniquely perfect self-expression.

Can we then penetrate at all the consciousness of Jesus Christ in
the days of His earthly ministry? Let us make the attempt, remind-
ing ourselves that just in the degree in which we accept the Church's
account of Him we shall expect to find ourselves unable to reach any
clear understanding of His Person.

Christian theologians have tried in various ways to represent the
Incarnation in the language appropriate to the thought of their day.
As we set out upon the same attempt let us remember that no one
theory has or can have the stamp of orthodoxy; and no theory is
heretical or heterodox unless it denies that Jesus Christ is both
Perfect God and Perfect Man.

First, then, let us be sure that the Incarnation was a reality and not a sham. He who lived among men and died on the Cross was the Second Person of the Eternal Trinity. But the life He lived on earth was a real human life, subject to all limitations that are the lot of humanity, and subject also to all temptations, save only such as arise from sin committed in the past. (This, I am sure, is the true meaning of Hebrew iv, 15.) He grew in knowledge as He grew in stature, and learnt by the same processes by which other men learn. But He was aware of the intimacy with God which He found that other men had not experienced. He interpreted this as a call to fulfil the promise of the Messiah who should come. The Voice that hailed Him at His Baptism called Him to begin the Messianic work. He comes among men healing and teaching, calling to repentance and proclaiming the Divine Kingdom which it was the function of the Messiah to found. The Divine is working through the human, and normally at least within its limitations. His prayers are real prayers. The agony in Gethsemane is a real agony, and the prayer then uttered is a real cry of humanity to its Creator. But all the while through the human channel comes flooding the Divine love and power and knowledge of the souls of men. He is conscious that He is something more than one sent by God. He knows that He is in the Father and the Father in Him. As He approaches the glory of the uttermost sacrifice, He remembers a like glory which had been His, before the world was (St. John xvii, 5). As the human personality reaches its complete development—being made perfect by suffering —it reveals itself as having never been the ultimate fact about this human life. Behind it, working through it, utterly expressed by it so far as human nature allowed, but transcending it as Godhead transcends humanity, is found the Divine Word Himself. In order to live and die and rise again as Man he had subjected Himself to all the conditions of our life. He had, as St. Paul said, "emptied Himself." We shall be wrong if we infer that during those years the Second Person of the Trinity was denuded of those Divine attributes for which there is no room in a human life. We have no data enabling us to draw inferences of that kind. What we may justly say is that from that moment there is in God not only a sympathic under-standing of our state and of death itself, but a real experience. He Himself hath suffered being tempted. This, I expect, is the impression left on the open-minded reader of the Gospels. They tell the story of a human life; but humanity is not the last word about it. He who so lived is not self-occupied or concerned with doctrines of His own Person. But spontaneously and with conscious appropriate-ness He does what only God can do. At times, as spiritual occasion arises, the implications of this come vividly before His mind. He is

F

not self-analytical, but self-revealing; and the Self that He reveals is more than human, more than superhuman—it is specifically divine.

And so, if it is true that God lived a human life, we know about God what otherwise cannot be known. We know His love in a way that is otherwise impossible. For first, His coming at all is a supreme act of love. We may say that the love was there before He came, and the reality of sacrifice which is self-giving. But self-giving is an act, not a mere state. If He has not given Himself as a matter of historic fact, He may be ready to do it, He may be going to do it some day; but it is because He has done it that we are sure of His readiness to do it. And further, if God lived this life, then in this life we have the one adequate presentation of God—not adequate to the eternal and infinite glory of God in all His attributes, for that would be unmeaning to us even if it were offered, but adequate to every human need, for it shows us God in the terms of our own experience. To me, at least, all spiritual experience finds in this act of God its focus and pivot, and those of us who have had the privilege of being brought to a belief in it find here the comfort of all sorrows, the grace that is sufficient, the basis of faith, the fountain of hope, the well-spring of love towards God and man.

(From *Fundamentals of the Faith*; four lectures delivered in Manchester Cathedral, January–February 1922)

Symbolism as a Metaphysical Principle

It is abundantly clear that one of the chief characteristics of contemporary philosophy is the place which it gives to the concept of Value. There is nothing unprecedented in this. Indeed it is not possible to give a higher place to Value than Plato did when he made the Good the supreme principle in reality or required of Anaxagoras that, in order to illustrate the supremacy of Reason, he should prove the earth to be either round or flat by showing which it is better that it should be. Aristotle, whom no one has yet censured for sentimentalism, similarly clinches his argument for the Unity of God or the governing principle with the maxim and the quotation: τὰ δὲ ὄντα οὐ βούλεται πολιτεύεσθαι κακῶς. "οὐκ ἀγαθὸν πολυκοιρανίη· εἷς κοίρανος ἔστω." But though not unprecedented, the prominence of Value in the thought of our time is characteristic. To the religious thinker, it is welcome. And yet there is a remarkable indefiniteness in the current use of the term, and the relation of Value to Reality or Substance is by most writers either not discussed or is very sketchily outlined. The aim of this paper is to offer a very small contribution to the discussion of these questions.

I

The structure of Reality, as it presents itself to us, seems to be as follows : It consists of many grades, of which each presupposes those lower than itself, and of which each finds its own completion or perfect development only in so far as it is possessed or indwelt by that which is above it. This seems to involve an infinite regress, and suggests an infinite progress. Whether there is in fact a lowest and a highest term in this scale of finite existences I do not know, and I do not greatly care. In a book of mine called *Mens Creatrix* I have tried to show that the infinite series is not necessarily meaningless in logic or futile in ethics. At present I am not concerned with the problem of lowest and highest terms, but with the facts before us, which may fall midway between such terms. I am rather tabulating impressions than constructing a system, though the tabulation is of interest because it suggests the principle of a system. To make my present meaning clear it will be enough to take the broad divisions : Matter, Life, Mind, Spirit. These grades may be for our present purpose indifferently regarded as various entities or as different modes of action and reaction. Matter is itself a term covering many grades; so is Life. But each has sufficient identity in itself and sufficient distinctness from the others for the requirements of the argument.

The term Matter is here taken to cover the substances or the modes of action and reaction which are studied in the sciences of Physics and Chemistry. It is at once quite clear that those sciences give no account of the self-movement which is one characteristic of Life, or of the comprehension of spaces and times which is one characteristic of Mind. The lower cannot explain the higher. But that is not all. The living organism has in its material constitution a unity of differences, a subtlety of co-ordination, a spontaneity of adaptation, that no knowledge of Physics and Chemistry would enable the observer to anticipate. The material only reveals its full potentialities when Life possesses and indwells it. The later development reveals what had all along been potential in the earlier; but no knowledge of the earlier apart from that development would have made possible a prediction of the development. Matter only reveals what it really is when Life supervenes upon it.

Similarly Life only reveals what it really is when Mind supervenes upon it. No study of zoology and biology will enable the student to predict the occurrence among living things of Shakespeare or Bach or Leonardo or Newton. The use of faculties, which at first are used for mere survival, in the interests of ends that have nothing at all to do with survival, must occur in fact before it can be anticipated in theory. So too Mind as intellect only shows what it can be and do when it is guided by Mind as Spirit. The existence of Art and Science, though they make upon Life an absolute claim, will not account for the self-sacrifice of the hero or the martyr. And, if Religion is to be trusted, even Spirit (as known in our experience) only reveals what it can be and do when it is possessed by that Highest Being, whom we call Spirit because Spirit is the highest grade of Reality known to us.

We begin then with the conception of Reality as existing in many grades, each of which finds its own completion or perfect development only in so far as it is possessed or indwelt by that which is above it. But we then notice that each depends for its actuality upon those which are below it. Matter itself as experienced by us can be reduced to what is simpler than itself, whether to α, β and γ particles or still more ultimately to Space-Time. Life is unknown apart from living organisms, which are Matter informed by Life. Mind is unknown except in reasoning living organisms. Spirit is unknown except in conscientious, reasoning, living organisms. Whether the higher grades can exist apart, there seems to be no means of deciding; in our experience they never do.

Thus we see each grade dependent for its existence on the grades below, and dependent for its own full actualization on the grade or grades above. Such seems, apart from any theory of its origin or *raison d'être*, to be in fact the structure of Reality.

II

At this point I must ask leave to assume that when we ask for an explanation of the Universe as a whole we are bound to formulate the answer in terms of Will. To summarize very briefly the argument by which I should seek to justify this assumption, I would submit that there is in our experience one, and only one, self-explanatory principle—namely Purpose or Will : no doubt, if anyone can believe in a purpose with no will behind it, we should have to say " Purpose " only, leaving " Will " as a precarious inference; but as it appears that Purpose and Will are terms that mutually imply each other, we may speak of either indifferently. There is a " problem of evil," but there is not in the same sense any problem of good. When we find as the cause of any phenomenon an intelligent will which chose to cause that phenomenon to occur, we raise no further questions, unless we fail to see how that will came to seek this occurrence as good. We may be puzzled by the way a man exercises choice; but our problem here is not as a rule a problem of efficient causation. When we sympathize, we are not puzzled. If I say of anyone " I cannot understand acting like that," I do not mean that I cannot give a psychological analysis of the motives of the action; I mean that I cannot imagine myself doing it. When in the causal regress we arrive at a will, the regress is at an end, and to understand means, not to give a casual explanation, but to sympathize. We have reached an ultimate term. And when we do sympathize, our mind raises no more questions. The only explanation of the Universe that would really explain it, in the sense of providing to the question why it exists an answer that raises no further question, would be the demonstration that it is the creation of a Will which in the creative act seeks an intelligible good. But that is Theism. Theism of some kind is the only theory of the universe which could really explain it. Theism may be untenable; if it is, the universe is inexplicable. Merely to show how it fits together as a rational system does not explain it, for we are left still asking—why does it exist at all? When once that question is asked the answer must be found in Theism or nowhere.

I need hardly say that I do not advance this outline argument either as the only defence of Theism or as a sufficient intellectual basis for it. The whole body of argument that is articulated by Professor Pringle-Pattison and Professor Sorley in their Gifford Lectures, or by Mr. Matthews in his recently published Boyle Lectures, is here presupposed. But the point which I have just mentioned, and which deserves more attention in my judgment than it generally receives, is the one most germane to the group of considerations with which we are now specially concerned. Other arguments seem to establish the principle that the universe must be interpreted by spiritual rather than by mechanical or other materialistic categories. Other arguments tend to establish the ethical character of the spiritual power or powers that govern the world. Philosophically everything is ready for Theism. But actual belief in a living God rests primarily, as I think, on religious experience, and finds its intellectual support in the reflexion that this belief is capable in principle of supplying an explanation of the very existence of the Universe, which no other hypothesis available to us affords any hope of doing. That is no proof. It cannot be laid down as an axiom that there must be some explanation of the existence of the Universe. If the existing scheme of things be internally coherent, it cannot be said that the mind imperiously demands more than this for its satisfaction. It is true that we have to choose between postulating a rational universe and accepting complete scepticism. It is not true that we have to choose between theism and scepticism. I should be very sorry to have to believe that Reality is what Mr. Bradley describes or even what Professor Pringle-Pattison describes. But I could not reject their accounts of it only on the ground that they do not explain its existence as a whole. For while it is an additional advantage in any theory if it can do this, it is not fatal to any theory that it should fail to do this, or even refuse to attempt it. It may be that there is no explanation of Reality itself, and that it is not self-explanatory except in the sense that all its parts support each other in constituting the whole. Or, again, it may be that there is an explanation of Reality, but that it is something wholly inaccessible to the mind of man. There seems no reason to suppose that mind, in its human manifestation, either includes, or itself is, the last term in cosmic evolution, and if there is more to follow, then though human mind would comprehend the lower forms it would not know at all what constituted the higher forms, and it would be in these, not in human mind, that the explanation of Reality might be found.

None the less, if there is an available hypothesis which is capable in its own nature of supplying the explanation of Reality, it is thoroughly scientific to experiment with it and see if it can make good its claim. Now Purpose, as the expression of a Will, is such a principle. But to seek the explanation of the Universe in a Purpose grounded in a Will is Theism; it is the acceptance, provisionally at least, of the doctrine of God as Creator. From religion there comes abundant support for this doctrine. To some religions, and notably to the Jewish and Christian religions, it is essential and fundamental.

III

Now if we assume the structure of Reality to be such as I have outlined, and if we accept (at least for purposes of enquiry) the explanation of it which Theism offers, certain consequences follow, which it is the main purpose of this paper to trace out.

Will acts always for the sake of value, or good, to be created or enjoyed as a result of the action. It is precisely as so acting that it is self-explanatory and intrinsically intelligible. This would lead us to expect that whatever Will creates is either itself good or is a means to good. Moreover, if what is created is good not (or not only) as a means but in itself, this means that its very being or substance is good. I do not, at present, go so far as to say that good is the being or substance of all that exists, but we are entitled and even bound by the hypothesis adopted to say that whatever exists must either be a means to something which is substantially good or else be itself substantially good. We seem therefore to be led up to a new enquiry into the relations of value and reality.

Now if I may take Professor Pringle-Pattison as an illustrious example of contemporary philosophy, and discuss, not the details of his argument, nor its claims taken as a whole, but the general impression created by it on my own mind, and also (as I find) on many other minds, I would venture to suggest that many of the anxieties with regard to it which that general impression arouses would vanish if he saw his way to a more thorough-going conception of God in terms of Will. For the general impression left on my mind by his great book on the *Idea of God,* and greatly strengthened by his essay in the volume entitled *The Spirit,* is that he accepts the Universe as somehow existing, and then finds that it reveals values, which are regarded all the while as being adjectival to it. That they appear at all is a determinant consideration for the philosopher, and yet they appear rather as appendices of an otherwise existing universe than as themselves its constitutive elements; and when we reach the Being in whom all values are realized, He hovers uncertainly between two positions, being at one time the Ground of all existence and at another a characteristic of a universe which would apparently continue to exist (though shorn of its values) if He were to cease. And it is the latter position to which He seems to be ultimately relegated. I have no doubt that this summary is unjust to Professor Pringle-Pattison. Almost any summary of a theory elaborated with so delicate a balance and an argument so closely knit would be unjust. But at the end of *The Idea of God* I was left with a sense that this book makes God adjectival to the Universe, and the essay in *The Spirit* removed all doubt on the question. And yet I was sure that in the main the Professor was dealing with the matter on right lines and had rendered a great service to philosophy, and especially the philosophy of religion, by following the method which he had chosen.

The question with which I am now concerned is this : should we conceive of things as existing independently and possessing value as an attribute, or should we think of value as itself the true reality which realizes its various forms through embodying itself in things —or through the creation of things for this purpose by the Divine Will?

Now I believe that our difficulty arises from the fact that Philosophy being an intellectual activity, always tends to depend more upon that search for an ultimate value which is conducted in science than upon the two kindred efforts of ethics and of art. In science the intellect is not only supreme but sole; it is natural for the intellect to take the methods and operations of science not only as its method but also as determining the subject-matter of its enquiry. That I take to be the essential feature of the heresy of intellectualism. Philosophy must be intellectual or it ceases to be itself. But the intellect always gets its subject-matter from outside itself; it is ready enough to accept it from the physical world, and from its own procedure and results in dealing with the physical world. It is less ready to accept as the material of its operations the procedure and results of human activities which are either not purely or not at all intellectual. Yet for a satisfactory metaphysic it must include these, and indeed (as I think) must give them a determining influence. The goal of Science is on the objective side Reality, on the subjective side Knowledge; the goal of Art is on the objective side Beauty, on the subjective side Creation and Appreciation; the goal of Ethics is on the objective side Society, on the subjective side enlightened Conscience and dutiful Action. It is apparent that whereas Science ends in Knowledge, which leaves the objective world as it finds it, Art and Ethics—and Religion—aim both at a comprehension of the object and at action which modifies the object. Now if the intellect is led by its own process to the affirmation, or at least to the supposition, that the explanation of the Universe is to be found in the activity of a Creative Will, it must go on to accept those human activities which include some creative energy as surer guides to the constitution of Reality than its own special activity of science.

Starting with the general outlook appropriate to science, philosophers have generally made Reality their substantive notion, while Value has become adjectival. It is quite true that Plato spoke of the Idea of Good as ἐπέκεινα τῆς οὐσίας—which the context proves to mean " above and beyond *objective* being " (*Republic*, VI, 509 *b*); but he does not follow this up by including ethics and politics in his propædeutic studies; he remains under the predominant influence of geometry. So St. Thomas Aquinas is quite thorough in the deliberate and reiterated identification of Good with Being—*Bonum et ens sunt idem secundum rem : sed differunt secundum rationem tantum (Sum. Theol.*, Pt. I, Q. V, A. I)—yet he goes on to treat Being as prior because it is the first object of the intellect, and thereafter the whole concept of Value almost disappears. Consequently his definition of Substance as that which exists of itself—*substantiae nomen . . . significat essentiam cui competit sic esse, idest per se esse (Sum. Theol.*, Pt. I, Q. III, A. V)—never leads him even to consider whether this is not the same as to say that Substance and Good (or Value) are synonymous terms : hence the chief difficulties of his sacramental theories.

But the identity of Substance (so defined) with Value follows inevitably from a thorough-going acceptance of the Theistic hypothesis. The Universe is to be conceived as deriving its origin and unity from a Creative Will. But the correlative of Will is Good or Value; therefore the most fundamental element in things is their Value. This is not a property which they have incidentally; it is the constitutive principle, the true self, of every existent. Aquinas says that a thing is perfect in so far as it exists: *Intantum est autem perfectum unumquodque inquantum est in actu (Sum. Theol.*, Q. V, A. I)—and that everything is good so far as it exists: *Omne ens, inquantum est ens, est bonum (Sum. Theol.*, Q. V, A. III). The inversion of this is the fertile truth: everything exists so far as it is good. Value and value alone is substance or has substantial reality.

IV

It is certainly true that Value is only actual in the various things that are valuable : and it is only fully actual (though this is of no consequence for our present purpose) so far as it is appreciated by some conscious being. And it is tempting to separate the Good from the good thing, and to demand either some account of it in such separation or else a method of apprehending it in separation. But to do this is to repeat the mistake made by the Hedonists in Ethics.

When I am hungry, I want food and not (except incidentally) the pleasure of eating. Desire is not of some one thing, such as pleasure. And yet it is true that when I am hungry what I want is the value or the good of food; but this is not separable from the food, and is not even properly distinguishable from it, though it is distinguishable from other aspects of the particular food in question which are irrelevant to my hunger.

So Will aims at Good in all its forms; and as God makes the world, He beholds it as very good. There is the problem of Evil of course, and it may be that it will wreck this whole fashion of philosophy; but we cannot embark upon the discussion of it here—I can only refer to an attempt to handle it in my book *Mens Creatrix*. Our concern just now is with the method which philosophy must pursue if it adopts this principle that only Value has substantial being.

It is clear at once that Ethics and Politics, and Æsthetics, will be exalted alongside of Mathematics, as the typical activities of Mind, and that on the whole they will be the more normative for Metaphysic. The Universe will be approached less as a problem (or theorem) in Geometry, more as a Drama or Symphony, and as a Society in process of formation.

Now if the structure of Reality is such as we described, and if the problem of Metaphysics is to be approached along the lines now indicated, we begin to see a great unification take place. The lower grades, we said, only attain to the fullness of their own being so far as they are indwelt and dominated by those above them. They exist then, ultimately, to embody or symbolize what is more than themselves. The universe is sacramental. Everything except the Creative Will exists to be the expression of that Will, the actualization of its values, and the communication of those Values to spirits created for the special value actualized through fellowship in creation and appreciation of values. Men can do some of this work themselves. Speech is a manipulation of sounds for just such communication and fellowship. By this doctrine the reality of the objects in the world is not divorced from our sense of their significance. A friend gave me during the war an illustration to show how familiar a fact is the transvaluation, which on this theory is the only true transubstantiation: Suppose a man comes to see me, finds some strips of coloured calico on the floor, and amuses himself by dancing on them to show his contempt for what he takes to be my interests; I may think him a tiresome fellow, but that will be all: now suppose those bits of calico have been sewn together to make my national flag, and he dances contemptuously on it; I shall kick him out of the house.

That is comparatively a trifling instance. In any case the symbolism of a flag is purely conventional. Yet even here it seems absurd to say that the reality of the flag is the same as the reality of the strips of calico. The accidents (as the schoolmen would say) are the same; the substance is changed.

Beginning with such a conventional symbol we may go on to fuller symbolism such as that of great Art. Here the principle emerges that to be a true or (as I have named it elsewhere) an essential symbol, a thing must be itself an individual instance of what it symbolizes. So Othello can symbolize jealousy because he is a very individual jealous man. In great art, at least, the symbol is unique, and there is no other way of saying what the artist has said. In Emerson's great phrase " The word is one with that it tells of." If after reading *King Lear* or hearing the Fifth Symphony a man asks what either means, we can only tell him that each means itself; but that is the extreme opposite of saying that either is meaningless.

In that highest sphere of creative art which we call human conduct, the good or value sought is that of Personality (or Character) in Fellowship, with all the varieties that this implies. Actions have their value as symbolizing and as producing this.

It is clear that as we advance from the purely conventional symbolism, represented by the flag, to the essential symbol of great art or of ethical conduct, the subjective element is reduced in importance, at least so far as it is variable. The Union Jack has value only for those who are familiar with a particular convention; and to those who do know this it may have very different values—for Lord Carson and Mr. de Valera, for example. Yet even here the value is constitutive in so far as the flag is only made for the sake of the value. But in the symbolism of Art and Conduct there is no such variability. Men may still react in varying degrees of intensity to the different embodiments of value; some are more stirred by colour; some more by line; some are more stirred by heroic energy, some more by patient humility. But at this level there is no doubt what is the value expressed in the work of art or the moral action.

If we start with this principle of symbolism as our basis, we shall not, I think, be led to any system very different in its structure from such as is set out, for example, by Professor Pringle-Pattison. The difference will be mainly one of emphasis and of detailed expression; but difference of this kind will be all-pervasive. In ways innumerable the statement will be (as I think) more luminous in detail, more sympathetic. There will be more understanding of the different phases of Reality from the inside. For it is the characteristic of æsthetic and moral appreciation that in them we become absorbed in the object itself, as a single whole, and understand it by letting it take possession of us, whereas in science we understand partly by setting the object in an ever-widening context and learning what forces mould it from without, and partly by breaking it up analytically into its own constituent elements. Of course, our method will not dispense with the processes and results of science; but it will depend quite equally, or rather more, on those of art and morality. We shall not dispense with the psychologist or sociologist; but we shall expect to learn still more of philosophic value from the dramatist and the statesman. We shall still seek rational coherence, but shall interpret it more as realized in the *Civitas Dei* than as represented by the solution of logical contradiction.

Above all we shall avoid two difficulties that are inherent in the other method. We shall not try to treat the merely physical as self-subsistent, leaving values to attach themselves to it in a rather vague manner, while still declaring that the explanation of the lower is in the higher; but making this declaration, we shall insist that the higher are the more nearly self-subsisting, while only the Highest is altogether so. And we shall not leave God to hover uncertainly between His function as the universal ground of existence and His adjectival attachment to the universe as the sum or realization of its values, but we shall confidently affirm Him as the sole self-subsistent Being, existing in absolute independence of all else, for whose pleasure and by whose creative activity all things are and were created.

(Reprinted from *Mind, A Quarterly Review of Psychology and Philosophy*, Vol. XXXI, No. 124)

The Genius of the Church of England

I

OUR CHURCH is in some respects quite peculiar among the Churches of the world; and the briefest expression of her peculiarity is to say that she holds together, in a degree not elsewhere paralleled, the continuous tradition of Christendom from the earliest period through the Middle Ages to the present, and the characteristics of that new birth in Christian history which is called the Reformation. To say this is in itself to say that her name is something more than a geographical description. For this effort to hold together apparently diverging forces is itself typically English, and the way in which our Church has set about it is typically English also. Other nations have other gifts, and the races of Asia and Africa will bring to the treasury of the Universal Church interpretations of the Gospel very largely their own. It is not to be desired that all Churches should come to resemble the Church of England; but it is most desirable that the Church of England should fulfil the destiny which providence, through the processes of history, has marked out for her. And this will only happen if her sons are not content merely to receive her benefits, but seek to understand her character and live by her tradition in all its fullness.

We do not claim, then, for the Church of England that she is a model for others to imitate, but rather that she has her own contribution to make to the wealth of the united Church, for which we pray, just as others have their own contribution for lack of which we should all be poorer. In politics we have ceased to suppose that the only alternatives are an exclusive nationalism and a cosmopolitanism which ignores national distinctions. We all accept today the ideal of internationalism, which regards all nations as comrades and co-operators, but rejoices in their diversity which enables each to bring its own special enrichment to the common life of all. This is, indeed, the principle of the family, where the interest and zest of common life arises from the differences, rather than from the likenesses, of those who share that life. And we are beginning to see that it must be so with Churches also. Reunion, when it comes, will not come by way of absorption (though Rome impenitently clings to that vain hope) nor by mere agreement to differ, but by the mutual understanding and mutual appreciation which make possible a real synthesis of all that is precious in all the uniting traditions.

The Church of England, then, is to be accepted in all the features of its actual historic development. Our loyalty is not to a remote ideal, but to a very definite, even if sometimes definitely vague, historic society. What is involved in such loyalty will be discussed in some respects a little later. But the special danger of any such body as the Church of England is that its members, in their various groups, may attach their loyalty not to the whole society, but to those aspects of its life, or elements in its life, to which they are especially devoted; they call this loyalty to their ideal of the Church, but it is in fact mere concentration on their personal preferences. Actual loyalty must always be loyalty to an actual body, capable of making up and expressing its own mind. If, then, it is true that the Church of England combines what for brevity's sake we may call the Catholic and the Evangelical traditions, and, indeed, that this is its most distinctive characteristic, loyalty to the Church must involve an acceptance of this combination and a desire to maintain it. If a man sets out to be loyal to the Catholic tradition, so understood as to rule out all that is distinctive of the Reformation, he cannot also be fully loyal to the Church of England. If a man sets out to be loyal to the Reformation so understood as to rule out any elements of the Catholic tradition which were not universally retained by the reformed Churches, he cannot also be loyal to the Church of England. The Church of England has always bridged the gulf (or sat on the hedge, if you like) that divides " Catholic " and " Protestant " from one another; no one section can claim that loyalty to its history favours exclusively the tradition of that section.

It has been said that this effort to combine apparently divergent traditions is typically English; and our foreign neighbours often twit us with our power to act on various principles all at once which they find incompatible. They call this illogical, though it would seem that the application of principles within, and not beyond, their proper spheres has as much claim to be called logical as a ruthless pursuit of some one principle to the exclusion of others that are just as relevant. Whether logical or not, the English method has always been to enjoy all kinds of excellence together as far as possible, retaining the glamour and unifying influence of monarchy with the steadying influence of hereditary aristocracy while welcoming the progressive impetus of democracy. Our mixed constitution is only the most conspicuous illustration of an almost invariable national method. It is not a method which leads to the loftiest heroism or to the basest villainies. Joan of Arc and Robespierre would both be out of place in the less highly coloured pageant of English History. But it is a method with its own very solid advantages, and perhaps it is because the normal tenor of our life is even and secure than in our men of genius imagination flies on an even stronger wing than elsewhere. The combination of our normal mediocrity with our unequalled galaxy of poets is no accident. Where the normal is romantic, romance must seek a little normality; where the normal has the security of pedestrianism, romance can soar into the empyrean free from care.

But if the enterprise is English, the way in which it has been attempted is English too. Nowhere was the Reformation accomplished with so little assertion of abstract principles as in England. By individuals indeed they were proclaimed loud enough; but the Church did not commit itself to them except on a very modest scale. Let anyone who doubts this compare the Prefaces to the Book of Common Prayer, the Catechism, and the Thirty-nine Articles with utterances of similar authority in other Churches, Lutheran or Calvinist. Just as in our political life we seldom proclaim general principles of the kind that become symbols of enthusiasm, but rather seek to do on each occasion what seems, all things considered, to be the best in the circumstances, so our Reformers, taken as a body and in their official action, were more concerned to do the best they could for the religious life of England than to advance this or the other special interpretation. Of course, their criterion of what was best was found in Scripture, and the practice or teaching of the Early Church; and as against those parts of current Roman doctrine which they repudiated, they asserted definite principles based on their understanding of Scripture. But their main concern, especially at the vitally decisive moment when the Elizabethan settlement ended the short Marian reaction, was practical more than theoretical; and the guiding conception of their practical policy was the comprehension within our Church of as many as could be or were willing to be so comprehended.

Now it goes without saying that the primary requirement of a Christian Church is that it be loyal to Christ; and just because He is supreme as no other can be supreme, there must be no shadow of compromise between His claim and any other. If, or in so far as, our national tendency to hold all types of thought and currents of feeling in combination has ever led us is practice to put His claims on a level with others, or to seek any adjustments of other claims to His except by way of their complete subordination, that is merely sin, to be confessed as soon as recognized and to be repented of with humiliation and contrition. That neither we nor any other Church in Christendom are free from this sin is certain, and God sends us prophets from time to time to warn us that we are acquiescing as a Church in an outlook which is sub-Christian.

But if we are on the look-out to avoid compromising the claims of Christ, we have no reason to regret or to apologize for the national character of our national Church. We do not claim to be or to do all that the Universal Church is called to be and to do; we cannot possess in its fullness all that the Church of other lands possesses; and we ought to be eager for that full union with all other parts of the Great Church which will enable us to receive all we can of their fullness while imparting to them all we can of our own. But we shall only do our best work for our own country, and we shall only bring our completest gift to the reunited Church, by being to the utmost degree what our history specially and uniquely enables us to be.

The Church of England, like other Churches, has often failed to be completely Christian—always, indeed, if we take those words in all their proper depth of meaning; but it has never failed to be utterly, completely, provokingly, adorably English.

This makes it, like the British Constitution, the despair of the systematizers; and in times of controversy it is sharply called upon to declare its position. Does it hold this view or that? Does it regard this or the other institution which it maintains as necessary to its character as a Church, or only as spiritually valuable or convenient? The Church of England has been slow to answer such questions, because it has steadily believed that those who give different answers none the less can, and ought to worship and work together in one body. It thus loses sharpness of definition, and therewith some of the zeal and zest and effectiveness in immediate action which sharpness of definition promotes. But in every generation it can rejoice in its former refusals to take sides as a body in controversial issues, and therein finds encouragement to persist in its traditional course.

Critics sometimes say that this is tantamount to a declaration that we prefer peace to truth. It would be a fairer account of the Anglican attitude to say that we have learnt from a full experience that nearly always peace is the best way to truth. It is the fact that we commonly put the peace of the Church before our personal convictions; and, just because we do this, our personal convictions undergo modification from the influence of our fellow-Churchmen, for each side in the controversy learns to value what is true and wholesome in the contention of the other. After all, no proposition was ever yet believed in with sincerity by any large number of people except because of some truth latent in it. The way of truth, no less than of charity, is to avoid wholesale repudiation of traditions or schools of thought just because another tradition has a greater proportion of truth, and to weld together as far as may be all the truth in all the traditions. Let individuals or groups within the body contend vehemently for the truth as they see it; that is their contribution to the life of the body; but let them not rend or break the body itself, and let the body rejoice in them all.

II

It is time to turn from these generalizations to the more particular consideration of the main streams of tradition which flow together in the Church of England in a process, still very incomplete, of coalescence.

The great river of Christian tradition has divided into three main streams. But it is well to remember that before its course was fairly begun the Church had already suffered mutilation by the refusal of Israel to accept the Gospel. That refusal led to the Church becoming European instead of European and Asiatic together from the start; and that same fact led to the excessive influence of Greek intellectualism over the moral and prophetic witness of the Church in the formative period of the Church's doctrine, which a strong Hebraic element would have counterbalanced. The European Church suffered two great divisions, the one of East and West, the other of North and South. With the division of East and West we are not now concerned; with the division of the Western Church by a separation of North from South we are very much concerned. For the Reformation involved the loss to the South of the traditional Teutonic local autonomy and so led to the intense modern centralization in the Papacy, and the whole legalistic regimentation to which the Latin genius tends; while it involved the loss to the North of the strong Roman principle of order, and left regional and congregational liberty as the sole possessor of the field, with the consequent infinite divisiveness which we find in American Protestantism.

The Church of England, by deliberate policy and choice, sought to combine the strong elements of both traditions. It has held them in rather unstable equilibrium; they have until lately rather existed side by side than coalesced into a real unity. But both have been there throughout, and in our own time there has been apparent a most manifest drawing together in mutual understanding, appreciation, and even assimilation.

Our Church, at the Reformation, retained the traditional Ministry of the Catholic Church, and the traditional creeds with their confession of faith in the One, Holy, Catholic and Apostolic Church. It made its service book—the Book of Common Prayer—out of the

G

old liturgies and offices. The Order of Holy Communion, in all versions of the Prayer Book, is based on the traditional Orders, of which the Roman Missal is the best known. It was modified in several most important particulars; but it was not a new Order; it was, and is, the old Order revised. Great efforts were made to avoid shocking that conservative instinct which is always strong in English religion. In Faith and Order the Church was to be manifestly not a new Church, but the old Church reformed.

Of course, some felt that the Reformation had changed the essential character of the Church, and remained loyal to Rome. To them and to their successors the Church of England inevitably appears to be a new Church, which began to exist at the Reformation. But it has never so regarded itself, and its answer to such critics is that Rome itself was the defaulter, leaving the standard of primitive purity and allowing superstitious accretions to become attached to the faith of the Gospels. The Church of England did not leap forward to grasp at novelties, but turned back to the Church of the Apostles and Fathers, striving in all ways to maintain their traditions unencumbered but intact.

Thus it sought, and still seeks, to offer to the world and to uphold before the world all that was fine and wholesome in the ancient tradition of Christendom. But its criterion of truth and wholesomeness was derived from the spiritual impetus which gave birth to the Reformation. It is possible to regard that great historic event from many angles. The medieval Church was worldly and corrupt, and the Reformation was a movement for spiritual purity according to the rule of the Gospel. That is the fundamental fact about it. But the form which this movement for spiritual purity took was determined by its whole historic context. If we go back to what is sometimes called the Golden Middle Age—roughly from about 1050 to 1250 or 1300—we find policy and thought alike dominated by the desire to bind all together in the unity of obedience to God. In policy the exaltation of the Papacy and its struggle with the Empire were inspired by the desire to assert the supremacy of Christ and His Rule over all departments of life. No doubt the motives were mixed, and worldly ambition played its part along with zeal for the Kingdom of God; but the latter was truly there. More fundamental is the complaint that the Church then attempted to achieve a spiritual result by essentially unspiritual means, so that the decay and corruption which followed were inevitable results of the method adopted with such lofty aims. Anyhow, this great attempt at politcal and international unification had only a limited success, though it was by no means altogether without success. Far otherwise was it in the field of thought. The great scholastic theologians, notably that supreme intelligence, St. Thomas Aquinas, really achieved a unification of the thought and knowledge of their time, under the sceptre of Theology, the Queen of Sciences, such as has never been regained in any subsequent age. The trouble about this effort was not that it failed but that it succeeded too well. Its very completeness laid fetters upon the intellect of later generations, and when progress came it was as by the bursting of a dam.

In reaction against all this the movement for the recovery of spiritual purity took the form of an insurgence of nationality against an internationalism which had come to be represented by foreign control, and an assertion of individual judgment against an authority felt to be mechanical and tyrannous. The former led to the establishment of the various national Churches. On the whole the Lutheran tradition subjected these to the secular authorities, while the Calvinist or Presbyterian tradition sought to subordinate the secular powers to the authority of the Ministers and Elders. It was a familiar thought in the seventeenth century that Papalists and Presbyterians, Jesuits and Calvinists, were agreed in their view of the proper relations between Church and State, only differing in their notion where the true Church is to be found, while Lutherans, English Royalists and French Politiques united to hold a theory of State Sovereignty, embodied at that time in the essentially Protestant doctrine of the Divine Right of Kings.

The spiritual essence, then, of the Reformation is that it was a movement towards spiritual purity; this characteristic it shared with every great religious revival. Its actual form was determined by three things: first, its appeal to Scripture, as the test of spiritual purity; then the two features determined by the historic circumstances, nationalism in religion and the assertion of private judgment. And all of these are conspicuous in the post-Reformation tradition of the Church of England.

It is not necessary to dwell on the supremacy of Scripture. By that the Church of England stands firmly. Of course, Scripture itself is variously interpreted in different ages according to the knowledge available at any time. But these variations are very slight as compared with the constant witness of Scripture when taken as the supreme standard of doctrine. There we find, first in divers portions and in divers manners (as the writer to the Hebrews puts it) in Law and Prophecy and Psalm, then in the Gospels in its fullness of its splendour, the glory of God's revelation of Himself. And our Church allows nothing to be taught as necessary to salvation but what is grounded in Scripture. There has never been any pretence that there is no true knowledge except through Scripture, as orthodox Islam claimed on behalf of the Koran. Nor is there any denial that it is permissible to teach as pious opinion what goes beyond the Scriptures; but the Scriptures and the Scriptures alone are accepted as the rule of faith for all.

Secondly, the Church of England is national, and allows no foreign dictation in religious matters. If it is open to criticism here it is for being too national rather than for not being national enough. But that fault is finding correction now when the Church of England finds itself the mother of Churches throughout the world, which are more and more leaving behind what was distinctively English in order to commend the Eternal Gospel to the consciences of other races.

Thirdly, the Church of England believes in the spiritual liberty of the individual; that is the full expression for what in the circumstances of the Reformation and its repudiation of an alien authority was acclaimed as private judgment. But it is worth while to remember that what the Reformers insisted on was not the right but the duty of private judgment. Each man, in virtue of that immediate access to the Father which Christ had opened for him, was called upon to exercise his own conscience and to appropriate for himself the truths of revelation and the blessings of the Gospel, not merely to acquiesce in what authority prescribed for him to do and believe.

But to this private judgment the Church of England presents all the treasury of the Catholic tradition and means of grace. It calls upon each member of the Church to determine how he will use these, but it offers them for his use in their completeness. The Anglican note is " You may " in contrast with the Roman " You must "; but the liberty so offered is a liberty to claim all the traditional privileges of the Catholic Church.

Liberty is always beset by temptations. We have to confess that the method of saying " You may " easily encourages slackness; a Roman Catholic who was told that Confession was possible in the Church of England but not obligatory said, " What an easy religion! " No doubt many take advantage of it in that way, and the more military or legalist methods of Rome may get better results out of the given human material in a short while. But there is a sacred principle at stake. Christ seems to have set no limits to His respect for the liberty of the individual in spiritual things; and the reason would seem to be that liberty is the indispensable condition of a truly spiritual response. Our method may be slower, but it alone is capable of reaching the ideal. To the indifferent it affords less stimulus or support, but perhaps this is balanced by the fact that it does not drive them away. To the truly devoted or to the sincere enquirer it is wholesome and bracing to be required to exercise his own judgment and conscience concerning the opportunities which the Church puts before him; and this is what must be the result of maintaining at once the Catholic and the Evangelical traditions.

That those two traditions should invariably be at peace together in one body is not to be expected. Nowhere except in the Church of England do they co-exist in one body in at all the same fullness of strength and conviction. It is inevitable that from time to time the adherents of one or other of these two great streams should wish to follow their own tradition to points which would seem to the other tantamount to breaking the conditions of fellowship. Anglo-Catholics sometimes desire practices, especially in connection with the Eucharistic elements, which Evangelicals find themselves unable to tolerate in a body to which they belong. Evangelicals sometimes desire action, specially in the way of intercommunion with non-episcopal Churches, which seem to Anglo-Catholics a repudiation of the Catholic doctrine of the Church and therefore entirely inadmissible. At such times the questions to be faced are these: Is it really important for the welfare of Christendom that there should be within it a Church specially pledged to the maintenance within one body of both these great streams of tradition? And is a Church with so typically English an aspiration likely to be a good medium for commending the Gospel to the English people? If so, it is worth while for adherents of either party to make at least some sacrifice for the sake of fellowship with the others. In the long run it is found that either the desire itself dies out in those that had felt it, or the resisting party withdraws its resistance; for there is a mind or spirit of the fellowship which ultimately prevails over sectional wishes and judgments, provided that these are not hardened by violence against them.

III

Once more we repeat that the conviction inspiring such a policy or outlook is not that peace at any price is preferable to truth, but that peace among sincere disciples of Jesus Christ is the first condition for learning fuller truth concerning Him.

No doubt this Anglican way is beset with peculiar difficulties. But they are the difficulties of the ideal. It is easy to grasp the various aspects of truth one by one, just as it is easy to cultivate certain virtues (such as the maintenance of a high moral standard) if others (such as charity for sinners) are ignored. But it is very hard indeed to see all sides of truth in a just proportion, or to acquire the whole series of the Christian virtues. Our beloved Church is still learning how to fulfil its divinely appointed mission, and is not always strong at the points where others are strong. But it is learning steadily. Momentary controversies may throw the points of difference into relief and make it appear that the Church is tending towards disruption. Those who are acquainted with its inner life know perfectly well that the permanent movement is steadily towards greater unity. The achievement of greater unity within itself is perhaps at this stage not only the condition of its effectiveness in England but the chief service that it can render to Christendom.

Just because of its comprehensive character it is regarded with the deepest interest by other Churches. Three recent international conferences—at Stockholm in 1925, at Lausanne in 1927, at Jerusalem in 1928—have supplied evidence of this fact. The position which history has given to our Church is one carrying an influence entirely out of proportion to its numerical strength. And the same is true of its strategic position in the campaign of World Evangelization. Partly because of the area covered by the British Empire, but also to an extent for which that does not at all account, we find that the key positions are in the hands of this one Church which seeks to hold Catholic and Evangelical together, each in full development yet each in harmony with the other, and which has learnt in that enterprise something of that secret of spiritual synthesis whereby racial varieties of apprehension may also be welded together in unity.

It is our English custom to belittle what we feel to be our own, and we are shy of glorying in our Church. But when we survey its history, its saints, its theologians, its statesmen; when we consider its expansion through the world and its position in Christendom; above all, when we contemplate the possibilities before it for which it seems to have received a Providential preparation, then we are bound to give glory to God for what He has done, and is summoning us to do, through this Church in which He has called us to serve Him. May He so kindle our devotion that we be not utterly unworthy of our heritage!

(Church Publications Board, 1928)

My Point of View

To state one's point of view with regard to any particular problem or enterprise is usually not very difficult; to state it with regard to life and experience as a whole is difficult, because it is plainly wise to try to see these in every possible aspect, and that seems to involve shifting the point of view as often as possible. But every man who thinks seriously at all must at a particular time have adopted some attitude or other to the age-long problem of the one and the many; either he believes that life is a single whole in which every activity has its own appropriate place in relation to all the others; or he does not. If he does, then either he believes that he knows in some degree its principle of unity, or else his main concern is the search for it; if he does not believe that experience is a unity, then he will find in one or other of its departments his dominant interest—it may be science, it may be art, it may be politics; there is a great variety of possible dominating interests for thoughtful people.

The Medieval Background of Modern Thought

The characteristic of modern thought and life, as distinct from medieval thought and life, has been sectionalism. It is important to see the modern movement against the medieval background, because its distinctive impulse has so largely been one of reaction. The great Middle Ages were a period of unification. The so-called Dark Ages which preceded them had been a time of chaos and disintegration following on the collapse in the West of the unifying power of the Roman Empire. Men were eager to bring purpose and system into life. From this point of view three names are of supreme importance: Hildebrand, who became Pope Gregory VII, Innocent III and St. Thomas Aquinas; and behind these three is the great genius, one side of whose mind supplied the leading ideas of all that period— St. Augustine of Hippo. The name of Hildebrand stands for a great reformation in which he was the central figure. Society was chaotic and the Church corrupt; Hildebrand had the vision of a purified Church giving order to the world. The name of Innocent III stands for the achievement of the Papacy by which this vision was most nearly realized. St. Thomas is the greatest of those scholastic philosophers who provided the intellectual expression of this vision and achievement by mapping out the whole area of thought and action in provinces, each with its own frontier, under the controlling sovereignty of theology, queen of the sciences.

Of course, the practical accomplishment lagged far behind the intellectual scheme. But the conception was a noble one, and the scheme most thoroughly worked out. From our modern standpoint it is open to criticism in two main respects, which are indeed intimately related to one another. Vast as was the intellectual energy and capacity employed in the construction of the scheme, it won its complete unity too easily. The scholastics are not to blame for this. The historic method, and the idea of evolution which goes with it so closely, had not yet become part of the furniture of men's minds; the notion that there were new facts yet to be learnt, new modes of experience to be appreciated, could not weigh with them. We know that our apprehension of the universe is bound to be in one way or another superseded in the generations that follow us; any unification that we attempt will be that of pervading principles, not of a completed system. If a philosopher produced a system of thought which fitted all existing knowledge together, but left no room for any more to come, we should know for that reason alone that he was in error. It was this apparent completeness of the scholastic system which made it resist new knowledge which it could not assimilate. Thus it became a mental tyranny, bound at last to be indignantly repudiated. For this reason also it could not be transformed by perpetual readjustment. When experience outstripped it, it could only break up.

The other failure was part of this. In the intellectual scheme of the Middle Ages we do not watch the progressive unification of experience by the apprehension and articulation of its own principles, revealed by its successive stages; we see a unity imposed from above by deductive argument from theological propositions, which were not themselves regarded as open to criticism or revision. And this is the intellectual counterpart of the use of persecution for preventing the growth of varieties of belief which would, as was supposed, be fatal to the unity of social and political life. It is true that St. Augustine had employed the text " compel them to come in " as a justification of persecution. But not even his great influence could have led to the Albigensian crusade or the Inquisition, if persecution had not belonged so closely to the prevailing habit of mind. And here it is possible and necessary for us to censure that habit of mind. For it supposed itself to assume the supremacy of Christ; and if one thing is more conspicuous than another in the teaching and practice of Christ, it is His absolute refusal to infringe the liberty of the individual. All response was to be free, and if no free response was forthcoming He would seek no other.

THE RENAISSANCE OUTLOOK

Whatever finally caused the Renaissance, its character is clear. It was a movement of emancipation. The significance of Machiavelli is not his lack of moral principle, but his quite clear assumption of the autonomy of politics as a sphere outside the control of theology. He made the State an object of man's allegiance, but left nothing to which the State's allegiance can be given. And in this all civilized nations have followed him, though illogically shrinking from his perfectly correct conclusions. Art began in practice to claim a similar autonomy. Science and philosophy equally set out upon their own investigations, ready to accept the conclusions to which their own processes conducted them. For a long time there was some acknowledgment of a universal sovereignty in God; but this became steadily weaker as an effective influence, until at last religion, which had been the public and universal concern *par excellence*, came to be regarded as of all private concerns the most intimately private, an affair between each man and his Maker, and affecting only what is purely individual.

In practice, of course, some principle of action was necessary. Various forces were at work all through the Middle Ages, substituting for the non-national relationships of Feudalism the self-conscious and self-distinguishing nations which already confront us in the sixteenth century. Nationalism, actual and ideal, took the place of actual Feudalism and ideal Catholicism as the governing factor in politics. It inspired great heroism in its service; it facilitated the growth of cultural traditions by which the life of the whole world is enriched; it supplied units of self-government so that men could learn the difficult arts of political liberty; and it led us, through its culminating self-expression in the Great War to the search for an internationalism which shall at once conserve its benefits and avoid its perils, in the League of Nations. In the political sphere we are quite evidently trying to find our way back to an all-embracing unity.

THE GLORIFICATION OF THE INDIVIDUAL

In the spiritual and intellectual spheres, there was no nucleus of new unification to which men could turn when the growing wealth of experience cracked the mould of the medieval unity, except the individual consciousness. This was assumed as a point of established, or given, unity, and from it the pioneers of the new adventure took their start. Luther's declaration at the Diet of Worms—*Hier steh' ich, ich kann nichts anders* ("Here I stand, I can naught else")—and Descartes' discovery that, in the effort to doubt all things, one certainty remains, namely, the doubter's assurance that he is doubting—*Cogito, ergo sum* ("I think, therefore I exist")—are the spiritual and intellectual expressions of the same principle—the autonomy of the individual in mind and conscience.

It would be impossible to enumerate what we owe to the practical assertion of this principle. All the wealth of art and literature, all the enterprises and achievements of science, all the equipment and organization of life which these have made possible, we owe in part at least to this principle. And yet the life so equipped and organized is felt by many to be purposeless. Our poets and novelists do not for the most part suggest that life as they see it has any goal before it, the reaching of which is helped or hindered by the characters which they depict. Everything is fugitive and futile. All discipline is repudiated, but the result is rather boredom than exuberance. To take the obvious example—few novelists of our time show any respect for the Christian ideal of marriage or the Church's law regarding it; but the picture they give us does not lead one to suppose that the abandonment of these is any guarantee of happiness. No doubt such generalizations are subject to exceptions: and one voice there is which calls to another way than that of individualism run wild—I shall refer again in another connection to the Poet Laureate's great utterance, *The Testament of Beauty*—but the impression made upon me by contemporary literature is broadly what I have described.

And now the heart of this glorification of the human individual is taken out of it by the discovery that the unity of the individual himself is not a fact of his original nature but an achievement of conscious and social life. Psychology leaves us in no doubt about this. It will have nothing to do with a central core of personality or selfhood, ordering all the elements of human nature by the power of something called a will. Each of us at birth is a mass of instincts and impulses—each ready to be stimulated into activity by its appropriate environment. The first business of our education, which begins at birth and is not finished at death, is to fashion all these into a unity which shall control every one of them. It often happens that during that process two, or even more, groups of elements are formed; it is for this reason that boys and adolescents sometimes seem to be hypocrites. Real hypocrisy is on the whole an adult failing. But it easily happens that young folk behave after one fashion in one company and after a very different fashion in some other company, without any hypocrisy. The boy who is a perfect little gentleman in the headmaster's drawing-room, and a perfect little fiend half an hour later, is behaving with complete sincerity and spontaneity on each occasion, but his character is not fully formed; he is, perhaps, no longer a multitude, but he is two inchoate personalities not yet fused together; and each becomes active when its own environment sets it going. Yet all the while there is the basis of unity in the fact that only one impulse or group of impulses can be active by means of his bodily organism at any one time. That fact sets up from the outset a rudimentary sense of continuity, personal identity and responsibility. As this sense of responsibility develops it becomes the chief means of unifying the whole personality.

The Need of a Unifying Principle

But if all this is true, then the chief need of humanity, now more urgent than ever before, is for some principle that may bring unity into life. It is possible to go a long way in unifying personality on the basis of self-interest. But you cannot go all the way; for there are generous elements in human nature which can never be brought under its sway. And so far as success is reached by that method it only prepares for deeper failure; for the self that is unified under the principle of self-interest will come into conflict with other selves governed by the same principle. No sectional principle will do. Self-perfection, self-expression, "Art for Art's sake." "Business is business," "My country right or wrong"—these are products of the modern departmentalism which has led us to moral bewilderment, æsthetic chaos, industrial class-war, international and interracial jealousy with the suicide of civilization as its inevitable outcome. The principle of unity which is to meet our need must be in its nature truly universal.

We are in search, then, of something which is wide enough to cover every human interest, august enough to claim an absolute allegiance, and connected by an intimate, but also an identical, relation with every individual and every race. That is what we want, if we can find it. But it is quite inconceivable that such an ideal should emerge out of the extremely various experiences and traditions of mankind. No English sketch of an ideal plan for life will appeal (say) to the Italian or the Frenchman. No European sketch will appeal to the Indian or Chinese. And if we try to imagine an international committee attempting to draw up a universal plan of life, we know that they could only reach agreement by confining themselves to platitudes, and that what they put forth could have no compelling force whatever upon the passions of mankind. There are

many problems, social and political, of which there is demonstrably
no solution until the parties concerned acknowledge one common
standard of judgment. But we cannot construct that standard. What
we want can only be found if the ultimate ground of all existence
is somewhere and somehow made known otherwise than in the
partial and fitful apprehensions afforded by the experience of
different men and races. In other words, if there is a God who is the
Father of all men, and if He has revealed His character in some
way that we can understand, then the crying need of the world can
be met; and if not, it cannot be met.

The Answer of the Christian Faith

Now the Gospel is precisely the proclamation of the good news that
God exists and is eternally what we see in Jesus Christ. That such a
faith is the answer to such needs as I have outlined needs scarcely to
be pointed out. But it is worth while to point to the importance of
the fact that the revelation is given in a Person and not in a set of
propositions—not even in a set of propositions about that Person.
It is to Christ, not to the Creed, that the world is to look for its salvation. The Creed is important because it points to the one hope of
redemption; but its importance is secondary, for it is not itself the
source of saving power. Remembrance of this will save us from the
central medieval blunder of imposing the rule of theology on science
or art, or *enforcing* a submission of conduct to religion. The unity
we seek must come from the all-pervasiveness of the influence and
spirit of a Person. The message of the Gospel to individuals, to
groups, to classes, to nations, to races, is "Let this mind be in you
which was also in Christ Jesus," and the same message is given to
statesmen, to economists, to scientists, to artists, to poets, to novelists,
to journalists. Moreover, it declares that this is possible just because
Jesus Christ is not only a historic figure like Socrates or Cæsar, but
is the manifestation of that universal and eternal spirit in whom we
live and move and have our being, and who is Himself the source
of our existence and sustainer of our life.

The Bases of Christianity

But is the Gospel credible? To complete the description of my point
of view, I must try to give you in the same sketchy outline what I
conceive to be the grounds for belief in God and in Christ as His
self-revelation. And first let me say that the strength of the case for
Christian theism is not to be found in any one line of argument, but
in the convergence of several independent lines of argument. First,
then, I take this. Science never attempts to explain the existence of

the Universe itself. It explains any given part of the Universe by showing its relation to other parts. This process is, indeed, very far from complete; but even if it could be completed, it would not explain the existence of the whole or (consequently) of anything at all. If that question is raised, and there can be no doubt about the intellectual impulse to raise it, no answer can be satisfactory if it is of such a kind as to require further explanation. The explanation of all things cannot be found in anything which needs itself to be explained. If, concerning the answer given, the mind can ask again the question, Why so? the answer is no final explanation. Now there is in our experience one principle, and only one, which does, so far as it is applicable, give such a final explanation; it is the purpose of living intelligence. It is therefore reasonable to make the hypothesis that the explanation of the Universe is to be found in the purpose of a living intelligence—or, in other words, in creation by God.

Secondly, whatever is to account for all particular existences must be adequate to the most highly developed. We may make a rough classification of existence as things, animals and persons. The thing is passive, moving as it is moved; it is not sentient; it has no feelings to be considered. The animal is self-moving and has feelings. But it has no purpose or plan of life. You do not say to a puppy, "What would you like to be when you grow up?" To have such a purpose in life is the distinctive mask of personality. So the principle invoked as the explanation of all things must at least be personal in the sense of acting by intelligent purposes.

Thirdly, the world as science presents it to us increasingly appears to exist in a series of grades or strata. A rough classification of these is matter, life, mind, spirit. But these are related to each other in such wise that the lower is necessary to the actuality of the higher, while the higher can direct the lower to conformity with its own ends. Thus life only appears as living matter—the organism; mind only appears as directing organisms; spirit only appears as guiding minds. Reality as a whole cannot be less than one of its own parts; so as spiritual being exist within it, spirit must be part of its own nature. But if so, and if spirit exists by guiding mind, mind by directing life, and life by possessing matter, then the system of reality as a whole must be spiritual. It is just this conception which the Poet Laureate has set forth with a noble combination of logical power and poetic beauty in his great poem *The Testament of Beauty*.

Fourthly, all this receives reinforcement from the religious experience of mankind and especially of the saints. If the general argument of philosophy seemed to me to incline towards atheism, I could not confidently reject the theory of some psychologists that all religious experience is illusion. If there were no experience which seemed to be a personal relationship with God, I should have to admit that the balance of probability in the general philosophic argument is not decisive. But the two converge and support each other; it is in the mutual support of general argument and religious experience that we find the main strength of the case for theism. There are other converging lines of argument from moral obligation and from beauty, which I have not room now to trace; this strengthens the case still further. But for me the convergence of the two lines already mentioned is the most important. For the philosophic argument points to creation by a personal spirit capable of personal relationship with persons; and religious experience appears, at least, to be the apprehension from our side of such relations with the infinite reality.

Significance of the Incarnation

Once more, in personality as we know it in ourselves, the process of evolution has produced a being capable of apprehending universal truth and absolute obligation; for though our range in these regards may be limited, yet in principle we are familiar with such apprehensions. The truth that $2 + 2 = 4$ is not dependent on circumstances; it is genuinely universal. But beyond the universal and the absolute it is self-evidently impossible to go. Man then, in respect of his reason and conscience, is akin to whatever is ultimate. Here is the image of God stamped on human nature. Here also is the condition making possible a personal revelation of God in human nature. The Incarnation is in principle possible.

But does that same principle of evolution allow us to believe that it has actually happened? Can the final revelation be already given? Men often ask this question. But it betrays great confusion of thought. Finality of principle and direction is not inimical to development and progress. No mathematician proposes to reconstruct the multiplication-table in the interest of mathematical advance. What is given to the world in Jesus Christ is not the goal of man's destiny, but the direction to be followed and the power to follow it. There still remains the task of bringing all activities into conformity with the mind " which was also in Jesus Christ "; there are infinite vistas of progress before the human race.

Visions of Progress

It is not possible now to describe the task awaiting us as we look down those vistas. But we may easily begin to envisage the difference that it would make if in international affairs the mind of Christ were always in control; if patriotism were always Christian, so that patriots always desired for their country pre-eminence in service rather than in power, and valued power only as a means of service; or again the change in our social and industrial life if men always cared more for justice than for gain, more for fellowship than for domination, more for what might link them to their fellows than for what enabled them to feel superior; or again the change in much of our literature and art if there were a constant loyalty to the mind, the spirit, the outlook of Christ, so that with complete freedom to handle all subjects and to handle them freely the artist were really delivered from the chaotic futility of mere self-expression, without regard to the question whether there is a self worthy of expression or only a talent for expressing it.

PRINCIPLES OF THE CHRISTIAN LIFE

Each group, and indeed each individual in each group, must work out the meaning of all this in the various departments of life. For the Church as a whole, or anyone in its name, to undertake this would be to repeat the medieval blunder, and to give up just what is best in the whole modern movement of mankind. But at least four principles can be stated as part of the Christian view of life, and calling for application in great things and small every day. First, personality is sacred; progress means the perpetually fuller recognition of the personal element in human beings in all relations of life; that personal element shows itself above all things in free intelligent choice. Secondly, we are not isolated individuals but members of a brotherhood; progress means the perpetually fuller realization in practice of this fact of fellow-membership in the family of God. Thirdly, the duty of man is to serve God by serving his fellows; progress means the perpetually greater number of those who put service before gain as the guiding principle of life. Fourthly, power is subordinate to love, and love exerts its power by self-sacrifice; this is the way of the Cross; progress comes mostly not through those who fight for it, but through those who suffer for it.

Now all this is not proved. We walk by faith, not by sight. Intellectually regarded, the Christian faith is a hypothesis to be tested by thought and practice. Spiritually regarded, it is a discipleship in which we rely at first on the testimony of others and progressively find the vindication in our own experience. But the charge to the Church is " make disciples of all the nations "; and the call to mankind is " Come unto Me and I will give you rest." The world can only know whether that promise is fulfilled, if it first fulfils the condition. I cannot offer proof; each individual and mankind itself must find the proof by the experiment of practical discipleship. But I hope I have succeeded in setting before you in a sketch that view of the world which from my point of view I seem to see, and which I now summarize as follows.

I believe that life and the world constitute a single whole; I believe that the Word of God—that is, the mind and character of God in self-expression—is the principle of its unity; I believe that this mind and character of God are fully expressed, so far as human nature allows, in the person of Jesus Christ as set before us in the Gospels and as known in the experience of the Christian Church; I think that the state of knowledge is beginning—though only now after a long interval of beginning—to make possible again the enterprise of seeing all life and the world as a unity having that revelation as its focusing point; and I am convinced that nothing is now so important—for indeed the alternative is in the long run the collapse of civilization—as to reconstruct our whole fabric of thought and practice around the self-expression of ultimate reality in Jesus Christ as its focus and pivot and dynamic source of power.

(Broadcast, February 10, 1930)

Archbishop Lord Davidson

" HE WAS A GOOD MAN, full of the Holy Ghost and of faith." (Acts xi, 24.)

On Sunday, May 25, 1930, a notice was fixed to the door of a house in Cheyne Walk, to which the thoughts of multitudes were already turned, saying that very early that morning "Archbishop Davidson entered into the larger life." It was deeply characteristic of her who wrote it, and in its simple faith it was beautifully appropriate to the man of whom it spoke. For that is the first and last impression of him—simple, confident faith in God and the things eternal. For the great mass of the public this might easily be obscured by other impressions—not the first or the last—of which I will speak in a moment. But those who knew him best remember him as chiefly great in his simplicity and in the nearness of his life to God.

I got my first impression of him when he attended, as Bishop of Winchester, my father's enthronement at Canterbury in January 1897, when I was just over fifteen years old, and from that time onwards he held my affection, for I had seen there the signs of the intimate relationship between him and my father. But it was almost six years later that the real revelation came. During my father's last illness his kindness to us all was wonderful. He was present at the last celebration of the Holy Communion in my father's bedroom; and when my father called for him, after saying his solemn farewell to Archbishop Maclagan and to the Bishop of London, the Bishop of Winchester had slipped away—most characteristically—lest the dying man's strength should be exhausted before he could speak to his own family. A few days later the end had come, and I remember how my mother and I were standing at the top of the flight of steps immediately inside the front door of Lambeth Palace, when the door opened, and he came running up with a radiant smile and saying, "Angels and Archangels and all the company of Heaven—that is what we are thinking of to-day."

It was just six years later still that I was ordained deacon by him at Canterbury, and I have often wondered if anyone really knew him who had not seen him through the days when he had in his house the young men who were by him to be admitted to the ministry. Already before this I had often been with him at Lambeth—

sometimes at historic moments; and immediately after my ordination as priest he made me one of his honorary chaplains.

You will forgive, I trust, these personal words which partly explain how it was that Archbishop Davidson was to me in a double sense my father's successor, for from the time when he succeeded him in office he also became most truly a second father to me. That is why I think first, not of the great Archbishop, but of the man who in faith, and simplicity, and charity, lived very close to God.

He was, indeed, not in the least mystical. I do not suppose that he spent very long times in private prayer. But no one with whom he prayed could doubt the directness or sincerity of his approach to God. He was most regular in all religious observances. Even in his eightieth year, when presiding each day through long sessions of the Church Assembly or other gatherings, he was punctual in his chapel for the celebration of Holy Communion at 8 o'clock in the morning —which was held daily during such periods. And these times of regular devotion were focusing points of what pervaded his life. He was perfectly natural and spontaneous; but he faced every problem and discharged every responsibility as in the sight of God, and when in the midst of some conference, such as those on the Prayer Book, he called us to prayer, it was with the sense of falling back on what had been present all the time.

His power of work was astonishing. He could absorb information at amazing speed, and then have it ready for use, apparently at any subsequent date. I watched him once getting the material out of the Report of a Royal Commission for an important speech in the House of Lords. He turned over the pages with a steady, slow swing, giving to each about the time required for reading aloud two sentences of average length. I asked him if he had really been getting what he wanted or only noticing where to find it later; he replied that he thought he had mastered the main points. And his speech showed that he had.

He was not in the least an orator, as that word is commonly understood. He used no artifice; he just said what he had to say with weighty deliberation. But few speakers have been so persuasive. His manifest sincerity, his fairness to all points of view, his vast range of knowledge, and his complete freedom from excitement or the bias associated with it, made his opinion appear to be identical with wisdom itself—and the event usually confirmed this impression.

In handling men, whether singly or in multitudes, he had consummate skill. Very often his chief concern was, not to secure success for views to which he inclined, but to secure unanimity in pursuit of the course which the common mind of the Church might choose. He belonged to no party. He appreciated the devotion shown by men of all parties. When some question arose which divided them, he did not try to reach by argument some common ground beneath their difficulties. He was not a philosopher; indeed for philosophy he had what I can only call a contemptuous admiration. He admired, because his own mind did not work that way, and he had generous admiration for those who could do what was not possible to him. But his admiration was in one sense contemptuous, though most genially so, for he was sure that no practical question is ever settled that way. His method was to bring the parties together; never appeal to, yet always take for granted, their common loyalty to Christ and His Church; learn by an almost magical instinct on what point they could be brought to converge; and then with equal magic lead them all towards it. The point reached would not represent any reconciliation in principle of divergent tendencies, but it would represent agreement about what should be done next. And as that is the only thing that can ever be done at all, that is also the only kind of agreement that is of practical use; when differences broke out again, they could be dealt with in the same way.

Now it is easy to criticize this kind of leadership. But the criticism usually omits the main consideration. To Archbishop Davidson all the matters about which Churchmen or patriots quarrel were secondary; he fully admitted their importance, but they remained secondary. Primary were the loyalty to Christ and the loyalty to country, which ought to exist, and nearly always do exist, on both sides of every dispute, ecclesiastical or political. His aim was to let this primary loyalty exert its control over concerns which, however, important, are secondary. He did not try to impose his solution; he wished the whole body—the body politic or the body ecclesiastical— to find its own adjustment. It is a method based on humility, and only made possible by wide sympathy; and its very essence is trust in the Holy Spirit who inspires and leads the Church. If the leader who resorts to it has no depth of personal loyalty, it will either fail or lead to a purely superficial and probably ambiguous formula. But the Archbishop could apply it safely and effectively because his own deep and devoted loyalty to his Master and to the common good led the disputants unconsciously towards that outlook for which their dispute no longer seemed a sufficient cause to be allowed to hinder united effort in the common service.

Of course this strange personal ascendancy which showed itself, not by subjecting men to his convictions, but by making them conform to their own deepest principles—in short by drawing the best out of them—was heightened in all affairs pertaining to the Church by his unequalled range of knowledge. No one has ever known the Church of England as he knew it. From the time that he became chaplain, as a young man, to Archbishop Tait, he was closely associated with Lambeth and with that central responsibility for the welfare of our Church throughout the world for which Lambeth stands. For a quarter of a century he bore that central responsibility on his own shoulders. As the various dioceses fell vacant, he informed himself of their various conditions, for often he had to nominate the new Bishop, and more often still he was consulted by those who had. It was quite a common experience for a Bishop of some area of which the very name is unknown to most educated people to discover, on returning to England, that in some respects the Archbishop knew facts about his diocese that he had not yet discovered himself.

Perhaps the greatest of his claims to honour in the sphere of public activity is found in his world-wide outlook. Most men of note who passed through England visited the Archbishop and drew on his wisdom; meanwhile he stored his mind with the impressions that they brought him. A friend of mine working in the Foreign Office during the later period of the war said that the Archbishop had a surer sense of the currents of opinion and feeling in the various European countries than anyone in the Foreign Office itself. His own convictions about the war were quite clear. He had no doubt that we were bound by our duty to fight, and to fight till victory was won. But he never said one word that would have to be withdrawn or forgotten before friendship with those who were then our enemies could be resumed. When the House of Commons went to St. Margaret's, Westminister, to join in the national intercessions, he took for his text the Third Commandment—" Thou shalt not take the Name of the Lord thy God in vain "—and said that if they came to pray with malice or hatred in their hearts they were breaking that Commandment.

After the war, when the World Alliance for the Promotion of International Friendship through the Churches met again and had to choose a President, only one name was considered. The meeting was held on German soil; there was some thought that a representative of a neutral country should be selected. But all turned to the Archbishop of Canterbury, and a German delegate assured the gathering that he had the most international understanding of any man alive. Throughout the war, while unwavering in his belief in the allied cause, he was looking to the time that would follow, when those who were fighting as enemies would have again to live together as neighbours.

Probably the most courageous action of his life was his intervention in the so-called General Strike. He knew perfectly well that by some of the very people whose judgment he most valued he would be accused of weakness—an accusation that only a very strong man can calmly face. He saw, of course, that the strike was in itself revolutionary in tendency. He also saw that the vast majority of the strikers had no revolutionary intention. Here were two facts, on either of which a policy might be based, for both were real facts. He believed that to treat the movement as revolutionary (which it was) would turn the men engaged in it into revolutionaries, while to ignore its revolutionary tendency would prevent that tendency from developing. No human judgment can make a secure estimate of the forces that mould history; but for myself I am persuaded that the peaceful issue of that crisis was largely due to the attitude which the Archbishop then adopted. Whether that be true or not, it is certainly true that only a very brave man could have adopted it.

Perhaps his courage in affairs, which was very real though as remote as possible from recklessness, found support in the continual courage with which he faced the results of the illness which nearly ended his life when he was Bishop of Rochester. From that time on, for more than thirty years, he lived with the knowledge that he had within him the seeds of a trouble, any return of which might bring speedy death. But that gave him no fear. His only fear was lest he might remain at his post when no longer able to meet its claims; and the noblest action of his life was his determination to resign while his power still showed scarcely any sign of abatement.

He was a great man—great in his public career, greater still in his own personality. But while he had powers beyond those given to most men, the greatest thing about him is not beyond our reach— the complete dedication of all the powers he had to God and duty. He had a clear knowledge of his own limitations. He rejoiced that others should do with success what he could not attempt; and he laboured in utter self-devotion at the service for which his talents supremely qualified him.

And all was done as in God's sight, and in the power of the Spirit. That is the deepest impression of all. " He was a good man, and full of the Holy Ghost and of faith." Thanks be to God for the life of His servant!

(A Sermon preached at Bishopthorpe Parish Church on the Sunday after the Ascension Day, 1930)

The Idea of Immortality in Relation to Religion and Ethics

IT IS NOT EASY to estimate the place which the idea of Immortality now holds in the actual religion of English people. Certainly it is nothing like so prominent as it has been in most previous ages of Christian history. And so far as it plays a part, it is a very different part. Here, as in other departments of life, we find ourselves at the end of a period of reaction from the Middle Ages. The medieval scheme, still presented by the Roman Catholic Church, is entirely intelligible in its broad outlines. Universal immortality is assumed; for those who are beyond pardon there is Hell; for those who are pardonable, Purgatory; for those whose pardon is accomplished, Paradise. And alongside of these, for the unawakened soul there is Limbo. The scheme presents certain administrative difficulties. It involves, in practice, the drawing of a sharp line between the awakened and the unawakened, and again, between the pardonable and the unpardonable. But unless it be held—as in fact I find myself driven to hold—that these difficulties are insoluble in principle, it may be urged that they are soluble to omniscience, which, ex hypothesi, is available for the purpose.

There are many of us, however, to whom the difficulty mentioned is so overwhelming as to make the whole scheme unreal, however watertight it may be dialectically. And I have not hesitated to speak of it in terms which indicate that sense of unreality. For the human soul is at once too delicately complex, and too closely unified, to be dealt with by any method of classification whatever into mutually exclusive groups. And how can there be Paradise for any while there is Hell, conceived as unending torment, for some? Each supposedly damned soul was born into the world as a mother's child; and Paradise cannot be Paradise for her if her child is in such a Hell. The scheme is unworkable in practice even by omniscience, and moreover it offends against the deepest Christian sentiments.

But this is a very modern reaction to it. What happened at the Reformation was very different. The doctrine of Purgatory was the focus of many grave abuses—sales of Indulgences and the like. These called for remedy, and thus set moving the normal method of Reformers—the method of referring whatever was found to call for remedy to the touchstone of Scripture. And Scripture supplied no basis for a doctrine of Purgatory. So the doctrine was not freed from its abuses but was eliminated, and the Protestant world was left with the stark alternatives of Heaven and Hell.

Now the medieval scheme, being easily intelligible as a theory, however difficult in practice, had great homiletic value. It presented vividly to the imagination the vitally important truth of the " abiding consequences " of our actions and of the characters that we form. And this homiletic value was if anything increased at first through the simplification effected by the Reformers. There, plain before all men, was the terrible alternative. Only by faith in Christ could a man be delivered from certain torment in Hell to the unending bliss of Heaven; but by that faith he could have assurance, full and complete, of his deliverance; and that faith would be fruitful in his life and character.

But there was much to set upon the other side. The new form of the scheme gave a new prominence to Hell, and whereas the popular mind in the Middle Ages was mainly concerned with Purgatory and with ways of shortening or mitigating its cleansing pains, it was now Hell that alone supplied the deterrent influence of belief in a future life. And this, while it lasted, reacted on the conception of God. For punishment which is unending is plainly retributive alone in the long run; it may have a deterrent use while this life lasts, but from the Day of Judgment onwards it would lose that quality, and it obviously has no reformative aim. And it requires much ingenuity to save from the charge of vindictiveness a character which inflicts for ever a punishment which can be no other than retributive. Certainly the popular conception of God in many Protestant circles became almost purely vindictive. We can read in the protests of such writers as Shelley and Byron what sort of picture of God had been impressed on their imaginations.

> Is there a God? Ay, an almighty God,
> And vengeful as almighty. Once His voice
> Was heard on earth; earth shuddered at the sound;
> The fiery-visaged firmament expressed
> Abhorrence, and the grave of Nature yawned
> To swallow all the dauntless and the good
> That dared to hurl defiance at His throne
> Girt as it was with power.[1]

No doubt Shelley was in violent reaction, and misrepresented by exaggeration what he had been taught, in addition to using the irony of indignation in order to satirize it. Yet a caricature depends for its

[1] Shelley, *Queen Mab*.

force on maintaining some resemblance to what it ridicules. And there are sermons of the eighteenth century which go far to justify the poet's indignant contempt.

But such conceptions could not permanently survive in the minds of people who read the Gospels. Steadily the conviction has gained ground that the God and Father of our Lord Jesus Christ cannot be conceived as inflicting on any soul that He has made unending torment. So Hell has in effect been banished from popular belief; and as Purgatory had been banished long before, we are left with a very widespread sentimental notion that all persons who die are forthwith in Paradise or Heaven. And this seems to involve a conception of God as so genially tolerant as to be morally indifferent, and converts the belief in immortality from a moral stimulant to a moral narcotic. There is a very strong case for thinking out the whole subject again in as complete independence as possible alike of medieval and of Protestant traditions. The reaction from the Middle Ages here as elsewhere has worked itself out.

It has often been pointed out that in the religious experience of Israel the hope of immortality is of late origin. In the earlier times there was an expectation of a shadowy existence in Sheol; but it was not a hope. " O spare me a little that I may recover my strength, before I go hence and be no more seen " is a prayer as far removed as possible from either the later Jewish or the Christian faith in the life to come. The hope of immortality as we understand it only dawned when faith in God as One and as Righteous was already firmly established. Those of us who believe in the providential guidance of Israel's spiritual growth will at once seek a divine purpose in this order of development, but those who start with no such presupposition may quite well trace a value in it which has permanent importance.

The great aim of all true religion is to transfer the centre of interest and concern from self to God. Until the doctrine of God in its main elements is really established, it would be definitely dangerous to reach a developed doctrine of immortality. Even when the doctrine of God is established in its Christian form, the doctrine and hope of immortality can still, as experience abundantly shows, perpetuate self-centredness in the spiritual life. If my main concern in relation to things eternal is to be with the question what is going to become of *me*, it might be better that I should have no hope of immortality at all, so that at least as I look forward into the vista of the ages my Self should not be a possible object of primary concern.

For as in order of historical development, so also in order of spiritual value, the hope of immortality is strictly dependent on and subordinate to faith in God. If God is righteous—still more, if God is Love—immortality follows as a consequence. He made me; He loves me; He will not let me perish, so long as there is in me anything that He can love. And that is a wholesome reflection for me if, but only if, the result is that I give greater glory to God in the first place, and take comfort to myself only, if at all, in the second place. I wish to stress this heavily. Except as an implicate in the righteousness and love of God, I cannot see that immortality is a primary religious interest at all. It has an interest for us as beings who cling to life, but there is nothing religious about that. It has an interest for us as social beings who love our friends and desire to meet again those who have died before us; that is an interest capable of religious consecration, and for many devout souls it has an exceedingly high religious value; but even this is not religious in itself. No; the centre of all true religious interest is God, and self comes into it not as a primary concern which God must serve, but as that one thing which each can offer for the glory of God. And if it were so, that His Glory could best be served by my annihilation—so be it.

But in fact God is known to us through His dealings with us. And if He left us to perish with hopes frustrated and purposes unaccomplished, He could scarcely be—certainly we could not know Him to be—perfect love. Thus our hope of immortality is of quite primary importance when regarded both doctrinally and emotionally as a part of, because a necessary consequence of, our faith in God. There is here a stupendous paradox; but it is the paradox which is characteristic of all true religion. We must spiritually renounce all other loves for love of God; yet when we find God, or, rather, when we know ourselves as found of Him, we find in and with Him all the loves which for His sake we had forgone. If my desire is first for future life for myself, or even first for reunion with those whom I have loved and lost, then the doctrine of immortality may do me positive harm by fixing me in that self-concern or concern for my own joy in my friends. But if my desire is first for God's glory, and for myself that I may be used to promote it, then the doctrine of immortality will give me new heart in the assurance that what here must be a very imperfect service may be made perfect hereafter, that my love of friends may be one more manifestation of the overflowing Love Divine, and that God may be seen as perfect Love in the eternal fellowship of love to which He calls us.

For these reasons it seems to me, so far as I can judge, positively undesirable that there should be experimental proof of our survival of death—at least of such survival in the case of those who have had no spiritual faith on earth. For this would bring the hope of immortality into the area of purely intellectual apprehension. It might or might not encourage the belief that God exists; it would certainly, as I think, make very much harder the essential business of faith, which is the transference of the centre of interest and concern from self to God. If such knowledge comes, it must be accepted, and we must try to use it for good and not for evil. And I could never urge the cessation of enquiry in any direction; I cannot ask that so-called Psychical Research should cease. But I confess I hope that such research will continue to issue in such dubious results as are all that I can trace to it up to date.

When we turn from the relation of this doctrine to Religion and consider its relation to Ethics we are confronted with a different but, as it were, parallel paradox. The expectation of rewards and punishments in a future life has certainly played a considerable part in disciplining the wayward wills of men. And of this as of other discipline it is true that there may grow up under it a habit of mind which afterwards persists independently of it. But so far as conduct is governed by hope of rewards or fear of punishments as commonly understood, it is less than fully moral. We are probably agreed in rejecting the extreme austerity of the Kantian doctrine that the presence of pleasure in association with an action is enough to destroy its moral character; but even more probably we shall agree that if an act is done for the sake of resultant pleasure or profit, so that apart from that pleasure or profit it would not be done, it is not a truly moral act. Consequently the ethical utility of Heaven and Hell, conceived as reward and punishment, is disciplinary and preparatory only. So far as true moral character is established, whether with or without their aid in the process, it becomes independent of their support and will only be injured by reference to them.

Moreover, the utility of Hell, so conceived, is very early exhausted, even if it be not from the outset overweighted by disadvantages. For in Ethics as in Religion the fundamental aim is to remove Self from the centre of interest and concern. But fear is the most completely self-centred of all emotions, and to curb irregularity of conduct by constant use of fear may easily make this aim harder of attainment than it was at the outset. I think it is good for most people to have an occasional shock of fright with reference to their shortcomings; there is no doubt that to live under the constant pressure of fear— in the sense of anxiety concerning one's self—is deeply demoralizing.

It is notorious that Kant, while excluding hope of profit from the motives of a truly moral act, yet found himself bound to postulate immortality as a means of securing that adjustment of goodness and happiness which he considered Reason to demand. I believe this line of argument to be substantially sound. But if it is, then we find that the hope of immortality is wholesome as an implicate in an independently established morality, though if introduced earlier it may hinder as much as help that establishment of morality, just as it has high value as an implicate in faith in God, though if introduced earlier it may hinder as much help the establishment of such faith.

All that has so far been said is introductory to our positive reconstruction, and has aimed rather at clearing the ground. We shall find that the authentic Christian doctrine of the future life is free from the objections which lie against the general notion of Immortality, while it contains all which in that notion is of religious value or of ethical utility. This Christian doctrine has three special characteristics:

(*a*) It is a doctrine, not of Immortality, but of Resurrection.
(*b*) It regards this Resurrection as an act and gift of God, not an inherent right of the human soul as such.
(*c*) It is not a doctrine of rewards and punishments, but is the proclamation of the inherent joy of love and the inherent misery of selfishness.

(*a*) The Christian doctrine is a doctrine not of Immortality but of Resurrection. The difference is profound. The method of all non-Christian systems is to seek an escape from the evils and misery of life. Christianity accepts them at their worst, and makes them the material of its triumphant joy. That is the special significance in this connexion of the Cross and Resurrection of Jesus Christ. Stoics teach an indifference to death; the Gospel teaches victory over it. Richard Lewis Nettleship said our aim should be to reach a frame of mind in which we should pass through the episode of physical death without being so much as aware of it. That is a splendid utterance; and yet it implies a detachment from wholesome interests and from the intercourse of friends which is a little inhuman. Surely it is true that death is a fearful calamity—in itself; and as such the Gospel accepts it; there is no minimizing of its terrors. Only its sting —its very real sting—is drawn; only its victory—its very real victory—is converted into the triumph of its victim. It is one thing to say that there is no real tragedy in the normal course of human life; it is quite another thing to acknowledge the tragedy and then to claim that it is transformed into glory.

We lose very much if we equate this hope of transformation, of resurrection whole and entire in all that may pertain to fullness of life, into a new order of being, with a doctrine of mere survival.

Incidentally, though the theme is too great to be developed here, this glorious Christian hope coheres with a totally different conception of the relation of Time or History to Eternity; for it both clothes History with an eternal significance and at the same time points to a conception of Eternity as something much more than the totality of Time; and Time becomes not so much the " moving image of Eternity " as a subordinate and essentially preparatory moment in the eternal Reality. But that fascinating and bewildering topic would require a whole Lecture to itself.

(*b*) The Christian conception of the life to come as a gift of God has affinities with the Platonic doctrine of Immortality. Plato had sought to demonstrate the inherent immortality of the individual soul. In the *Phaedo* he fashioned an argument which seems for the moment to have satisfied him. But in fact it is invalid. What Plato proves in the *Phaedo* is that the soul cannot both be, and be dead; he does not prove that it cannot pass out of existence altogether. In the *Republic* he advances an argument of which the minor premise seems to be simply untrue. He says that what perishes does so by its own defeat; but the essential disease of the soul—injustice—does not cause, or tend towards, the decay of the soul; therefore the soul is imperishable. But there is every reason to deny the second proposition. When once the essential nature of the soul as self-motion is established, it is at least open to question whether injustice is not a negation of that quality. No doubt the wicked man may display great activity; so may metal filings in the proximity of a magnet; that does not mean that they are endowed with self-motion.

It is in the *Phaedrus* that Plato first reaches the clear conception of the soul as characterized essentially by self-motion, and argues from this its indestructibility. But not each individual soul is completely self-moved, and the argument, supposing it to be valid, as I think it is, only establishes the indestructibility of the spiritual principle in the universe, not the immortality of each individual soul. Plato seems to have accepted that result, for in the *Laws*, where we find his final conclusions, he declares that only God is immortal in His own right, and that He of His bounty bestows on individual souls an immortality which is not theirs by nature.

That this is the prevailing doctrine of the New Testament seems to me beyond question as soon as we approach its books free from Hellenistic assumption that each soul is inherently immortal in virtue of its nature as soul. That is a view which is increasingly hard to reconcile with psychology. But psychology is still a nascent science and cannot as yet claim any great degree of deference. I do not claim that in the New Testament there is a single doctrine everywhere accepted; on the contrary it seems to me that here and there a relapse into the Hellenistic point of view may be detected. But its prevailing doctrine, as I think, is that God alone is immortal, being in His own Nature eternal; and that He offers immortality to men not universally but conditionally. Certainly we come very near to a direct assertion of the first part of this position in the description of God as " the blessed and only Potentate, the King of them that reign as kings, and Lord of them that rule as lords, who only hath immortality " (I Tim. vi, 16). The only approach to an argument for a future life of which our Lord makes use is based on the relationship of God to the soul: " He is not the God of the dead, but of the living: for all live unto Him " (Luke xx, 38). And in close connexion with this saying in the Lucan version are the words, " they that are accounted worthy to attain to that world and the resurrection from the dead " (Luke xx, 35). It is in consonance with this that the Resurrection of Jesus Christ is constantly spoken of throughout the New Testament as the act of God himself. No doubt St. Paul explicitly states that " We must all be made manifest before the judgment seat of Christ " (II Cor. v, 10), but that settles nothing, unless we make, with some followers of " psychical research," the entirely unwarrantable assumption that the survival of physical death is the same thing as immortality. Quite clearly it is not; for a man might survive the death of his body only to enter then upon a process of slow or rapid annihilation. And St. Paul elsewhere declares that he follows the Christian scale of values " if that by any means I might attain to the resurrection of the dead " (Phil. iii, 11).

Are there not, however, many passages which speak of the endless torment of the lost? No; as far as my knowledge goes there is none at all. There are sayings which speak of being cast into undying fire. But if we do not approach these with the presupposition that what is thus cast in is indestructible, we shall get the impression, not that it will burn for ever, but that it will be destroyed. And so far as the difficulty is connected with the terms " eternal " or " everlasting," as in Matt. xxv, 46 (" eternal punishment ") it must be remembered that the Greek word used is αἰώνιος, which has primary reference to the quality of the age to come and not to its infinity. The word that strictly means " eternal " is not frequent in the New Testament, but it does occur, so that we must not treat the commoner word as though it alone had been available, and when a vital issue turns on the distinction it is fair to lay some stress upon it. And after all, annihilation is an everlasting punishment though it is not unending torment.

But the stress in the New Testament is all laid upon the quality of the life to come and the conditions of inheriting eternal life. It is not to a mere survival of death that we are called, while we remain very much what we were before; it is to a resurrection to a new order of being, of which the chief characteristic is fellowship with God. Consequently the quality of the life to which we are called is determined by the Christian doctrine of God.

(*c*) What is abundantly clear throughout the New Testament is its solemn insistence upon what Baron von Hügel spoke of as " abiding consequences." Language is strained and all the imagery of apocalypse employed to enforce the truth that a child's choice between right and wrong matters more than the course of the stars. Whatever is done bears fruit for ever; whatever a man does, to all eternity he is the man who did that. Moreover, evil-doing entails for the evil-doer calamity hereafter if not also here, while for him who gives himself to the will of God there is stored up joy unspeakable.

Further, there can be no question that our Lord was prepared to use a certain appeal to self-interest to reinforce the claims of righteousness: " It is good for thee to enter into life with one eye rather than having two eyes to be cast into the hell of fire " (Matt. vii, 8). But these passages are mostly connected with cases where loyalty to righteousness involves some great sacrifice or self-mortification; they are not so much direct appeals to self-interest as counterweights to the self-interest that might hinder the sacrifice or mortification required. And the positive invitation to discipleship is never based on self-interest. He never says, " If any man will come after Me, I will deliver him from the pains of hell and give him the joys of heaven." He calls men to take up their cross and share His sacrifice. To those who are weary and heavy laden there is the promise of rest; but the general invitation is to heroic enterprise involving readiness for the completest self-sacrifice, and concern for the mere saving of the soul is condemned as a sure way of losing it.

We are all called to fellowship with Christ, in whom we see the eternal God. It is fellowship with Love, complete and perfect in its self-giving. How weak is the lure which this offers to our selfish instinct! There is in the Gospel a warning that the way of self-will leads to destruction, so that prudence itself counsels avoidance of it. But when we turn to seek another way there is none that commends itself to prudence only. For the reward that is offered is one that a selfish man would not enjoy. Heaven, which is fellowship with God, is only joy for those to whom love is the supreme treasure. Indeed, objectively regarded, Heaven and Hell may well be identical. Each is the realization that Man is utterly subject to the purpose of Another —of God who is Love. To the godly and unselfish soul that is joy unspeakable; to the selfish soul it is a misery against which he rebels in vain. Heaven and Hell are the two extreme terms of our possible reactions to the Gospel of the Love of God. " This is the judgment, that the light is come into the world, and men loved the darkness rather than the light " (John iii, 19). " This is life eternal, that they should know thee the only true God, and him whom thou didst send, even Jesus Christ " (John xvii, 3).

If with such thoughts to guide us, and paying regard to what seems the best help that contemporary thought can give us, we try in any way to schematize our belief in the future life, I suggest that the result is somewhat as follows.

God has created us as children of His love, able to understand that love in some degree and to respond to it. In the psycho-physical organism of human personality there is the possibility for a development of the spiritual elements, in response to and communion with the eternal God, which makes these capable of receiving from God the gift of His own immortality. Unless there has been such degeneration that only animal life continues to exist, it must be presumed that this possibility remains; and as it is hardly conceivable that any human being descends altogether to the level of the animal during this mortal life, it is further to be presumed that every personality survives bodily death. But that is not the same as to attain to immortality. And here we are confronted with a dilemma, which I expect will remain insoluble so long as we have available only those data which are afforded by experience on this side of death. On the one hand is the supreme significance of human freedom, which seems to involve the possibility for every soul that it may utterly and finally reject the love of God; and this must involve it in perdition. God must assuredly abolish sin; and if the sinner so sinks himself in his sin as to become truly identified with it, God must destroy him also. On the other hand, this result is failure on the part of God; for though He asserts His supremacy by destruction of the wicked, yet such victory is in fact defeat. For He has no pleasure in the death of him that dieth. The love which expressed itself in our creation can find no satisfaction in our annihilation, and we are prompted by faith in God's almighty love to believe, not in the total destruction of the wicked, but rather in some

> sad obscure sequestered state
> Where God unmakes but to re-make the soul
> He else first made in vain; which must not be.

As I have said, I do not think the dilemma can be resolved by us here on earth. At one time I confess that I was almost confident in accepting Universalism. Later I began to waver, and was much interested, when I told von Hügel that I was moving away from Universalism, to receive his reply that he found himself moving towards it. But while I am now by no means confident, I will offer what slender hope of a solution to the difficulty I am able to entertain.

There is one condition on which our conduct can be both free and externally determined. It is found wherever a man acts in a certain way in order to give pleasure to one whom he loves. Such acts are free in the fullest degree; yet their content is wholly determined by the pleasure of the person loved. Above all do we feel free when our love goes out in answer to love shown to us. Now the Grace of God is His love made known and active upon and within us; and our response to it is both entirely free and entirely due to the activity of His love towards us. All that we could contribute of our own would be the resistance of our self-will. It is just this which love breaks down, and in so doing does not override our freedom but rather calls it into exercise. There is, therefore, no necessary contradiction in principle between asserting the full measure of human freedom and believing that in the end the Grace of God will win its way with every human heart.

But this must be interpreted in the light of the doctrine of " abiding consequences." If I allow myself to become set in self-centredness the love of God can only reach me through pain; and when it has found me and stirred my penitence and won me to forgiveness, I am still the forgiven sinner, not the always loyal child of God. And this general truth has application to every act of moral choice.

Again, because God is Love, the universe is so ordered that self-seeking issues in calamity. Thus we are warned that even when judged from its own standpoint self-seeking is unprofitable. But while mercy in this way gives to selfishness the only warning it is capable of heeding, there is no way offered of avoiding the calamity while the selfishness remains. The fear of future pain or of destruction may stimulate a man for his own self's sake to seek salvation; but the only salvation that exists or can exist is one that he can never find while he seeks it for his own self's sake. The warning is a warning that while he remains the sort of man he is, there is no hope for him; it is a call, not merely to a grudging change of conduct for fear of worse or hope of better; it is a call to a change of heart which can only exist so far as it is not grudging but willing. Thus it is a call for surrender to that Grace of God which alone can effect such a change of heart. It is Love that keeps aflame the hell of fire to warn us that in selfishness there is no satisfaction even for self; and Love then calls the soul which heeds that warning to submit itself to the moulding influences of Love by which it may be transformed; and the promise is of a joy which only those who are transformed into the likeness of Love can know, while to others it is the very misery from which they seek deliverance.

In such a view there is neither the demoralizing influence of a cheery optimism which says, "Never mind; it will all come right in the end," nor the equally demoralizing influence of a terrorism which stereotypes self-centredness by undue excitation of fear. There is an appeal to self-concern in those who can heed no other, but it is an appeal to leave all self-concern behind. Again there is no promise for the future which can encourage any soul to become forgetful of God, for the promise is of fellowship with God, and therein, but only therein, of fellowship also with those whom we have loved. It is an austere doctrine, more full of the exigency than of the consolations of religion, though it offers these also in gracious abundance to all who submit to its demands, for to be drawn into fellowship with God is to find that the Communion of Saints is a reality. And the core of the doctrine is this: Man is not immortal by nature or of right; but there is offered to him resurrection from the dead and life eternal if he will receive it from God and on God's terms. There is nothing arbitrary in that offer or in those terms, for God is perfect Wisdom and perfect Love. But Man, the creature and helpless sinner, cannot attain to eternal life unless he gives himself to God, the Creator, Redeemer, Sanctifier, and receives from Him both worthiness for life eternal and with that worthiness eternal life.

(The Drew Lecture for 1931)

Christian and the Way to Peace

I: The Claim

The world is bewildered as seldom before. There may have been at previous times as many problems demanding solution; there was never a time when the same people were confronted by so many problems at once and conscious of some measure of responsibility for them all; and the same causes which have brought this about have also led to the reciprocal interrelation of all these problems, so that whatever is attempted in respect of one is liable to produce unexpected results in connexion with another. Consequently the world needs, as never before, some guiding principle which men may follow in adjusting their conduct to the bewildering complexity of the situation. But this is conspicuously lacking. We are surrounded and beset by prophets proclaiming remedies for this trouble and for that; but their witness agrees not together, and as a rule their suggestions for action in one field are inapplicable or worse in another. So we drift on in actual distress towards threatened calamity.

There are two groups of people who believe themselves to have found in the same allegiance the guiding principle of which the whole world so evidently stands in need. The one group consists of those who accept the full doctrine of the Christian Church, believing that in Jesus Christ the eternal truth of God and of Man is disclosed. These, if they have any consistency, must needs believe that in that revelation they have direction for all their actions, personal or political. They believe that the world was created and is sustained by God, whose character and purpose are made known in Christ; and though the world as it is has been deeply infected by evil, it yet remains His creation; moreover He has taken action for its redemption; and it is by obedience to Him who created it, and in the spirit of Him who redeemed it, that the evil from which it suffers can be overcome.

The other group starts from considerations of moral value and obligation, and reaches the conviction that in the life and teaching of Jesus of Nazareth, as recorded in the New Testament, there is offered an expression of the ethical truth which can save the world. They find their groping apprehensions met by a reality which satisfies, and their certainties heightened by an achievement which at once vindicates and surpasses them. Here then, whatever is to be the ultimate interpretation of the Figure who thus constrains their homage, they trust that they have found the direction which they need for threading the maze of human perplexity.

There will come times and occasions when these two groups may be unable to co-operate without some adjustment of their differences. But the area of possible co-operation is large and the call to united action is urgent. The former group—the fully " orthodox " Christians—should not hesitate to make common cause with the latter on any ground of fear lest the faith which they uphold should be compromised. The latter should not hesitate to join with the former through anxiety lest they be credited or discredited with more traditional beliefs than they accept. Both acknowledge the lordship and leadership of Christ in practical life; let them unite in loyalty to Him and His teaching. No doubt Christians are under a grave disqualification for exercising a healing influence in the world as a result of their own divisions. The trouble is not only the lack of united testimony; indeed, ways have been found of giving united testimony in spite of ecclesiastical divisions. The trouble rather is that men are little disposed to heed the exhortation, " Sirs, ye are brethren," when it is spoken by those whose own exhibition of fraternity seems to have made little moral advance on that of Cain and Abel. Christians ought to be deeply ashamed and manifestly penitent for their divisions; but we cannot withhold Christian testimony until be have achieved Christian reunion.

There are thousands who would like to believe in Christianity but are unable to do so. They cannot be won by being told of the beauty of the love of God, because that is exactly what they want to believe and for which they doubt the evidence. They could be won by being shown that the way of Jesus is a practical way, and by seeing men follow it and so solve problems that had seemed baffling.

The first necessity is for study, realistic thought, and vigilance. For study, because much Christian sentiment is rendered ineffective through lack of any accurate apprehension of the facts—but it must be Christian study, that is to say, study conducted with the object of promoting effectively that brotherhood among men which answers to the universal Fatherhood of God; for realistic thought, because those who dwell on principles often erroneously suppose that the rational exposition of these is sufficient to control human impulses and passions, whereas the Christian life has to be lived in a world where its principles are largely repudiated or ignored, and it is often hard to describe what will in fact secure expression for those principles; for vigilance, because the Christian claim may be challenged at any time in any part of the world, and if it goes by default anywhere it is weakened everywhere. Many English Christians at this moment [1935] are oppressed by shame and indignation at what seems to them the betrayal by our Government of a definite trust on behalf of the Assyrian Christians in Iraq. But the Government, subject to many other pressures, was not subject to any decisive pressure from a great volume of Christian opinion. The Archbishop of Canterbury has been untiring in his personal efforts in this cause, but the Christian opinion of the country has remained dormant, and our influence on the side of righteousness and of peace has been greatly damaged by what has appeared to be a breach of promise.

This is mentioned only as illustration. There are many fields where Christian opinion ought to be well informed and energetic. One of these is the economic field, where the twin evils of unemployment and exploitation present a perpetual challenge. About certain aspects of this I have taken another opportunity to express some convictions born of experience gained in recent work on behalf of the unemployed. But dominating all other concerns today is the supreme issue of Peace or War, and in what follows attention will be concentrated upon this. Has Christian belief any clear guidance to offer here?

In this connexion it is important to be clear on every occasion when it is demanded that " the Church should do something about it " what precisely is intended by " the Church." It may be any of four things:

(1) It may be the authoritative Councils of the Church laying down what is to be accepted by all members on pain of disloyalty to the Church. All agree that in this sense the Church should only declare what is universally requisite for Christian faith and practice.

(2) It may mean the Councils of the Church as guides to the conscience of its members, who are yet left free to follow their own judgment. Such action should be confined to matters where the judgment of a Christian ought to be affected by his faith—e.g. the obligation to see that no citizen is left to starve, as distinct from the question what the amount of assistance to unemployed persons should be.

(3) It may mean that individual Bishops and Clergy should make pronouncements. The value of these will depend on their personal qualifications for forming a judgment on the matter in question. If they are so qualified, it is not unreasonable that they should use their position as a means of reaching the public, and it may be stimulating to the public conscience that they should do so. But it must be understood that when they act thus, they act as prominent Christian citizens, not as spokesmen of the Church.

(4) It may mean that all Christian citizens ought in the inspiration of their faith to study the matter and act courageously upon the convictions which are thus conscientiously formed. In this sense the Church ought in our time to be active in many directions in reference to which it had no such obligation in previous generations, because the ethical quality of so many public questions is now a main factor determining the answer to be given. But activity of this sort will not necessarily result in united action by Christians apart from their union in study. It will, however, result in a different attitude towards each other on the part of those who differ in policy. For they will know that they differ only with regard to the most effective application of principles which all agree to uphold.

II: FAITH AND LOYALTY

If God exists, absolute allegiance is due to Him alone. The Christian owes loyalty to his State, but it is not an absolute loyalty; it may be his positive duty to disobey the State, as the instance of the Christian martyrs is alone sufficient to prove.

There can be no doubt about the claim of Christ in this respect. It is deliberately expressed in terms of violence. All particular ties of natural loyalty, gratitude and affection are to be ruthlessly ignored when they are incompatible with obedience to Christ.

Normally it is a Christian's duty to obey the State and its laws. It has its function in the promotion of that good life—the life of fellowship—which is the Christian's goal; and that function is indispensable. The Christian recognizes that the civil authority—even though its spokesman and executive agent be Nero—is " ordained of God." It is a great mistake to suppose that only the virtuous can be instruments of God. The vices of the wicked only have real power to harm us so far as we are alienated from God, and then they become, as Assyria was to Israel, " the rod of God's anger "; such was Lenin to the old régime of Russia. And it is to the ruler as ruler, not as virtuous or wicked, that allegiance is due. Most kinds of lawlessness arise from the self-centred passions which law exists to curb. In the conflict between these the Christian must be on the side of law, especially when the self-centred passions are his own. But the State cannot claim an obedience unconditional and unlimited. And there is urgent need for fresh examination of the limits of political obligation. Here only the main factors of the new problem can be mentioned, and some of the principles affecting it.

The primary function of the State is to secure by law those external conditions of well-being which can well be settled by universal regulations. Where individuality and spontaneity are of the essence of the matter, law is out of place; it is out of place therefore in art and (for the most part, at least) in religion. On the other hand universality is of the essence of property-rights, which are therefore especially suitable for legal determination. If the State as creator and upholder of law steps out of its proper province and prescribes to artists how they shall paint, or to scientists what they shall discover, or to physicians how they shall heal, or to worshippers how they shall pray, it becomes a duty to resist, at first by protest but, if the outrage continues, by active disobedience.

The whole problem has lately become complicated by the immense extension of the State's activity in promoting welfare otherwise than by coercion. Power of coercion is indeed a part of the State's necessary equipment. Force is entrusted to the State in order that the State may effectively prevent the lawless use of force; and from the moral standpoint the use of force to uphold a law designed for the general well-being against any who try to use force contrary to the general well-being, is in a totally different class from the force which is thus kept in check. If the police draw their truncheons to quell rioters they do not thereby become rioters. Because the State aims at the general well-being it should not use more force to control violence than is necessary; but it is still more important that it should use enough. If once the State has recourse to force at all for the maintenance of law the primary requirement is that it should employ sufficient force; otherwise it leaves lawless force triumphant.

But the State now does much in which coercion plays a very minor part, and even in which the aim is to substitute other methods for coercion. Of such activities the most important is education. Parents are required to send their children to school; so far, coercion plays a part. And inside the school coercive discipline exists as a last resort. But few parents are often conscious of coercion, and the aim of teachers is to avoid recourse to it. The Probation System is a deliberate attempt to substitute persuasion and influence for coercion in the treatment of offenders. Thus the State enters the field not only as the source of law, but as the dominant moral influence in the lives of citizens. No one can question the reality of progress thus secured. But with this a new danger emerges. For while the State which held the force confined itself to coercive action, and the agencies aiming at the exercise of influence were without force, the latter might keep one another in check, and the State itself could intervene if occasion arose. But if the State absorbs into itself the cultural activities, who is to rectify errors or disproportions in the minds of those who manipulate its enormous powers?

If any respect is to be paid to the spiritual character of man the

claim of the Totalitarian State, whether Communist or Fascist, must
be resisted. But the only ground of such resistance and the only
guarantee of man's spiritual character is the reality of God as alone
entitled to absolute allegiance, and the relation of sonship which
every human being bears to Him. If God reigns, and if each man is
His son, then every individual has a significance and value which
are prior to and independent of citizenship in any earthly state. If it
is in many respects a duty of the citizen to serve the State, this does
not exhaust his duty. If ever the claim of the State conflicts with
obedience to God, the State must be defied; and in the last resort
it is more completely the function of the State to serve its citizens
than it is their function to serve the State, for they have an eternal
destiny and the State has not.

The question when a conflict of loyalties has arisen such as to
require disobedience to the State can only be answered by the individual Christian himself; and he is not infallible. Upon him as a child
of God there rests the ultimate responsibility for determining what
duty to God requires. He must not complain if the State treats him
as a criminal; it treated his Master so. But, of course, he will use his
own influence and power as a citizen to prevent the State from treating thus others who resist it for conscience' sake. The formal recognition of conscientious objection to military service during the Great
War was a Christian act on the part of the British State, whether or
not the conscientious objectors were right in their objection and
whether or not the State was right to be engaged in war.

III: THE FAMILY OF MANKIND

God is the Father of all men and the King of all nations. It is impossible to doubt that His will for nations is that they should learn to
live together in the fellowship of one family. Patriotism can be a
noble Christian virtue, if it subordinates narrower to wider loyalties
or takes the form of pride in priority in service; on the other hand
that form of Nationalism which involves regarding all other nations
primarily as potential enemies is incompatible with Christianity. It
is of the essence of the Christian Church that it should be supra-
national, uniting men in a fellowship to which all natural divisions
are irrelevant. The Christian citizen is bound by his faith to direct
his political influence and to use his share of political power in
accordance with this principle of world-fellowship.

IV: PRACTICAL POLICY

Hitherto we have been concerned to state principles which no
Christian can loyally dispute; we do not pretend that our formulation

of them is perfect, but we believe that it represents them sufficiently for recognition. Let any one who can, formulate them more adequately; but let no one regard defect in the formulation as excuse for ignoring the principles.

We pass now to the field of application. Here differences may arise between Christians equally loyal, for at least on many of the urgent questions there is dispute concerning the probable effects of various proposed courses of action.

There are some Christians who hold that loyalty to Christ forbids all participation in fighting. We respect that view, but we do not share it. If it is not adopted, a distinction must at once be drawn between the duty of a Christian in time of peace and his duty when war has broken out. When that calamity has happened, so that the international order has collapsed, he has to judge what will best effect its reconstitution on a sure foundation. But that is not our problem now. What we have to consider is the Christian's duty as a citizen in regard to international affairs in time of peace.

He is called upon to foster justice, peace and goodwill and to promote that fellowship among the nations which may enable them to live together as members in the family of God. But how is he to do this?

The question is far from simple. Two outstanding factors which create great difficulty must be mentioned. First, there is the difference in level of cultural attainment and in ethical principle which is characteristic of different peoples. It is not certain that justice or goodwill is best served by such agreement on policy as could now be reached between, shall be say? France and Turkey or between the United States and Persia. There is difficulty in determining what States may be admitted to any League or Pact, and also in determining the relations between them when admitted. It cannot be said that all Christians are bound to agree in their judgment on such matters.

Secondly, there is the fact that all natural societies or groupings of men are animated by a measure of corporate egoism more intense than that which animates their component members as individuals. Christians cannot admit that this is a necessary characteristic of all societies. If Pentecost means anything it is that there can be a Fellowship of the Spirit animated by pure love; and there is in experience abundant evidence to the fact that a fellowship based on adherence to some ideal can rise to ethical heights transcending the moral capacity of its members acting singly. But these are fellowships of the elect—of those, that is, to whom the ideal in question makes effective appeal and whom it thus selects and draws into its own fellowship. When all men are truly Christians, so that the nations which they compose are consciously parts of a Church truly Christian and truly Catholic, we may expect nations to be free from corporate egoism; to expect this on any other terms is to be false alike to experience and to the purpose of God as Christians believe it to have been declared.

The problem of Christian statesmanship is therefore to find the way in which national egoism may be subordinated to, and if possible made to serve, justice, peace and goodwill. For such a task we have no infallible guidance and what is proposed is not so much a distinctively Christian policy as apparently the only rational means to the Christian end.

First, then, it seems to us necessary that every nation should abandon its claim to be judge in its own cause. Englishmen are accustomed to claim that their armed force will never be used except to maintain justice and freedom. Foreigners are not always able to feel confident of this. In any case, why should the French or German peoples be expected to accept without more ado the British estimate of what is just, especially where British interests are involved? There should be an unshakable determination to submit every dispute to the appropriate form of arbitration and to accept the award.

Secondly, inasmuch as fear is now the chief source of danger to peace, the chief causes of fear should be removed. Our first demand —acceptance of arbitration in all disputes—would carry us far in this direction. Another requisite is the ending of all competition in armaments. It is not more wicked to kill men with a big gun than with a small gun, but the knowledge that a neighbouring nation is equipping itself with guns of unprecedented range is a great occasion for panic. Our own country has been as conspicuous a sinner as any other in this respect; the building of the Dreadnought appears in retrospect as a most lamentable action. The purpose of seeking to limit armaments by international agreement is mainly to put an end to competition in armaments and the fear excited by it. It is because it seems certain that private armament firms encourage that competition that the abolition of private trade in armaments is recommended.

Some Christians would go so far and no further. We urge the necessity of further steps.

The first need is to strengthen and develop the machinery which provides the civilized world with a central co-ordinating organization. The institution of the League of Nations did not involve any new principle but represented the extension of an old, well-tried and generally accepted system of government from the individual nation to the community of nations.

No civilized community can exist or ever has existed without some form of central government. The world in recent years has developed from a series of isolated and self-supporting units into a community bound together by common interests of trade, industry and finance, so that the welfare of each part has become the concern of the whole. With whatever feelings we may view this change, we are faced by the alternatives of developing a central organization or reverting to what is truly described as International Anarchy.

The organization of the community on the basis of law requires the acceptance of three fundamental principles. The first of these is the point made above, that every nation should abandon its claim to be judge in its own cause. The claim to judge the merits of a dispute by one party automatically robs the other party of a similar right. It is often urged against the system of international arbitration that no nation can be sure of getting justice at the hands of an international court. There would appear to be some substance, although not much, in this claim, but the choice lies between accepting a system of justice devised by man and therefore imperfect, and having no system of justice at all.

Individuals have long realized that it is infinitely better to surrender their freedom and submit to judicial decisions which are not always in accordance with abstract justice; they willingly pay this price in order to obtain the benefits of an ordered community and freedom from the impossible task of endeavouring to enforce upon others their own views. However imperfect may be the decision of an international court, it cannot inflict more than a tithe of the disaster and chaos which result from trying to settle disputes by war—the only alternative means. But in fact experience has shown that the Permanent Court of International Justice has maintained a very high level of impartiality.

The second principle which is involved is that the defence of the individual should be undertaken by the community. This does not mean that an individual nation, any more than an individual person, is not entitled to defend itself if attacked until such time as the forces of the community can come to its help; but in practice, if it is known in advance that to attack an individual is to challenge the community, such attacks rarely or never take place. When once the principle is established they will probably, in the case of nations, never take place at all, since individuals who defy the community hope that their misdeeds will never be traced to them, but such a hope could not be entertained by a nation.

The third principle which follows necessarily from the second, is that individuals should defend the community, since only so can the community defend the individual. Within the confines of a nation, this duty is in practice delegated to paid servants—the police —but the reason why a small handful of men can keep order among a large population is that behind the authority of the police there is, in the last resort, the whole force and power, first of the armed forces of the Crown, and eventually of the whole body of citizens. The chief argument against applying this system to nations is that it would represent an endeavour to suppress war by making war. This is not the case; there are essential moral and practical differences between the abuse of, and the restraint of, violence, as is shown by the example already given of the use of force by the police for the suppression of a riot.

The basis of collective action is " the strength of all for the defence of each "—a conception which, once generally accepted, makes the defence so overwhelmingly strong in relation to any possible attack that the resultant feeling of security transforms a state of fear and uncertainty into one of safety and enterprise.

" But all this," it may be said, " is mere prudential politics. Christianity only begins where all this leaves off." Well, we have already not only admitted but clearly affirmed that what we have put forward is not a necessary inference from the Gospel but only a reasonable means to a Christian end, though apparently the only means to this end. Yet there is more to be said than that. It is strictly congruous with the divine method as Christians have been taught to understand it. It is no accident that the Law precedes the Gospel. That is part of the providential ordering of History. The revelation of the New Testament completes that of the Old, but also presupposes it. The great Counsels of Perfection in the Teaching of Christ which look at first like contradictions of the old Law are introduced with the words, " Think not that I came to destroy the law or the prophets; I came not to destroy but to fulfil." It is to characters already disciplined by Law and its sanctions that the Gospel of love can make its appeal, carrying them on to stages of spiritual attainment to which no law or sanction could ever raise them.

And the Law remains, providing the firm basis on which the Gospel can call men to build their spiritual habitation. It is not abrogated by the Gospel, but assumed as supplying and ensuring the basis from which the Gospel starts. We know in our own lives that we need the coercive control of law as well as the uplifting appeal of the Gospel. The Law is influencing us every day; it is not active only when men are brought before its Courts. As A. L. Smith, the late Master of Balliol, used to say, " We may be reasonably honest folk who prefer to pay for our seats when we travel by train; but probably there are occasions when the existence of the ticket-collector just clinches the matter."

Our present measure of liberty has not been reached by diminishing the relative volume of force available to the central national authority, but by increasing it until it is incomparably great and resistance to it is futile. The first necessity was for the Crown to gain control over the feudal nobility. Till that was done, national life was a chaos of private wars. Those wars ceased when the Crown was strong enough to call both parties to book. Now order is tolerably well established, but it rests on the force at the disposal of the Crown as central authority to suppress all disorder. That force is relatively so overwhelming that no one, broadly speaking, challenges it. So we forget it, and enjoy the orderliness which it guarantees, and the liberty thus made possible. Our freedom and capacity to enter on the intercourse and aspirations which spring from freedom, rest on the fact that the State has at its disposal lawful force sufficient to control all exercise of violence which is lawless force.

It can be so also among nations. There is not reason to suppose that order and liberty can be secured in any other way. Especially is there no reason in Christian revelation for hope by any other way than this.

V : Congruity with Christian Faith and Hope

What is first asked for is a big sacrifice of pride; this at least is thoroughly congruous with Christian ethics. We have to call upon our nation to forgo its unlimited Sovereignty and to regard itself as subject to the Law of Nations and to the authority—be it the League or some freshly constituted body—which is the source and upholder of that law. This is likely to be unpopular in principle; it is certain to be highly unpopular in practice when we have to accept an award given against our interests as we see them by people whom some of our fellow citizens will describe as Dagoes. National pride must humble itself or be transmuted. The latter is not impossible. We are already proud of British justice; we have only to develop that sentiment to its logical completion.

Further, we must be prepared for a revision of the public law of nations now embodied in so-called Treaties imposed by victorious upon vanquished peoples. In many respects the Treaties of Versailles and Trianon are not bases of peace but a prolonged act of war. By no system of law is a contract binding if entered into under duress. The Treaties may be binding *de facto*; they have legal authority; and no one who stands for international order can regard lightly a deliberate breach of international law. But they are not binding *de jure* by any system of ethics, human or divine; they have no moral authority binding upon conscience except that which belongs to any particular law because it is part of the whole body of law. A recognition of this may involve sacrifices for all the lately victorious nations. It is likely that in a general readjustment our own country will be called upon to give up some territories allotted to it after the war. We must be ready for that. Again, it is hardly to be expected that in the long run it will be found compatible with international civilization that one State should retain control of narrow seas. If all forces are subject to international control this may survive for a while; but it is hard to regard as permanently compatible with an international guarantee of order our own control of Gibraltar and Aden. We certainly shall not voluntarily give them up till order is fairly well secured, so perhaps it is idle to discuss whether we ought; but there will come a point where this is the test of our loyalty to our proposed ideal of international authority.

In all of this we shall be acting on the principle that " we are members one of another "—the basic truth about human life which proves that even now, and from the beginning, it is in essence subject to the Kingdom of God.

The prominence of the Kingdom in the teaching of Our Lord is the great discovery of recent study. To us it is most obvious; but till the middle of the nineteenth century it was little noticed. When attention came to be directed to it, two extreme views of it were taken. One represented it as something alien from our existing state, which would one day be inaugurated by the miracle of a cosmic catastrophe. The other conceived it in terms of personal and civic virtue and led men to speak of their own actions as extending or building the Kingdom of God. If either of these views were right the other would be impossible. The Kingdom of God is indeed established by God alone. In part it is here already, for with all our self-will we never escape from the Sovereignty of God; in part it is yet to come through God's action in His own time. But the Church is the Body of Christ, the vehicle and organ of the Holy Spirit. God can and does effect the increase of His Kingdom by His own activity in the society of Christian people. Our duty is to put ourselves under the control of that Spirit and to let Him guide our action private and public, individual and corporate. Thus we become His agents in increase of His Kingdom as it is, and in preparation for its perfect coming.

(Published by the S.C.M. Press under the auspices of the League of Nations Union, 1935)

Christian Democracy

AT A MOMENT when the Christian tradition is challenged as never before since the conversion of Constantine, and when in many regions Reason is openly decried as a guide inferior to the intuitions due to impulse, and even to prejudice, it is worth while to consider whether there is any connexion between these two phenomena. Christianity and Rationalism (in any interpretation of that term) are not simply identical; there is in Christianity that which Reason could never have discovered, and, even after it has been revealed, can never prove. It therefore makes a claim which only Intuition can either repudiate or accept. But most champions of Reason would admit, or perhaps rather insist, that Reason itself has a wider scope than " reasoning," and must always in the last resort base itself on judgments of value which are incapable of proof or of serious support by argument; indeed Reason is essentially a special kind of Intuition —the Intuition of Totality or of the Whole and of every fact in its place in the Whole. But no one actually grasps the Whole in its entirety; consequently reliance upon Reason manifests itself as a free play of interchange between different minds; and " reasoning " is the process of reaching an intuition of the Whole or the closest possible approximation to that; all rational argument takes the form of setting particular facts or beliefs in relation to others with which they must be adjusted or fitted to make up the Whole. What is urged in the following pages is the intrinsic kinship between the ultimate intuitions of Christian faith and the attitude towards life which is both expressed in and encouraged by reliance upon Reason. We shall consider this first in the political sphere and then turn to some more general considerations which point in the same direction.

I

One of the most conspicuous features of the present time is the reversion of great numbers of people from reason to violence as the determining force in politics. The causes for this are many, and some of them will be mentioned later. But one is so relevant to the purpose of this essay that it must be discussed at the outset: it is the bewildering complexity of life. It has always been true that things were going on all over the world at once; but it is only in recent times that we have had to think about them all at once. Not very long ago a European Government, hearing of disturbances in China, would send a representative to ascertain the facts and do the best he could about them. He could not receive many instructions, because these would be out of date by the time that he arrived. His Government at home might wonder what he was at, but they could not act and were therefore relieved of the obligation to acquire knowledge and form judgments for the guidance of their action.

Now all the world is one neighbourhood. As soon as any important event takes place, it is known in all other places. Not only does our Government know what happens in China as soon as it occurs, but all other European Governments know also, and all those of both Americas. Consequently there is a necessity to define a policy in relation to the events in China, which is also and at the same time a policy in relation to the policies being formed or likely to be formed by all the other Governments. All political questions are interlocked, so that the handling of any one of them is a matter of vast complexity.

The same is true of the economic world. Here too we have the spectacle of a world which is one neighbourhood, but is administered by a multitude of Governments related together in every variety and degree of co-operation and rivalry. And here the complexity due to the varying relations of national States to one another is further complicated by the relations—co-operative and competitive—of various international firms active alike in commerce and in finance. It is very few who can disentangle these threads. The public at large is utterly bewildered. It tends to seek a leader who for some reason inspires confidence and to follow him blindly.

For it cannot merely stand aside. In the days of absolute monarchies, super-imposed upon a feudal system, the monarch, with some of his feudal magnates and a selected group of conspicuously able men, determined national policy while the peasants cultivated the soil and pursued their personal interests. But the coming of Democracy has altered all that. Now the people is sovereign—of course it always was so in a quite ultimate sense, but now it exercises sovereignty—and has suffered a heightening of national self-consciousness in consequence. If the people is sovereign alike in France and in Germany, those peoples must become aware of their difference from one another in a degree that had no relevance to the older system. Nationalism, as we know it today, is a by-product of the democratic movement. It is quite true that some nations have lately dispensed with democratic methods, but they have not reverted to the systems of the eighteenth and earlier centuries. Louis XIV led his people; but he did not derive his title from their support. Hitler and Mussolini are in many ways more despotic; but they are also more dependent on popular favour, which accordingly they spend much energy and skill in maintaining.

It is, in part at least, this new sense of responsibility in the masses of the people, coupled with the complexity of modern problems, which constitutes the temptation to despair of reason and to follow blindly a chosen Leader—chosen because of an immediate sense of affinity between him and the people, not because his policy is deliberately approved by the people. For when Italians follow Mussolini or Germans follow Hitler, they have no sense of abdicating their responsibility; rather, this discipleship is felt to be the exercise of that responsibility.

But where a man fulfils his obligations by practice of an uncriticized faith, his reaction to those who deny that faith will always be one of violence. He cannot reason with them, for his faith is independent of reason, and he cannot be sure that the application of reason will not corrode it. Consequently his only resource is violence of some kind—violence of speech if that is likely to be sufficient or is alone available, violence of action if what he regards as right or even sacred can be protected in no other way. For the same reason criticism must be suppressed; to question is as damaging as to deny. Questioners must be silenced.

Now it is quite possible for men to embrace a faith uncritically yet in a completely idealistic spirit. The aspect of Fascism or National Socialism which appeals to high-spirited youth is its demand for self-sacrifice on behalf of their country. They have a purpose in life, and they know that it is not a selfish purpose. It can be fulfilled only by self-abnegation. Yet in this appeal there is a subtly pernicious element. For although it is a call to self-sacrifice, and the conscious mind has nothing else before its attention, it is also a call to serve what for each patriot is his own country in distinction from others. Nor is it conceivable that such leadership should be successful on any other grounds. The driving force of Communism, where it secures the support of the masses, is not so much the ultimate hope of the class-less society as the immediate assertion of the Proletarian Class as dominant. Thus there is a stimulus offered to all the motives in human nature—self-devoting, gregarious, egoistic. Most if not all of the appeal to conscious thought is directed to the generous and self-devoting impulses; thus conscience is at once enlisted and drugged; but all the time the egoistic impulses are also pressed into service, for it is My leader whom I am to follow, My country that I am to serve, My race that I am to exalt, My class that I am to uplift.

Such an appeal must of necessity be anti-rational. It may be encased in an argumentative shell of great intellectual complexity, as with Marxian Communism; or it may present itself as a form of natural mysticism, as with the National Socialism of contemporary Germany. But it cannot permit the free play of reason upon its presuppositions. For the first axiom of reason is that each one counts for one, whether it be one citizen or one nation or one race or one class. It is marked by, indeed it is in its own very nature, an aspiration towards totality, towards a grasp of the whole wherein each part is seen for what it is as one part. Thus, for example, its interest in justice will never present itself as a demand from the citizens of this country or of that for justice for their own nation, but always as a desire for justice for all nations. This universalizing tendency, inherent in reason by its very nature, is abhorrent to any political system which rests upon appeal—skilfully concealed—to sub-conscious egoism. For rational criticism must reveal the quality of this appeal and must also condemn it. Consequently the new regimes openly disavow and repudiate the authority of reason, of science, and of any religious society or creed which sets all upon an equality and binds all in a single fellowship.

It has repeatedly happened in the history of Europe that Christian people have become conscious of the meaning of their own principles only when these are challenged. Indeed that is the way in which, speaking broadly, mankind most commonly becomes aware of its beliefs. It cannot be claimed that the Christian Church has stood steadily or consistently for the authority of reason or the free play of critical intelligence. We shall return before long to the causes for its anxiety in regard to these. Yet from the time of those Apologists, such as Justin Martyr, who were the first Christian theologians, as that term is now used, Christian theology has been deeply committed to the appeal to reason. And though in practice the Church has not uniformly relied upon that appeal, yet it has never abandoned it or compromised it. Indeed the extreme rationalism of medieval theology is the ground on which it is nowadays condemned by a dominant school of continental theologians.

Of course there is a vast difference between the appeal to reason in general and the appeal to your reason or mine. No one tries to control children only by an appeal to their reasoning powers; and the question whether, and if so when, we cease to be children in mind is not easily answered. The Church which broadly rested its case on reason, as that might be apprehended by St. Thomas Aquinas or St. Bonaventura, might also say to most of its members that they were forbidden to think for themselves because they were sure to do it badly and to arrive at conclusions both mistaken and calamitous. There is no self-contradiction in such a position. But there is extreme

K

psychological difficulty; for those who in dealing with others, even though they be children, appeal to other grounds of belief than reason, easily find themselves neglecting the appeal to reason in themselves. The risk of this is less when those concerned are children, for their dependence in other respects prohibits the analogy between them and their elders. But those who resort to non-rational methods of creating belief in grown-up people—such as persecution, or mass-suggestion, or individual suggestion—are liable to cease from critical enquiry into the rational grounds for the beliefs which they seek, by these non-rational methods, to impart. Consequently, when we find the same Church and even the same religious Order giving birth to scholastic theology and to the Inquisition, we have no ground to charge it with inconsistency, but we have very good ground for anxiety.

For the psychological tendency likely to result from the free employment in relation to adults of non-rational methods of persuasion has been reinforced in the history of the Church by the natural but usually unchristian love of power. Having found that spiritual authority can often be maintained by treating people as children, the Church has sometimes tried to keep them children in order that such treatment may be appropriate. The double Pauline injunction " in malice be ye children, but in understanding be men " is hard to observe with full regard to both of its requirements. Probably it is worse to fail in the first than in the second; and it may reasonably be held that a secular civilization and an education which has trained the intellect without any accompanying increase of discipline of the desires and emotions has done more harm than good. But the undoubted existence of that risk is a very insufficient ground for refusing the enterprise to which the whole course of the modern world is calling us—the enterprise of developing the resources of individual life in the activities of the mind and in control over nature, while deepening at the same time the experience of fellowship with men and communion with God. Moreover, the inevitable result of refusing that enterprise is in the long run a revolt in the name of reason and progress against religion and the institutions associated with it. A Christian Church which provokes that revolt has betrayed one of the distinctive features of the faith entrusted to it.

For Christianity is unique among religions in that it is in itself a spring of continual progress. For two reasons religion is as a rule a conservative force. One reason is provided by its own nature as religion. This is more intimately concerned with feeling than with thought, though of course it can only be " true " religion if thought takes a great part in it. And feeling is more easily stirred by old associations than by future possibilities, especially among the comfortable classes. Consequently religion clings tenaciously to all that is bound up with its sacred associations.

The other reason for the conservatism of most positive religions is that the precepts of the founder can be obeyed only under conditions similar to those which first occasioned the form of the precepts. Consequently, changing conditions always seem to imperil the practice of the religion, and those to whom that practice is sacred are bound to resist the change of conditions.

But Christianity is not primarily a religion at all; it is primarily a Revelation. As a religion it is essentially and at all times a response to that Revelation—not an aspiration towards an unknown or inscrutable God, but a responsive surrender to a divine self-disclosure. And this disclosure is not in a system of thought or morals but in a Person, so that the response of the disciple is not a careful fulfilment of precepts, but a life governed by loyalty to that Person. What Christ left in the world as fruit of His ministry was not a system of theology or a code of rules for life—a new Pharisaism—but a living fellowship of men and women united in His Spirit because of their loyalty to Him.

That Spirit within the Christian fellowship is a permanent ferment of unrest. For neither the world outside nor the soul of the disciple himself ever corresponds to that Spirit in more than fragmentary ways. Thus the Christian, who has an unshakable serenity in his eternal hope and inner communion with God, is a factor of perpetual discontent with all else than God and His Kingdom, as he forgets the things which are behind and stretches forth to those that are before, pressing on towards his goal, the prize of the call upwards which God gives in Christ Jesus.

This energy of perpetual progress cannot be limited to a purely " spiritual " sphere, while the world of history and experience is left to go its own way. Christianity is the most materialistic of the great religions. Its central affirmation is that " the Word was made *flesh*." Many religions seek to make men " spiritual " by calling upon them to turn their backs upon the material world and think only of " spiritual" things. Christianity teaches that spirit is actual in its control of the material. Not by ignoring the world but by conquering it does the Christian manifest the power of the Spirit in his life.

Consequently the Church is called to welcome material developments in civilization and the secular knowledge on which they rest, in spite of the temptations which these bring, and to try to balance development on that side with a corresponding growth in the knowledge and love of God, so that newly acquired powers over nature may be used for service and increase of fellowship, not for avarice and increase of enmity.

The Christian faith in God as Father of all men involves two consequences which are directly contrary to some powerful modern tendencies: these two consequences may be called Universalism and Individualism—but if so these words must be understood in a rather special sense.

If God is Father of all men, all men are His children, and brothers and sisters in His family. This forbids an exaltation of our own nation or state in any such way as to be damaging to others. There is a form of religion in some parts of the world today which, resting on the doctrine of Creation, declares that a man best serves God by absolute devotion to the nation of which God has made him a citizen. Apart from the word " absolute " that is true. A believer in God as Creator and Providential Ruler of the world cannot avoid the belief that nations exist by the will of God. It is by His appointment that one man is British, another French, a third German, and so forth. And the Englishman best serves God by being a good Englishman. Yet the national loyalty of a Christian cannot be absolute, just because it is an expression of, and subordinate to, his loyalty to God who is the Father of Germans and Frenchmen as truly as of Englishmen. The Christian's ideal, therefore, is neither an exclusive nationalism, nor a flaccid cosmopolitanism, but a family of nations, where each one develops its own qualities and yet gains from the qualities of others. His service to God is rendered in promoting the welfare of his own country, but this welfare is conceived in a manner which precludes its incompatibility with the welfare of others: for the fundamental principle is unity in the family of God. It is evident that these considerations call for a drastic revision and mitigation of that extreme nationalism which is rampant in Europe today.

All such considerations point to the democratic principle as best fitted to carry into human affairs the Christian conception of man. Among nations, each nation has its place, and none seeks to oust it. Within the nation, each citizen has his personal and independent value, which the political constitution does not create but recognizes. Everyone therefore may freely form and express his opinion; and government is conducted according to the upshot of reasonable discussion.

" Phew! What sentimental rubbish! " exclaims the man of the world. And indeed what has been described is more of an ideal than a fact. Democracy has not worked out like that. Sometimes its precious " greatest number " exercises effective control, and then you get mob-rule. Sometimes the power of wealth takes the place that properly belongs to collective wisdom, and in most capitalistic democracies there is a very large element of plutocracy working through democratic machinery. Sometimes (as was alleged to be the case in Germany under the Weimar Constitution) there is endless talk and no action, because there is not enough common feeling to lead the various sectional interests to combine on any policy, so that there is a majority against all proposals. This lack of common feeling may be due to a real deficiency of public spirit, or to a degree of individualization which frustrates united action. The political result is the same.

Moreover the human family is not a divine family. When Clemenceau was asked if he did not agree that brotherhood is the root principle of all human relations he answered, "Yes, certainly. Brotherhood, brotherhood; Cain and Abel, Cain and Abel." If men are free they will seek their selfish ends; these are often incompatible, and they will be led to fighting. The politicians of a democratic state will increase the evil by their method of buying votes with promises, which encourages citizens to think of the State as a reservoir of supply for their wants rather than as an object of their loyalty and service.

The politics of every actual state are determined by one form or another of selfishness in the citizens. It is claimed by Fascists that their system is less selfish than democracy because instead of putting up the Government for sale by appeals to the cupidity of electors, it bases its security on the spirit of self-devotion in its subjects. But this self-devotion is not in any true sense unselfish, for each one is encouraged to give devotion to *his* country in sharp distinction from others. This kind of self-devotion is selfishness writ large. It may be ethically superior to a purely individual self-seeking, but that is not quite evident. For our present purpose it is enough to insist that selfishness, being a prominent quality of human beings, is bound to be an important factor in the State.

But it may take many forms—individual or collective, enlightened or unenlightened. It is part of the political advantage of a developed scheme of national education that it tends to produce a greater capacity for a sane estimate of values and a subordination of immediate but transitory to more abiding interests. Selfishness itself gives rise to a real form of social justice, because each can have security only so far as he respects the security of others. The political discussions characteristic of democracy have a powerful educational effect and tend to the substitution of enlightened for unenlightened selfishness.

There is even a certain sense in which the Christian way of life itself is the way of "enlightened self-interest." There is nothing arbitrary in the God disclosed by Christ, nor is our acceptance of His revelation a surrender to an alien authority irrespective of our own self-realization. Rebellion against God or neglect of Him is a severance of the self from its own root in reality. The rebel hopes to gratify himself, but in fact he excludes himself from the way of joy and peace. The Christian's aim is not so to behave as to avoid provoking the arbitrary retribution of God, but so to behave as to conform to the real principles of human life, which are recognized by reason, if it be true to itself, as true and just. In pursuit of this aim he must be ready for sacrifice. Yet it remains true that the aim itself is the life in which men can find satisfaction.

Nevertheless there is no prospect that men will follow that way of life on grounds of enlightened selfishness alone or because it is the sensible thing to do. For men are more passionate than they are sensible, and the passions of avarice and ambition, personal and national, can only be overcome by a passion stronger still—the passion of devotion to a leader who claims the allegiance of our whole being. That is why Christian faith is indispensably necessary to the Christian life.

It is certainly true that every political constitution is open to abuse and the corruption of democracy is peculiarly odious. It is also true that more high-flown nonsense has been talked about democracy than about any other political system: *Vox populi, vox Dei*—and so forth. The reason for letting the majority govern is not that it is sure to be right; on the contrary, on any new and intricate issue it is sure to be wrong. But there is no means, till afterwards, of settling which minority (if any) is right. And the majority will seldom go as far wrong as some minorities often go. But the reason for letting the majority govern is not even that it is nearly sure not to go very far wrong. It is that the exercise of political responsibility is good for the citizens who practise it, so that a community trained in democratic politics is likely to be a more richly developed and more securely stabilized community than any other. And this in turn rests on the fact that it is the form of constitution which does most justice to the nature of man as God made him.

" As God made him "—not as he has made himself. Some communities are unfit for democracy; and none is perfectly fit for it. It does give a universal outlet for selfishness in the political sphere such as is offered neither by Communism, nor by Fascism, nor by the ancient caste system of India. Thus it presents a massive and multitudinous temptation which no country that has tasted democracy has completely resisted, and before which some have collapsed either in headlong ruin or in crumbling decay. Adherents of democracy do it ill service if they suggest that the establishment of democratic institutions is a remedy for all ills, or that in all circumstances it is desirable to establish or even to maintain them. Democracy makes greater demands on the moral resources of a nation than any other form of constitution. What is contended in this paper is not that democracy should everywhere be established, but that more than any other form of constitution it corresponds to the full Christian conception of man—man "fallen," i.e. selfish, and therefore needing to be governed, and that, too, by force; but man created "in the image of God," and therefore capable of responding to moral appeal and of living as a good member of the whole family of God.

The most sensitive point is freedom of opinion and of speech. The two go together. Only if facts and thoughts are freely communicated can opinion be freely formed; only if when formed it may be communicated will men take trouble to form real opinions. Liberty of speech and of the press is thus the most vital of all concerns to the believer in Christian democracy and government by appeal to reason. No doubt the "free" press appeals to much else besides reason, and deliberately may appeal to reason little or not at all. But passions and prejudices are ephemeral and tend to eliminate one another. The judgments of reason are enduring. Out of what seems to be a mere welter of appeals to prejudice and passion a very sound judgment may emerge, provided only that all passions and all prejudices are allowed to express themselves. As soon as any is denied verbal expression there is danger.

But it is not only true that Christianity best expresses itself through democracy; it is also true that democracy can only survive if it is Christian. It needs alike the inspiration and the check that Christianity can supply—the inspiration that leads each citizen to desire a fair deal for his fellow citizens, and the check that hinders each from using his liberty to exploit that fellow citizen. Our own democratic practice shows large traces of these in some departments, but very little in others. So far as democracy becomes a mere welter of competing self-interests it is on the way to perish and will deserve its doom.

Those who believe in Christian democracy as the best hope of the world are called upon to do all in their power to think out its implications for our time in great matters and in small. What does it require of us in relation to:

> The League of Nations
> Distribution of Colonies
> Access to Raw Materials

Ownership and Control of Industry
Commercial Competition
Social Fellowship in our Neighbourhood?

The list might be indefinitely expanded. But warning on two sides is needed. (1) It cannot be right for Christians to do more harm than good. Therefore they must do their best to know the facts to which they will seek to apply their principles: and this must include a wholesale recognition of the material selfishness of all men and a refusal to expect idealistic conduct except under the immediate pressure of known idealistic motives—whether religious or other. (2) On the other hand, it cannot be right for Christians to be content to let ill alone, so that, having tried to recognize the facts and to allow for the selfishness of men, they are bound to work as they have been taught to pray that God's Name may be hallowed, His Kingdom come, and His Will be done, on earth.

II

There is some danger that those who follow with sympathy the argument so far developed may suppose that democracy or its political forms is the matter of fundamental concern. In fact democracy was introduced as an illustration of a principle that extends far beyond it. Democracy with its freedom of thought and speech can be the best and most natural means in the political field of giving full scope to reason. It is not always this, as we have already seen; and it is never the perfect embodiment of reason pure and unalloyed. But it can give to the exercise of reason what no other system can give, and where it has not merited condemnation by its failure it should be valued for this potentiality. But the principle with which we are concerned is that of the necessary alliance of Christianity, when true to itself, with reason and with rational methods.

Such methods may—indeed they must—imply rational deference to authority. There is no greater delusion than to suppose that there is a necessary antipathy or antagonism between reason and authority. If I believe something " on the authority of the Church " or of the British Medical Association, or of the Third International, it is because I suppose that the authority in question is certain or likely to be right. Thus I believe the monstrously paradoxical proposition that the earth goes round the sun. I have never worked out the arguments for or against this view. But I understand that all students of astronomy hold it, and it would be quite unreasonable that I should regard it as false even though I am quite unaware of any ground (other than their authority) for thinking it true. My acceptance of that belief on authority is an entirely rational procedure. And all acceptance of belief "on authority" has that quality, though there may easily be mistakes about the degree of authority to be attributed to any person or society, and about the sphere in which it may be rightly exercised.

The appeal to authority is always a rational appeal in its own nature. Many people confuse with this what is in fact quite different, namely obedience or profession of belief under pressure of threats. If the Government calls upon me to act in a certain way and I obey because the Government has the right and the duty to determine my action in that matter, I am acting out of respect for its authority; if I obey, though inwardly protesting, only because the Government will fine, imprison, or kill me if I do not, there is no respect for authority but only a surrender to fear of consequences to myself. It is sometimes right that the Government should (as we say) uphold its authority by use of force through the law and the police. But this force does not constitute its authority, and the more true authority it has the less it will need to use force. It is a commonplace among schoolmasters that a good disciplinarian rarely sets punishments; he is obeyed because his authority is respected.

But if an authority is thus to win respect and effectiveness by the fact that reason supports it or responds to it, it must itself be based upon and directed by reason. Arbitrary authority is, strictly speaking, a contradiction in terms. In order, therefore, that there may be real authority in a community, there must be reliance on reason, just as reason often expresses itself by reliance on authority. Failure on either side provokes failure on the other. If subjects try to obtain by force what constitutional authority refuses to give them, that authority must resort to force in order to control them: but then its interest should be not primarily its own maintenance but rather the prevention of the surrender of the agents of reason to the non-rational pressure of force. In the same way, if those who hold authority fail to commend it to the reason (which includes the moral judgment) of their subjects, they provoke these to resist by force what is being forcibly imposed; and then the first concern of the "rebels" should be, not the assertion of their policy or even of their rights against others, but resistance to the usurpation by force of what rightly belongs to reason. As a rule, however, the due order of priority is ignored; those who are feeling outraged seldom adopt a reasonable or even a reasoning attitude, with the result that every failure to rely on reason begets a whole progeny of irrationalities. And that is not the end; for those who are actuated by outraged feelings rather than by reason are driven to keep alive their emotions of hostility and hatred because these supply the impulse for the course of conduct which they have chosen. So outrage breeds outrage, oppression breeds assassination, atrocity breeds massacre, and there is no end to the tale of horror till sheer exhaustion terminates it. We can see today in Spain the whole rake's progress; and our tendency to condemn the one side or the other will mainly depend on the point at which we begin to read the record. It makes a lot of difference whether we begin with the Spanish Inquisition or with the murder of Señor Calvo Sotelo or at any intermediate point. But though the starting-point of enquiry may determine our sympathies, the principle involved is unaffected. Outrage breeds outrage; hate breeds hate.

The Christian answer to this is the love which suffers all that hate can do, yet remains pure love. The Christian answer is the Cross of Christ. What does that mean for the Christian disciple in a hate-entangled world? Is he to show that spirit? to use that method? and admit into his conduct nothing else? In all ages this question of the Christian's duty in a selfish world is the most important that he can ask. It has presented itself afresh to our generation with staggering force.

There can be no doubt about the standard of judgment—it is Christ and none other. So far as our lives are conducted on principles alien from His they are involved in sin. But to say this only sets the problem and does not solve it. For the fundamental alienation of our lives from His is not the use of force or fraud or any other external method; it is that we are at heart self-centred. If we set ourselves to act conscientiously on His principles by the resolute determination of our own wills, we are likely to appear priggish and to be a source of additional irritation. No doubt this will be due to our failure to follow His principles completely, for prominent among them is the condemnation of all self-righteousness. But it is supremely difficult to play the part of *Athanasius contra mundum* without developing self-righteousness. Indeed it is impossible except in the power of radical evangelical conversion. Most of us cannot do what Christ did or commanded, because His spirit does not possess us; and while that remains true, even if we performed His outward acts, these would not have the effect of His. So far as they were contaminated with self-righteousness, they might have the very opposite effects.

But this is not all. The whole Gospel is concerned with the Redemption of the world—the winning of it by whatever cost is needed from its entanglement of hate to the true community of love. Is this the whole of the Divine intention for the world? Or does this follow on a Divine activity of creation and preservation? In other words, have the political order, the commercial and industrial

CHRISTIAN DEMOCRACY 149

order, and the like, any place in the Divine scheme of which
Redemption is the crown? It would take too long to argue this
question fully and no more is possible than the indication of a
personal view.

The natural order of society with its reciprocal needs and services
is part of the Divine plan and is the arena within which the drama
of Redemption is played out. The system of mutualities, which is
the structural principle of society, is, at its own level, a manifestation
of that spiritual unity of persons which in its highest development is
called love. Normally it has in it a strong self-regarding element, but
this need not go beyond the measure of self-love implicitly sanctioned
in the commandment " Love thy neighbour as thyself." The essential
principle of social life in all its forms is fully compatible with the
Gospel, though it is lower in the spiritual scale. The social life of
man is part of the Divine purpose in Creation, and what is requisite
for its maintenance is part of the Divine activity in preserving what
Creation has called into being. This is the theological justification
of the State and all its apparatus; and for anyone who approaches
the whole matter from the theological side it is of supreme importance that the State has a theological justification, which also prescribes the limits of the proper activity of the State, outside which
this justification would not hold.

The ordinary concerns of men—family life, industry, commerce,
politics—are all such as can in their own nature be conducted on
principles wholly compatible with Christianity. But even when they
are true to those principles they introduce complications in the expression of the Christian spirit. There are sacrifices which it is right
for an unmarried man to make, but wrong for a married man,
especially if he has children. Each of these concerns involves claims
of its own which are not directly the claims of the Kingdom of God.
St. Paul put the matter with great clarity, but perhaps with lack of
some needed qualification, when he said, " He that is unmarried is
careful for the things of the Lord, how he may please the Lord: but
he that is married is careful for the things of the world, how he may
please his wife." The contrast, we must insist, is real but not absolute.
For the husband's duty to God includes due care for his wife, and
to neglect her for " the Lord's work " could not be in accordance
with the Lord's will. Jesus of Nazareth was unmarried; a direct and
thorough imitation of His actions, even so far as different circumstances permit, would be neither right nor even possible for the
married.

Even apart from anything wrong, therefore, we have to recognize
a divergence of claim which has its source in the divine ordering of

the world. It is the divinely appointed duty of men to carry on their occupations whereby they contribute their share to the life of the world; and this will mean a refusal of many heroic renunciations! There is obviously a very insidious temptation inherent in this situation; and apart from any corruption of the social system, there would be moral problems for the Christian citizen.

But that system is deeply and pervasively corrupt. The self-interest of those who work it has corrupted it. Instead of being a system of reciprocal needs and services it has been perverted into a welter of competing selfishnesses. This is true of the social life within nations; it is even more evidently true of the life of nations in their dealings one with another. It is in this mad world that the Christian is set to give proof of his discipleship. And what is he to do? Every choice seems bad. If he consents to take a part in the activities of the world, he must share in some measure its contamination. If he refuses, he leaves these activities to be directed by those who have no ideals. The only way for him to avoid the contamination is to become a hermit and live on the roots and fruits that he grows himself. Is that God's will for him? Is he, like Plato's philosopher, to wait for the ideal state before he will take part in politics, and meanwhile to " cower under a wall to avoid the storm and sleet, happy if he can escape unspotted to the other world "? Christendom has faced that alternative and rejected it. The only other alternative is to enter the turmoil, keeping the absolute standard of Christian ethics steadily in view as the only criterion of real worth, and to conform the conduct of men in the world to that standard as closely as the conditions presented by the historical situation permit.

But here is need for the most searching exercise of reason, and for that culminating insight of reason which assures us that others may have as good grounds for judgment as ourselves when the conclusions that they reach are diametrically opposed to our own. A man or a party who is maintaining an established custom may resort to violence against any who assail it. But the Christian who is never primarily concerned to maintain any earthly thing but is always pressing on to " the goal of the call upwards," cannot use violence as his method. It must always frustrate his purpose. He may have recourse to force in order to prevent lawless violence from destroying what has been achieved, just as the civilized State is endowed with force precisely in order that lawless force or violence may be repressed and all force in practice be subject to law. Now Law, by its own essential quality as universal, is an expression of reason. Con-sequently the exercise of force for the maintenance of Law against law-breakers is in principle the subjection of force to reason.

Reason is not a term synonymous with Christianity. But Christianity by its own nature claims reason as its ally, its interpreter, its agent in the application of the principles of the Gospel to the affairs of life. Apart from that use of force which has already been described as the subjection of force to reason, Christianity abjures all use of force. Its adherents are committed to the application in life of such principles as necessitate the use of reason and reliance upon reason. There may be differences of policy or of interest between Christians. But their faith forbids them to settle these by force. They must reason with each other till agreement is reached, or failing that must submit their dispute to the more impartial reason of a judge or arbiter. This principle applies to Christian nations also. Force rightly comes in as between individuals, or groups, or classes, or nations, only to check aggression on the part of one who will not submit the question to the arbitrament of reason or refuses to accept its award.

Judges are not quite impartial; arbitration is seldom quite unbiased. In the international sphere it is especially difficult to find or to establish a tribunal which may have the respect of all possible disputants as certain to be quite fair. Here as elsewhere we have to do the best we can, using as our criterion of " the best " the absolute standard of the Christian ethic. But to determine this " best " is a work of reason.

In practice this reliance upon reason works out as a positive desire to hear the best that can be said for the other side. That side is sure to represent some truth which must be incorporated into a wise policy. And so far as its view is false, refutation of this is only possible when it is fully understood. Reliance upon reason is at once an expression of the spirit of charity and a generating source of it. Charity for the opponent makes us wish to know the best that he has to say; hearing this makes us think better of him than if we had only heard an inferior presentation of his case. Charity and humility combine to convince the Christian that in so far as others differ from him this is likely to be due in part to some error or defect in his own view. All Christian qualities combine to exalt reason and the reasonable habit of mind against prejudice and passion, even though they be the prejudice of national tradition and the passion of national loyalty. When Christianity ceases to regard reason as its chief ally it is false to its own genius; when reason is decried and passion exalted, Christianity is, for that time and people, imperilled.

III

It may be well to state in summary form the main contentions of this paper.

There is undoubtedly at the present time a widespread distrust of reason. This is partly due to the complexities of modern life, which tends to produce a feeling of despair before the task of unravelling them or of forming a reasoned judgment upon them.

The result is a tendency to fall back on a purely spontaneous judgment expressing a personal reaction. This is more likely to take the form of passionate loyalty to a leader than of acceptance of any policy. But such reactions are specially liable to perversion by unregarded emotions, and it is essential that they should be spiritual in quality. This makes supremely important the presentation of Christ Himself as the leader to whom loyalty is due, and calls for a careful review of the principles of life which express that loyalty.

But the urgent importance remains of preserving and increasing the activity or reason in relation to the affairs of the community. This cannot be done by the effort of every individual to understand every problem. It can best be done by individuals studying the broad issues which are involved, and, in particular, by perfecting a system of Christian democracy.

This seems to call for the building up of a body of opinion, based on Christian principles and agreeing on a series of broadly defined objectives. Such a project requires the employment of a specific method. It involves the willingness of a large number of people to devote considerable time, energy and zeal to what must be a long and arduous task. It also involves—perhaps still harder—a willingness to subordinate prejudice to reason and to believe in the good faith of those whose views do not coincide with our own.

The greatest question in this field today is that of the Christian attitude to war. Here there is a sharp and apparently fundamental difference of opinion. It is here that it is most important to exercise charity and restraint. It is also vital that differences here should not prevent co-operation in other fields—e.g. social and economic questions. It may be that a common Christian policy in these fields would go so far towards removing the causes of war that the disagreement about pacifism would become relatively unimportant.

(Published as a pamphlet by the
Student Christian Movement Press, 1937)

Christian Unity

"TILL WE ALL ATTAIN unto the unity of the faith and of the know-ledge of the Son of God unto a fullgrown man, unto the measure of the stature of the fulness of the Christ." (Ephesians iv, 13.)

The unity of the Church, on which our faith and hope is set, is grounded in the unity of God and the uniqueness of His redeeming act in Jesus Christ. The "one body and one spirit" correspond to the "one God and Father of all." The unity of the Church of God is a perpetual fact; our task is not to create it but to exhibit it. Where Christ is in men's hearts, there is the Church: where His Spirit is active, there is His Body. The Church is not an association of men, each of whom has chosen Christ as his Lord; it is a fellowship of men, each of whom Christ has united with Himself. The Christian faith and life are not a discovery or invention of men; they are not an emergent phase of the historical process; they are the gift of God. That is true not only of their historical origin, but quite equally of the re-birth to that faith and life of each individual Christian. Our unity in dependence for our faith upon the unique act of the one God is a perpetual and unalterable fact. If we are Christians, that is due to the activity of the Holy Spirit; and because He is one, those in whom He is active are one fellowship in Him—"the fellowship of the Holy Ghost."

But there is no human heart possessed wholly and utterly by the Holy Spirit; and most of us, "who have the first-fruits of the Spirit," are still governed also by self-will. Our surrender is not absolute; our allegiance is not complete. Consequently the historical form and out-ward manifestation of the Church is never worthy of its true nature. What marks it as the Church is the activity within it of the Holy Spirit—the Spirit of the Father and of the Son. But in the Church as an actual society in history this is not the only power at work; the various forms of human selfishness, blindness and sloth are also characteristic of those who by the activity of the Spirit are united to Christ. It is as though a lantern were covered with a dark veil. It is truly a lantern, because the light burns in it; yet the world sees the light but dimly and may be more conscious of the veil that hides it than of the flame which is its source. So the world may see the sin

153

of Christians more clearly than the holiness of the Church, and the divisions which that sin has caused more clearly than the unity which endures in spite of them.

When that happens, and in whatever degree it happens, the witness of the Church is weakened. How can it call men to worship of the one God if it is calling to rival shrines? How can it claim to bridge the divisions in human society—divisions between Greek and barbarian, bond and free, between white and black, Aryan and non-Aryan, employer and employed—if when men are drawn into it they find that another division has been added to the old ones—a division of Catholic from Evangelical, or Episcopalian from Presbyterian or Independent? A Church divided in its manifestation to the world cannot render its due service to God or to man, and for the impotence which our sin has brought upon the Church through divisions in its outward aspect we should be covered with shame and driven to repentance.

We do not escape from sin by denying the consequences of our sin, and we cannot heal the breaches in the Church's outward unity by regarding them as unimportant. To those who made the breaches, the matters involved seemed worthy to die for; it may well be that in the heat of conflict, such as tormented the sixteenth century, men so zealously upheld what seemed to them neglected truths that they became blind to supplementary truths which were dear to their opponents. It is seldom that in any human contention all the truth is on one side. We may look back with a calmer wisdom and see how here or there a division which occurred could have been avoided by a more conciliatory temper and a more synthetic habit of mind. But it does not follow that we should now take all the divisions as they stand and merely agree to co-operate while still maintaining separate organizations. For in practice those separate organizations are bound to become competitors, however much we wish to co-operate; and the separation will hinder the free interchange of thought and experience which should be a chief means of the process whereby the Body of Christ " builds itself up in love."

So we come to the second great evil of our divisions. The first is that they obscure our witness to the one Gospel; the second is that through the division each party to it loses some spiritual treasure, and none perfectly represents the balance of truth, so that this balance of truth is not presented to the world at all. God be thanked—we have left behind the habit of supposing that our own tradition is perfectly true and the whole of truth, and are looking to see what parts of the " unsearchable riches of Christ " we have missed while others have them; and so we are learning increasingly one from another. This mutual appreciation is the way alike of humility and of charity; and it is leading us to perpetually fuller fellowship.

In part our progress is due to the pressure of the needs of the world. It is not the task of the Church to solve political problems or to devise contrivances for mitigating the effects of human sin. But it is the Church's task to proclaim that the most oppressive evils under which the world groans are the fruit of sin; that only by eradication of that sin can these other evils be averted; and that the only Redeemer from sin is Jesus Christ, " Very God of Very God begotten; Not made, being of one substance with the Father; Who for us men and for our salvation came down from heaven, and was made Man." To Him, the Conqueror of death and sin—to Him, the Lamb of God who taketh away the sin of the world—we call the world that its sins may be removed, that its divisions may be healed, and that it may find fellowship in Him.

That proclamation, that invitation, we are bound as a Church to make. And the world answers: " Have you found that fellowship yourselves? Why do your voices sound so various? When we pass from words to action, to what are you calling us? Is it to one family, gathered round one Holy Table, where your Lord is Himself the host who welcomes all His guests? You know that it is not so. When we answer your united call, we have to choose for ourselves to which Table we will go, for you are yourselves divided in your act of deepest fellowship, and by your own traditions hinder us from a unity which we are ready to enjoy."

What is our answer to that retort? Is it not true that Christians who have lately been converted in heathen lands, and even the ordinary lay-folk who are rather detached from our denominational preoccupations, are more ready to come together in face of the resurgence of paganism than are the leaders of ecclesiastical organizations, intent upon the maintenance of their tradition and upon keeping their organization in being and in working order? If it is true that in its deepest nature the Church is always one, it is also true that today it is the so-called " Churches " rather than any forces of the secular world which prevent that unity from being manifest and effective.

Here is matter for deep penitence. I speak as a member of one of those Churches which still maintain barriers against completeness of union at the Table of the Lord. I believe from my heart that we of that tradition are trustees for an element of truth concerning the nature of the Church which requires that exclusiveness as a consequence, until this element of truth be incorporated with others into a fuller and worthier conception of the Church than any of us hold

L

today. But I know that our division at this point is the greatest of all scandals in the face of the world; I know that we can only consent to it or maintain it without the guilt of unfaithfulness to the unity of the Gospel and of God Himself, if it is a source to us of spiritual pain, and if we are striving to the utmost to remove the occasions which now bind us, as we think, to that perpetuation of disunion. It should be horrible to us to speak or think of any fellow Christians as " not in communion with us." God grant that we may feel the pain of it, and under that impulsion strive the more earnestly to remove all that now hinders us from receiving together the One Body of the One Lord, that in Him we may become One Body— the organ and vehicle of the One Spirit.

While there is much on our side for which we must repent, there is also much wrought by God for which we should give thanks. The record of the last ten years, since the former Conference on Faith and Order met at Lausanne, has been a time of progressive unification. That period can fitly be called, in the title of the Report presented on that subject, " a decade of objective progress in Church Unity." The consummated unions are chiefly, as is natural, between Churches of similar polity; but there is also a growth of understanding and appreciation among Christians of deeply sundered traditions. We shall speak of these things later in our Conference; but let us here at the outset take note of them and give thanks to God; for we enter on this second World Conference with great encouragement from what God has done for us since the first.

Moreover, side by side with progress in the specific task entrusted in part to us, we must rejoice in, and give thanks for, the perpetual growth of other manifestations of the *Una Sancta* despite its divisions. The sister Conference at Oxford has profoundly impressed the world; and it has approved a method whereby, if we are also led to approve it, the *Una Sancta* will be provided with a more permanent and more effectual means of declaring itself and its judgment than at any time for four hundred, perhaps for eight hundred years. We deeply lament the absence from this collaboration of the great Church of Rome—the Church which more than any other has known how to speak to the nations so that the nations hear. But the occurrences of the two World Conferences in one Summer is itself a manifestation of the *Una Sancta*, the holy fellowship of those who worship God in Jesus Christ and look to Him as the only Saviour of the world.

In this world movement of Churches towards fuller unity and more potent witness we have our own allotted task. In what spirit do we approach it? How shall we seek to express in this enterprise the graces of faith, of hope and of love? Of these love is the greatest, but in part at least it is rooted in faith and sustained by hope. Love, for us who are assembled here, means chiefly two things—an ardent longing for closer fellowship, and a readiness both to share our own spiritual treasures and to participate in those of others. Ten years ago our main concern was to state our several traditions in such a way that others should understand them truly; and that must still be our aim. But the divisions which we seek to overcome are due to the fact that our traditions are just what they are and none other; division cannot be healed by the reiterated statement of them. We are here as representatives of our Churches; true, but unless our Churches are ready to learn one from another as well as to teach one another, the divisions will remain. Therefore our loyalty to our own Churches, which have sent us here, will not best be expressed in a rigid insistence by each upon his own tradition. Our Churches sent us here to confer about our differences with a view to overcoming them. As representatives of those Churches each of us must be as ready to learn from others where his own tradition is erroneous or defective as to show to others its truth and strength. We meet as fellow pupils in a school of mutual discipleship. The Churches desire, through us, to learn from one another. That is the humility of love as it must be active among us here.

It will be sustained by hope. Hope springs from the experience of the last ten years. But even were it otherwise, hope should be strong in us because the goal which we seek is set before us by God Himself. The hope which arises from that knowledge is altogether independent of empirical signs of its fulfilment. Even if our cause were suffering defeat on every side, we should still serve it because that is God's call to us, and we should still know that through our loyal service He was accomplishing His purpose even though we could not see the evidence of this. But in His mercy He gives us not only the supreme ground of hope, which is His call, but also the manifest tokens of His working in the Churches that are spread throughout the world.

Let us never forget that, though the purpose of our meeting is to consider the causes of our divisions, yet what makes possible our meeting is our unity. We could not seek union if we did not already possess unity. Those who have nothing in common do not deplore their estrangement. It is because we are one in allegiance to one Lord that we seek and hope for the way of manifesting that unity in our witness to Him before the world.

Thus our hope is based upon our common faith. This faith is not only the assent of our minds to doctrinal propositions; it is the commitment of our whole selves into the hands of a faithful Creator and merciful Redeemer. If the word be thus understood we are already one in faith, but also alas!—and this, perhaps, is the more relevant to our purpose—one in the weakness and incompleteness of our faith. We are one in faith, because to commit ourselves to Him is the deepest desire of our hearts; we are one in the weakness of our faith, because in all of us that desire is overlaid with prejudice and pride and obstinacy and self-contentment. " Lord, we believe; help Thou our unbelief."

Meanwhile our witness is enfeebled: the true proportion and balance of truth is hidden from the world because we cannot unite in presenting the parts enshrined in our several traditions. We still wait in hope and faith for the movement of the Spirit which shall bring us all to a perfect man—the " one man in Christ Jesus " grown to full maturity—who shall be the measure of the stature of the fullness of Christ.

Our faith must be more than the trust which leads us to rely on Him; it must be the deeper faith which leads us to wait for Him. It is not we who can heal the wounds in His Body. We confer and deliberate, and that is right. But it is not by contrivance or adjustment that we can unite the Church of God. It is only by coming closer to Him that we can come nearer to one another. And we cannot by ourselves come closer to Him. If we have any fellowship with Him, it is not by our aspiration but by His self-giving; if our fellowship with Him, and in Him with one another, is to be deepened, it will not be by our effort but by His constraining power. " The love of Christ constraineth us." To that we come back. Because He died for all, all are one in His death. Not by skill in argument, not even by mutual love that spans like a bridge the gulf between us—for the gulf though bridged is not closed by any love of ours—but by the filling of our hearts with His love and the nurture of our minds with His truth, the hope may be fulfilled. It is not by understanding one another, but by more fully understanding Him, that we are led towards our goal. We can help each other here, and learn one from another how to understand Him better. But it is towards Him that our eyes must be directed. Our discussion of our differences is a necessary preliminary; but it is preliminary and no more. Only when God has drawn us closer to Himself shall we be truly united together; and then our task will be not to consummate our endeavour but to register His achievement.

O Blessed Jesu, Love and Truth of God incarnate, cleanse us from all that hinders or distorts our vision of Thee. So fill us with trust in Thee that we cease from our striving and rest in Thee. Thou Light of the world, so shine in our hearts that the rays of Thy brightness, now known to us in our separation, may be gathered into the pure radiance of Thy glory manifested through us in our unity in Thee. Thou Lamb of God, that takest away the sin of the world, wash our spirits clean from sin. By the mystery of Thy Holy Incarnation, by Thine Agony and Bloody Sweat, by Thy Cross and Passion, by Thy glorious Resurrection and Ascension, and by the Coming of the Holy Ghost, unite us with Thyself and in Thyself one with another, that we may be one with and in Thee as Thou art one with the Father, that the world may believe that Thou art its Saviour, God-blessed for ever.

(The sermon preached in St. Giles's, Edinburgh, on August 3, 1937, at the opening service of the Second World Conference on Faith and Order)

In the Beginning—God

" IN THE BEGINNING, GOD." So the Bible opens. So, we may say, it was bound to open. For the distinctive character of Biblical religion is rooted in the conviction that God is completely independent of the world. The world is dependent for its existence upon God: God is not dependent on the world. With perfect sureness of touch the author of Genesis says precisely what needed to be said without involving himself in metaphysical tangles. " In the beginning God created. . . ." He does not say that God existed before the world, which would raise questions about the relation of Time to the movement of created things. He does not embark on any speculation concerning the question how the gulf is to be bridged between the Infinite and the finite, the Immortal and the mortal, the Holy and the sinful. He lays down in precisely accurate terms the stark proposition, " In the beginning God created the heavens and the earth."

There are two, and only two, types of religion which are capable of claiming our adherence. For no modern person is going to worship the finite gods of the ancient world or of primitive tribes. As the modern world makes its impact on the more primitive races, their faith in tribal or departmental deities is undermined. We do not have nowadays to learn with difficulty that there is only one God. What we mean by the word God forbids the possibility of more than one. We do not say that there might quite well be several, but as a matter of fact there is only one. We say that if anyone supposes that there are more gods than one, this proves that his notion of deity is inadequate. There cannot be more than one Creator " of all things visible and invisible "; there cannot be more than one principle of the whole world's unity. We do not ask, " Is there one God or are there many? " We ask, " Is there any Being who corresponds to what we mean by the word God? " or, briefly, " Does God exist? "

Some deny that He exists; those are the Atheists. Some say they cannot answer; those are the Agnostics. We are not at this moment concerned with either. Of those who affirm the reality of God there are today two, and only two, main groups. There are those who mean by God a purely immanent power or principle, which is the ultimate explanation of everything, but has no independent existence apart from the world of which he or it is the explanation. This view finds its most complete expression in the great religions of India.

But what we have to notice is that it is broadly speaking characteristic of all religions which have risen above Polytheism but are not a
product directly or indirectly of the Bible (Zoroastrianism in its
primitive form is an exception. That seems to have been a religion
of the Biblical type which arose independently of any Biblical influence.) This Pantheistic type of religion has great difficulty in accepting the idea of any specific revelation. All the world is a revelation of
the God who is the ground of its existence, the principle of its unity,
the explanation of it in whole and in part; if we really understood
it, we should understand Him. Still greater, and probably insuper-
able, difficulty is felt from that standpoint as regards any supposedly
unique or final revelation. God, so understood, does everything in
general but never does anything in particular.

Over against any such conception stands, in sharp contrast, the
religion of the Bible, which finds expression today in three forms—
Judaism, Christianity, and Islam. Here God is the primal Reality,
existing in sovereign independence of all else, and having His own
character, which He reveals as and when He pleases. He is the
Creator of the world; and inasmuch as He made it, including ourselves and our minds, we may learn something of Him from His
work (Psalm xix, 1; Romans i, 20). But all that the created universe
reveals, even if we could understand it, is still far less than His
infinite glory; and our capacity to apprehend is not only limited by
our natural finitude, but also vitiated by our sinful, that is our self-
centred state. If His glory is to be made known, it must be through
His own divine act, at once disclosing His nature and enlightening
our hearts and minds to perceive the reality disclosed—in other
words, by His own intervention in history and by the illumination
of His Spirit. This is what the Bible gives us, both in the Old Testament and in the New. In the Old Testament we read the record of
God's acts, in dealing with His people, through the eyes of prophets
enlightened by the divine Spirit to know those acts for what they
were. In the New Testament that record of God's mighty acts
culminates in the Birth, the Life, the Death, the Resurrection, the
Ascension of Jesus Christ, and in the Coming of the Holy Spirit who
enabled the disciples to see and understand those acts of God and so
to become witnesses to Christ " unto the uttermost parts of the
earth."

This is the Biblical doctrine of God—not of a spirit or principle
immanent in the world with no existence apart from it, but of a
Living Being, supremely real in Himself apart from all else, Creator
of the world and regnant over it, making Himself known by revealing acts, which He performs in order to deliver the world from the

hopeless condition in which it is sunk. The Gospel is a cry of joy and triumph; it is emphatically not an expression of satisfaction with the world as known in our experience. It does not say "God's in His heaven, all's right with the world." It does say "In the world ye shall have tribulation; but be of good cheer; I have overcome the world."

"In the beginning, God." That is where, as Christians, we start. Here is the difference between faith and philosophy. For philosophy God is the ultimate problem, or at best the solution of the ultimate problem; he is reached, precariously, at the end of the argument. For faith He is the starting point, the subject of our initial assurance with which we set out to understand and to direct experience.

What we believe concerning God, who was in the beginning, who created the heavens and the earth, is to be set forth at other times. Here we must assume it in order to consider what is the meaning for us of this absolute priority of God. We assume, therefore, that by the Name of God we mean "the God and Father of our Lord Jesus Christ," so that in Jesus Christ we see Him who "was in the beginning."

So let us leave general reflections and consider what these words mean to us—to each one of us—to me : "In the beginning, God."

(1) Is God the starting point of our thoughts, either about the world, or about our neighbours, or about whatever most occupies our leisure?

(a) As we think about the world, do we try to understand it in the light of our knowledge of God—that is to say, in the light of God's revelation of Himself? That is one main concern of the Bible. The Prophetical Books, which include, let us remember, the Historical Books, are a reading of History by the light of the knowledge of God. We have a knowledge of God greater than was given even to Prophets who lived before Christ came. We are called to use the knowledge given through Him to interpret History. The Book of Man's destiny is in the hand of the Heavenly King (Rev. v). It is subject to His decree. But it is close-sealed with seven seals, and no man can open those seals. But there is One who can. The "Lamb that was slain " can "take the Book and open the seven seals thereof." In other words, Christ by His sacrifice interprets History; on the Cross He both put forth the power that controls it to its final goal and also, in the same act, supplied its interpretation. Are we trying to think out the History of the world, and our own share in the fashioning of that History, by the illumination of the Light of the World? That is our task in this day of crisis—of judgment. We must test our political thoughts, and the schemes of our statesmen, by reference to the touchstone—" In the beginning, God."

(*b*) By the same test we try our thoughts about our neighbours. Do we habitually think of them—especially those whom we naturally dislike—as other children of God, fellow members with us of His family? What a different thing the structure of society would be, if we all did that! And what a different thing our own social intercourse would be, if we did it ourselves. Next time you feel resentment against anyone, or contempt, stop and remember that Christ died for him; your bitterness or your contempt will just wither away.

(*c*) Once more, let us try by the same test our leisure thoughts. On what does your mind run, when there is nothing to claim its attention? Are your leisure thoughts such as you can go on with when you remember God? These leisure thoughts—as, for example, your thoughts when you wake in the morning before it is time to get up—are very powerful in influence on character, both because they are spontaneous and because they so easily become habitual.

(2) Besides thoughts, we must must bring under this discipline our desires, hopes, and ambitions. What do you most desire for your nation? for your family? for yourself? In your plans for your life or choice of your profession, what really controls your wishes? If you say of a friend, " He is doing very well," do you mean that he is giving good service, or that he is getting a large income? Happily the two are not incompatible; but assuredly they are not the same. If you choose your life's work with a view primarily to your own enjoyment of life, you are denying the principle " In the beginning, God." To be true to that principle you must ask, " What does God want me to do? "

Sometimes He will make that clear by an inward assurance that comes to you as you wait on Him in spoken or silent prayer. Sometimes circumstances produce a practical necessity, which must then be accepted as His providential leading. Very often He calls through the strength of our own inclinations. For a man usually does well what he likes doing and likes what he can do well. These inclinations may be the channel of a real vocation, but then we have to be specially careful that our sense of God's call through our inclinations takes precedence of our own desire to gratify those inclinations. It is a good thing to like your work; but it is a very bad thing to do your work only so far as you like it. Anyhow, the main point is to put first God's claim upon the use of your time and strength, and whatever your work is, to do it " as unto the Lord."

(3) There is no chance whatever that you will in fact be true to that principle in the realms of thought and desire unless you are true to it in your prayers. Indeed it becomes more and more clear that the real solution of our own and of the world's problems is to be found through worship, if only we remember what that is.

It is always easy to make fun of our necessary methods of worship. Why should the Creator of a myriad stars desire us to gather together and sing songs about Him? Truly our best expressions fall short of our meaning; and our meaning falls far, far short of the Reality. Yet if God is Love and our worship is real, then worship is what God most wants of us, and is the chief means of gaining strength to serve Him worthily. For what is worship?

It is the quickening of conscience by the Holiness of God—which finds expression in confession of sin. It is the feeding of our mind upon the Truth of God—as we listen to His Word and rehearse our belief. It is the cleansing of imagination by the Beauty of God—as we join in praise by means of psalms, and canticles, and hymns. It is the opening of our hearts to the Love of God, as His Truth and Beauty come home to us in the Gospel. It is the submission or surrender of our wills to the purpose of God—expressed in intercession according to the manner of prayer taught by our Lord. It is the gathering up of all these in adoration—the most selfless emotion of which our nature is capable: " We give thanks to thee for thy great glory."

All these elements are present in real worship. Of course it is true that if, when we go to Church, we are purely passive and let the successive parts of the service merely pass over us, that is not a way of occupying time very acceptable to God, or profitable to us, or important to the world. But if we regularly draw near to God and in His presence quicken our conscience by His Holiness, feed our minds with His Truth, cleanse our imaginations by His Beauty, open our hearts to His love, surrender our wills to His purpose, and offer our inmost selves in adoration—that is more than any other thing possible to us acceptable to God, profitable to us, and important to the world.

The testing point is petition. For what do we pray? Which comes first—God or ourselves? " In the beginning, God." Therefore the outline of a Christian prayer is never " Please do for me what I want " but " Please do with me—in me, through me—what you want."

Then, of course, the test of our sincerity in prayer is found outside our prayers in our life in the world. Are we doing all that we can to bring to fulfilment the prayers which we offer? If not—then the prayer is either hypocritical or, at best, half-hearted. But though life tests prayer, the power to live is won by prayer.

Our modern world is fond of pointing to the two Great Commandments as gathering up all that God requires of us; and then it goes on to suppose that only the second is of real account. It is quite true and most important that if we love God with all our hearts, we must love our neighbours as ourselves; for we have given our hearts to God, who loves all His children, among whom we are; in His sight they and we are on a level. So St. John tersely says, " If a man say ' I love God ' and hateth his brother, he is a liar." If I love God I must love my neighbour, so my relation to my neighbour is the test of my love to God. But it is also true that I can come to love my neighbour only if I first love God. Of course I can love my friends. Anyone can do that. But my neighbour? Everyone that I have anything to do with—even the members of a despised class or race? Only love of God who loves all will lead me to that.

Love of men is the fruit of the Christian life; love of God is the root—hidden, but the source of all that is seen. " In the beginning, God."

As from Him we must begin, so with Him we hope to end— Alpha and Omega, the beginning and the ending, the Almighty.

(An Address to the World Conference of Christian Youth, Amsterdam, July 24, 1939)

The Perils of a Purely Scientific Education

ONE OF THE SERIOUS EVILS arising from the religious controversy connected with education has been the withdrawal of interest from some questions still more fundamental. It is indeed true that no question can be more fundamental than that of the place of religion in education generally; but it is not about this that controversy has been excited. The advocates of secularism in education are, in our country, few; and secularism will never prevail unless the disputes of religious people among themselves lead the public mind to fall back upon it from sheer irritation and weariness. Those disputes have claimed so large a share of our interest chiefly because they have concerned matters which had for practical purposes to be settled one way or another quickly. It is not seldom that the need of deciding at once what must be so decided prevents the giving of proper attention to matters which are less urgent but in the long run even more important.

This has happened in connexion with the national system of education. Religious people have been occupied about the rights and wrongs of Non-provided Schools, about the Cowper Temple clause, about children transferred from Church Schools to Council Senior Schools. That has been quite necessary, for the decisions about these matters cannot wait. But meanwhile there has been developing in ever more menacing proportions a peril far greater than any Undenominationalism could ever be, the peril of a purely scientific education.

The recent increase in the number of Secondary Schools in the country is a source of gratification to all who care for educational progress. We still have much leeway to make up. But it is seldom realized how completely the scientific side of these schools preponderates as against the literary; nor is the effect of this preponderance upon the pupils often appreciated. We are training a generation expert in certain departments of science, but utterly undeveloped in imagination, in sympathy, in social and political instinct, in moral discrimination. It is easy, especially in the new urban Universities, to find many men, and no small number of women, who are really able, taking high honours in their science examinations, but are mentally puerile so soon as questions involving value—moral, social, aesthetic—are brought into discussion. Their technical attainments

will secure for them positions of influence and leadership in industrial and other fields; but they will not be qualified to use those
positions to the best advantage either of the people with whom they
are specially concerned or of the country as a whole.

The danger comes from the combined influence of school or
college curriculum and home circumstance. The people who direct
education were mostly brought up in homes where books are part
of the ordinary furniture of the house, where they are one main subject of conversation, and where they are the recognized resource for
leisure moments. Books, as they are used for those purposes, are not
solely or chiefly scientific treatises; they are specimens of all the
varieties of literature. But the population of the new Secondary
Schools does not for the most part, come from homes like that. Not
long ago I heard Dr. Grant Robertson, the Principal of Birmingham
University, say that according to his estimate 75 per cent of the
students entering that University had never owned a book in their
lives, except text-books of the subject of their study and, if their
families were religious, a Bible and a Prayer Book. The majority of
these would be science students, so that their text-books would be
science text-books.

Now it is a real loss to a man if he have no books and no school
education. But at least such a man will retain the natural variety and
balance of interests and mental faculties. There have been very
thoughtful men before now who could neither read nor write. Such
men by observation, by conversation, by the experience of life, may
become truly wise. And even if they remain simple, they are open to
appeal on the various sides of their nature. But a one-sided education
may destroy this natural balance, and result in the practical oblitera-
tion of some interests and faculties. At one time education was one-
sided through neglect of science; that was a great evil. It is becoming
one-sided through neglect of the " humanities "; that is a still greater
evil.

It is a greater evil for several reasons. First, the scientific habit of
mind tends to exclude the artistic or literary, more than the latter
excludes the former. Some of the aspects of experience which are
dealt with in science are so perpetually pressed on our attention that
it is very hard to lose touch altogether with the scientific interest and
attitude. The Law of Gravitation may not be known to us in its
Newtonian or Einsteinian formula; but we know that if we drop
things they fall, and that if we " tread on a stair that isn't there," we
give ourselves a nasty jolt. All such reflections belong to Physics. Our
digestions remind us that the subjects studied in Organic Chemistry
are perfectly real. And no artistic or literary attitude is relevant to

these subjects. But to the subjects which supply the proper material
of artistic or literary interest, the scientific habit of mind is appropriate in some degree. Human beings are susceptible of arithmetical
treatment, in statistics, for example; they can be counted, they can
be weighed. And a mind trained on purely scientific lines is more
likely to let slip the sense of value, than a mind trained on purely
literary lines is to let slip the sense of quantity.

For there are two main ways of understanding the world; and if
they are practised in isolation they seem to offer us two different
worlds altogether. Josiah Royce called them " the World of Observation " and " the World of Appreciation." Canon Streeter, rather
more illuminatingly, distinguishes the realm of Science as Quantity,
and the realm of Art as Value or Reality. He puts Religion with
Art; and this is right if it is allotted to either exclusively; I should
wish to make it the crown of the series—Science, Art, Religion.
Anyhow, there is here a very clear and a very important point. There
is one kind of understanding which may be gained in a laboratory,
by dissection, classification and the scientific process generally; there
is another kind of understanding—applicable only to human beings
or what is alien to them—which comes from sympathy. When a man
says " I cannot understand doing a thing like that," he does not
mean that he cannot give a psychological analysis of what went on
in his neighbour's soul before he so acted; he means that he cannot
in the least degree imagine himself acting in that way. This kind of
intelligence, which is so closely allied to sympathy, is far more important in all human relationships than mastery of scientific method.
It is told of Kepler, the astronomer (whether truly or not, I cannot
say), that having been unhappy in a first marriage he chose a second
wife on scientific principles; he eliminated all but eleven of his
feminine acquaintances, and then analysed these eleven, setting out
the merits and defects in parallel columns. He then married the lady
whose analysis displayed the greatest predominance of merit over
defect. When this venture also proved a failure, he pronounced the
problem insoluble to human reason. So, no doubt, it is, if by reason
is meant exclusively the use of scientific method.

We need an education which shall enable us to understand and
act wisely in relation to our environment. Leaving aside for the
moment things divine, the most important part of our environment
consists neither of planets nor of chemicals, but of human beings.
No doubt the wisdom that we need in our dealings with them is
mainly won by the experience of social life. That is why the fundamental element in a school is not the instruction given in classrooms,
but the life of the school as a society of young people. But it is also

true that, while sharing in such a life develops the social instincts, the development of the mind in relation to human beings, their needs and problems, comes by study of what are called the humanities : the great movements of mankind, their achievements and failures, in History; their loftiest aspirations and deepest feelings, in Literature. And education which does not give great place to one or both of these is dangerously unbalanced.

The balance was once wrongly inclined the other way; we needed the introduction of the scientific factor. But we have done more than make an even balance; we are as one-sided in favour of science now, as we were once in favour of the humanities; and year by year matters grow worse; and the error in which we are sinking deeper and deeper is more dangerous than that from which we have rather suddenly been delivered.

Mathematics and Science are not only of incalculable value in their utility for life, but are among the noblest disciplines of mind and soul. It is not the study of these great subjects, but the almost exclusive study of them by so many of the rising generation that gives ground for alarm. This exclusive attention is bad for citizenship, but is still worse for religion. It creates a type of mind which is clumsy and blundering in relation to all questions of Value—of Beauty and Ugliness in nature, art, or conduct; of Right and Wrong in all their less obvious manifestations. It creates a tendency to deal with men in the mass, by generalizations, rather than as individuals. Marxianism is, I believe, bad science; but half its viciousness consists in its attempt to treat the problems of human life on purely scientific lines. An exclusively scientific training leads men to demand crucial experiments with spiritual forces, such as are familiar in physical or chemical laboratories, forgetting that those forces can only be apprehended by the intuitions that are born of loyalty and sympathy.

Religion has its close affinities with Science, for it depends on the veritable truth of its convictions; and Science is an invaluable purge of Religion, cleansing it of illusion and superstition. But the actual life of Religion is far nearer to Art than to Science, and nearer still to human relationships. Faith in God is not belief in a demonstrated, or probable, proposition, though it is allied to this; in itself it is confident loyalty towards the Maker and Ruler of the Universe, before whom we are always as children before their father. The child does not practise scientific experiments on his father's love; but he understands it, and relies on it, and day by day more completely verifies it. There is an analogy here with the scientific but the difference is as important as the likeness; for the child does not put his father in a category of " loving beings " nor draw his expectations from any generalization. His understanding is not the classifying comprehension of science but the intuitive apprehension of sympathy; or, to put it simply, it is not the understanding by which Kepler tried to guide his matrimonial selection, but the understanding which every man has who falls in love.

When left to itself the human soul uses its two methods of understanding on the right occasions; but then it uses them clumsily. It needs education to get the full control of them. This education ought to be such as to preserve the natural balance. Then the citizen when trained will be chiefly scientific in dealing with all inanimate things, chiefly sympathetic in dealing with living things, and, all his faculties being alert, will be open to receive the vision of God.

(From the *York Quarterly*, 1932)

A Conditional Justification of War

WAR IS A MONSTROUS EVIL; of that there can be no doubt. Its occurrence is a manifestation of the sin of men. If there were no sin there would be no war. Then ought not any good man, still more any Christian man, to refuse to have any part in it?

I

If we are to think about such a question, we must try to think accurately. If a nation goes to war, a citizen cannot, strictly speaking, keep out of it. If he refuses to fight, for whatever reason, he is not simply doing nothing. He is withholding help that he might have given to his country.

A man is responsible for the consequences of his inactivity as surely as for those of his acts.

This is the reason why those who are upholding a nation's cause in war are liable to feel bitter against those who refuse their share. It is felt that these are letting down their fellow citizens.

The moral question is not settled by this consideration; but if this consideration is left out of sight, the moral question is wrongly envisaged. The British pacifist at this moment is not merely taking no part; he is weakening the British capacity to fight and so far is increasing Hitler's chance of victory. He may be right to do this; but let us—and let him—face the fact that he is doing this.

II

If it is admitted that war is a monstrous evil, it certainly follows that we ought all to be doing our utmost to abolish it. We ought to desire and work for established peace, and the settlement of all conflicting claims by peaceful means. So far as we have not done that—and who among us can claim that he has done all he could—we are guilty of the sin of war. Let all of us—and especially those who offer moral justification for taking active part in a war—face the fact that, whatever our duty after war has broken out, we are in part responsible for its outbreak.

III

There are two different questions which are often confused but should be kept carefully apart except so far as it is clear that the same

M

considerations apply to both. There is the question whether it is ever right for a nation to resort to war; and there is the question whether, when a nation does this, its citizens are bound to take a share or, again, are bound to refuse to take any part. Various positions with regard to these two questions are tenable with perfect consistency. It could be held that it must always be wrong for a nation to resort to war, but that if it does the citizen must take his share, at any rate if he is convinced that, war having broken out, the welfare of the world will be better served by the victory of his own country than by the victory of its enemies. It could be held on the other hand, that it may be right for a nation to resort to war, because the bulk of its citizens are capable of no higher course, but that those citizens who are capable of rising to a higher claim must refuse their service.

These are mentioned as two extreme combinations of view which are in themselves tenable with perfect consistency. But it is neither of those views which will be advocated here. We shall begin by considering whether, as is sometimes alleged, the highest moral considerations forbid a nation to go to war, so that the Government which declares war is always guilty of committing its nation to a morally wrong course.

The question cannot be answered without some enquiry into what is meant by calling acts or policies right or wrong. If we follow Christian principles in dealing with that enquiry we shall say that our highest ethical maxim is this : " Thou shalt love thy neighbour as thyself."

(It is true that within the Christian community there is a still higher maxim—the " new commandment "—" that ye love one another as I have loved you." But even if it be proposed, mistakenly as I think, to treat this as a precept for all, whether Christians or not, it will not affect the result; for the whole question is this : What action does love require?)

Now if we isolate a particular moment, it is clear that to shoot a fellow man or to institute a blockade of a nation is not a direct expression of any sort of love. But the question is not simply : How can we show love to Germans? The question is : How can we show love to Frenchmen, Poles, Czechs, and Germans, all at once?

Of course we very easily deceive ourselves when we speak of our aims in a war, and we ought to be very resolute that we will really serve the high purposes which we rather easily profess. But if it is at all true that we fight to resist and overthrow the Nazi tyranny and to secure for all whom our action may affect a greater measure of freedom than they can hope to enjoy under the Nazi rule, then it can fairly be said that our resistance of Germany by force at this time is a way of loving Germans themselves, as it is certainly a way of showing love to all others directly affected by the war. In the world which exists, it is not possible to take it as self-evident that the law of love forbids fighting. Some of us even hold that precisely that law commands fighting.

IV

" But that is a desperate paradox. How can love command you to kill a man who is one woman's son and another woman's husband? " We have already said that fighting is not a direct expression of love; it becomes an expression of love only because every alternative is worse.

" Then let us put it another way. Killing is bad; can it be right to do bad things? " Of course our whole case is that it can, and often is, right to do things which in isolation are bad. What things it is right to do may be very much affected by circumstances. Murder is always wrong; because murder is the taking of another man's life for personal and selfish ends. To kill a man, if that is the only alternative to being killed by him, is not murder; it is usually classed as justifiable homicide. Even if it is arguable that a perfect Christian would allow himself to be killed rather than kill his would-be murderer in self-defence, it is not arguable that he should allow a human brute to kill a child rather than kill that brute himself. Of course he should stop him without taking his life if that is possible; but if it is not possible, he is not only at liberty, he is under obligation, to kill; and that obligation is rooted in love.

People sometimes become confused by this recognition that the rightness of most acts is relative and not absolute; but this does not mean that the rightness is in any way doubtful. To take Plato's example, the third finger is both short and long—short in relation to the second and long in relation to the fourth. But in relation to the fourth it really is long. The general principle is that relative terms are absolute in the appropriate relations. To kill is right, if at all, relatively and not absolutely; that is, it can only be right in special circumstances. But in those circumstances it is absolutely right.

It is doubtful if any act is right " in itself." Every act is a link in a chain of causes and effects. It cannot be said that it is wrong to take away a man's possessions against his will, for that would condemn all taxation, or the removal of a revolver from a homicidal lunatic; neither of these is stealing—which is always wrong; though high authority has held that a starving man should steal a loaf rather than die of hunger, because life is of more value than property and should be chosen first for preservation if both cannot be preserved together.

The rightness of an act, then, nearly always, and perhaps always, depends on the way in which that act is related to circumstances; this is what is meant by calling it relatively right; but this does not in the least imply that it is only doubtfully right. It may be, in those circumstances, certainly and absolutely right.

Sometimes it looks as if an act were right apart from all relativity —as when a father gives a present to his child, or a man lays down his life for his friends. But it is possible to " spoil " children! And while the giving of life for others is always a sign of noble unselfishness, it only becomes right if the interest of the friends which is served in this way is the highest. A man ought not to put his life in serious danger in order to provide for his friends some momentary amusement, though this might be accurately described as laying down life for those friends.

The fact, then, that for a nation to engage in war can never be more than " relatively right " need not give us any anxiety lest it must always be doubtfully right. To do it light-heartedly must always be abominably wrong; but so far as we have seen yet, there may be circumstances in relation to which it becomes absolutely right.

V

But we must go farther. It is sometimes urged that war may have been justifiable in its simpler forms as known in earlier ages, but that modern warfare is always unjustifiable because of its indiscriminate character. The history in this argument is rather precarious. A regular feature of earlier warfare was the siege of fortified cities; this operation caused indiscriminate suffering of a horrible kind. But that is a small point. Is the fact that war causes indiscriminate suffering a proof that it is unjustifiable? Certainly to cause suffering to the innocent is an evil; whether or not it is wrong to bring that evil into the world depends on the nature of the evils which may be checked as a result. And it must be recognized that all citizens have their share in the national life. To claim for war that it distributes suffering with any regard for justice would be patently absurd; but it cannot be said of any citizen that he or she is wholly innocent of the crimes committed by the nation, especially if that citizen derives any share whatever of material benefit or patriotic pride from the results of those crimes. If it were possible to settle the matter by dealing only with the most responsible individuals, that way should be taken; but in fact it is not possible; and no citizen can claim to be altogether innocent of his country's wrong-doing. The suffering inflicted by war is not justly distributed; but neither is it a mere injustice. The indiscriminate character of modern war does not make it necessarily wrong in all circumstances to have recourse to it.

VI

" But is not all this talk pure humbug? We are ourselves guilty as a nation of contributing to the state of things from which the war arose. If our hands were clean we could perhaps come forward as champions of justice and freedom. But we are disqualified."

I should go farther than many in agreeing with the charge that we carry a heavy load of responsibility. To me it seems that we have incurred this in two ways. First, the method of peace-making in 1919 was bad, and the actual peace in some vital particulars shared the badness. The Versailles Treaty was in many ways one of the best peace-settlements in the history of Europe. It had more regard to justice for peoples as distinct from dynasties than any of its predecessors. It has the credit of restoring Poland to the map and of putting Czechoslovakia upon it. But it was imposed by the victors on the vanquished, and its economic clauses expressed the spirit of conquest. Worse than the Treaty was the policy of the ensuing years, and the continued refusal to welcome Germany into the fellowship of nations. This policy helped to create in Germany the mood that welcomed and enthroned Hitler. If Hitler is immediately responsible for the war, we are in part responsible for Hitler.

Alongside the treatment of Germany must be put our failure fully to operate the Covenant of the League. We disarmed in a mood of selfish relaxation when we should have maintained our full strength till general disarmament should become practicable. We followed a certain interpretation of British interests rather than the claims of the Covenant in the Manchurian crisis; we were not prepared to go all lengths on behalf of the Covenant in the Abyssinian crisis. Those failures are partly—largely, I think—responsible for the course of events which culminated in the war.

That is one individual's reading of the history; others read it very differently. I mention my reading here because I must insist with all possible emphasis that it does not carry with it the conclusion stated at the beginning of this section. The fact that we failed to do our duty at an earlier date is no reason why we should fail to do it now.

" But we only come in now because our own interests are now involved." That is partly true; but it still does not affect our duty. It is not wrong for a man to act justly on occasions when it is to his interest to do so; on the contrary, it is still his duty. There is nothing noble about it; but it is still right. We may wish that our champion-

ship of freedom and justice had been more consistent than it has;
it would be foolish as well as wicked to betray them merely because
now we are defending them for ourselves as well as for others.

VII

The whole question, then, comes down to this : Is the Nazi threat
to civilization so serious that the evil of allowing it to develop is
greater even than the monstrous evil of war?

About the answer to that question I have no doubt. Most of the
elements in life which we reckon as of highest value are incompatible
with Nazi rule. What is happening in Bohemia and Poland illustrates the principles and temper of that rule; and its characteristic
institutions are the Gestapo and the concentration camps. Far better
some years of "total war," with all its misery and waste and increasing bitterness of spirit, than the riveting of that diabolic system upon
more and more peoples.

Our civilization is not Christian in more than a rudimentary
sense; but it allows free course to the Christian message and to Christian experiment. We are fighting to keep open the opportunity of
making civilization increasingly Christian; we are fighting for this
against a system ruthlessly opposed to any such enterprise.

VIII

" Might not all of this be said by a pagan moral philosopher? Have
not you, as a Christian minister, a distinctive and different note to
sound? "

Yes, certainly. But Christianity does not sweep aside and render
obsolete all wisdom attained apart from it. It accepts this as its starting-point and goes farther. The Gospel was not to be the destruction
of the Law and the Prophets but their fulfilment.

Our Lord recognizes the right of kingdoms of this world to fight.
Those kingdoms have their place by God's appointment. They are
not the same thing as the Kingdom of God, which cannot be directly
served by fighting. But they are subject to the universal sovereignty
of God and must use their powers and exercise their rights in obedience to His laws. To check the aggressor and to set free the oppressed
are ways of doing this; and success in those aims opens a way for
that spiritual activity whereby men may be called to something
higher than justice or earthly loyalty.

The State must be very sure that it is doing this if it is to justify
before God its resort to war; but it must be ready to resort to war
when this is the claim made upon it.

IX

" But, even so, should the individual Christian, conscious of his own vocation to respond to that higher call which was mentioned, take part in this horrible business? "

The Gospel fulfils and does not destroy the law. We must not so respond to the Gospel as to fail to discharge elementary obligations. We must pay our debts before we give away our goods in reckless generosity.

There have always been two ways of Christian obedience—the way of withdrawal as far as may be from the world in order to follow as perfectly as possible the Christian precepts, and the way of living in the world by those precepts and by the Christian spirit, so as to bring the world itself nearer to the Christian standard. These two ways are those of the monk and of the Christian citizen.

It seems that some Christians are called to withdraw from any participation in war so as to bear a special witness to the supremacy of love and to the world-wide family of God. It seems doubtful, indeed, whether this can effectively be done by a mere refusal to fight accompanied by no renunciation. If a man is to enjoy the immunity which the Royal Air Force provides, and eat the food which the British Navy enables to reach him, his mere refusal to fight is a very slender witness to the supremacy of love. That witness, given in that form, seems to require the contracting out, so far as may be, from the advantages as from the obligations of the secular order of society. Those who do this—who, for example, choose to live in poverty among the very poor that they may share their lot and thereby bring them new strength and hope—are indeed pioneers of that better order for which we hope, wherein love alone and not self-interest will be the motive of all action.

But just as truly pioneers of that far-off age are those who accept the common obligations of men and strive to live in the spirit of Christ as they discharge them. The soldier who accepts the call of his duty and performs it with no hatred in his heart—still more, perhaps, the father or mother who sends a son to fight without allowing bitterness to spoil the sacrifice—is also showing the way to permeate the world itself with the Christian spirit. The Kingdom of God uses the service of both—of the Good Samaritan and the Good Centurion.

X

But one thing is certain. If we are to use such justification of joining in war as has been offered without becoming involved in horrible hypocrisy, we must be in deadly earnest. Only if we are determined to see that our victory really does serve justice and freedom; only if we are determined in our own national life to promote justice and freedom where now they are imperfectly attained; only on these conditions dare we come forward as their champions in war.

Especially must we remember that it is very hard to extract justice from strife. The passions evoked by war blind the vision and distort the judgment. We dare not hope to make our victory result in pure justice. We can, indeed, make it result in something far nearer justice than a Nazi domination; that alone would justify our fighting. But we must not ignore the perils inseparable from our enterprise; and we must steadfastly determine that we will resist, so far as by God's help we can, these corrupting influences, so that if He gives us victory we may be found faithful to the principles for which we have striven.

(Hodder and Stoughton, 1940)

The Sealed Book

ONE OF THE MARVELS connected with the Bible is the way in which it supplies our need in every new emergency that arises. For many years it may be that some Book seems remote and strange; it has no message for us, and we are puzzled that it should be there. Then a new set of circumstances confronts us and we find that precisely this Book appeals to us more directly and poignantly than any other. The moment for which it was written and included among the other Books in the Bible is come. So it is now with that great Book which is printed last in the Bible. Let us try to recover something of the experience which came to the Seer of the Apocalypse in the first vision in the Book of Revelation after the specific messages to the seven Churches of Asia were ended.

" After these things I saw, and behold, a door opened in heaven " (iv, 1). I suppose a modern writer would say that he received in a blinding flash an apprehension of the true secret of reality—or something of that sort. The old language is more suggestive : " a door opened in heaven "; only he does not mean that there was a hole in the sky and he looked through it. In this apprehension all attention is held at first by the figure of the Heavenly King—a figure altogether made of light and glory, the white light of the jasper stone and the red light of the sardius, and, round about, the green light of the emerald (iv, 2, 3). This figure is as little anthropomorphic as any visual image of the Heavenly King could be; it is a figure of light and glory.

" And round about the throne were four and twenty thrones; and upon the thrones I saw four and twenty elders sitting " (iv, 4) : the Church of all the ages; the Church of the Old Covenant or Old Testament, before its redemption in Christ, represented by the twelve Patriarchs, the sons of Jacob; and the Church of the New Covenant or New Testament, after its redemption in Christ, represented by the twelve Apostles; the four and twenty elders are the Church of all the ages.

" And in the midst before the throne and round about the throne were four living creatures " (iv, 6) which the passage in the Book of Ezekiel, from which the imagery is taken, shows to be the spirits who preside over created nature. They are " full of eyes," for nature is so vigilant that she never let one of her laws be broken. These

179

spirits of nature are engaged in ceaseless adoration. " They have no rest day and night saying ' Holy, holy, holy is the Lord God, the Almighty, which was and which is, and which is to come ' " (iv, 8).

So far perhaps we feel that we can understand. When we look up at the sky on a starry night and reflect upon the majestic order of this vast universe, or when we study the intricate and delicate beauty of a wild flower or an insect's wing, and recollect that all is due to the artistry of the Creator, then we realize that in very truth " the heavens declare the glory of God " and are ready to acknowledge that Nature exists to show forth His divinity.

And so far as we have any experience of worship we find that in it we are lifted above the chances and changes of circumstance; the worshippers with whom we join are not the people, many or few, who are gathered in the same building, but when we lift up our hearts to the Lord, forthwith it is with Angels and Archangels and with all the company of heaven that we laud and magnify His glorious Name.

That Nature exists for God's glory, and that there is an unceasing worship offered by an eternal Church, in which at our own best moments we can join—this we can believe. But what of the secular life of man, his age-long history with its wars and crimes? Does not this stretch as an ugly blot across the fair face of God's creation? Is there any way in which we can understand this?

" And I saw in the right hand of him that sat on the throne a book written within and on the back, close sealed with seven seals " (v, 1). The story is too long for the allotted space, and must run over, as we should say, on to the binding. For it is the long story of man's history and destiny. It is in the hand of the Heavenly King; but that is all that can be said—so far—about it. No one can interpret it; no one is " worthy to open the book or to loose the seals thereof " (v, 2, 3). It is God's decree and there is no more to be said. That is Mohammedanism; Kismet—it is fated; to which the only human reaction is resignation—Islam. St. John tells us that he "wept much " when he thought that was true (v, 4). But one of the elders —a spokesman of the eternal church—bids him not to weep. There is an interpreter of that book; it is the Lion of the tribe of Judah (v, 5). Judah was the Lion among the tribes in Jacob's blessing and was also their sole survivor. The Lion of the tribe of Judah is therefore He in whom all the meaning and hope of the Old Covenant is gathered up.

St. John looks to see this Lion—this figure of might. But there is no lion there. It is a Lamb—standing, and therefore alive, but with the marks of death upon Him, " standing as though it had been slain "; for this is He who in an earlier vision said " I am the first and the last and the living one, and I became dead and behold I am alive for evermore."

He takes the book, and forthwith the four living creatures and the four and twenty elders—Nature and the Church—fall down before the Lamb and sing a new song : " Worthy art thou to take the book and to open the seals thereof, for thou wast slain " (v, 8, 9). That is what qualifies Him. The death of Christ upon the Cross is the clue to the interpretation of human history. Then the whole universe boils over, so to speak, in an ecstasy of adoration.

And I saw, and I heard a voice of many angels round about the throne and the living creatures and the elders; and the number of them was ten thousand times ten thousand, and thousands of thousands; saying with a great voice, Worthy is the Lamb that hath been slain to receive the power, and riches, and wisdom, and might, and honour, and glory, and blessing. And every created thing which is in the heaven, and on the earth, and under the earth, and on the sea, and all things that are in them, heard I saying, Unto him that sitteth on the throne, and unto the Lamb, be the blessing, and the honour, and the glory, and the dominion, for ever and ever.

What is left but that Nature should give its solemn assent? " The four living creatures said ' Amen '." What is left but that the Church should adore the Heavenly King and the Lamb? " The elders fell down and worshipped " (v, 14).

Perhaps at this point we are disposed to say that all this may have been credible in those roseate days before 1914, or even in the first few years after 1919; but not now. At those times it might be possible to believe that the course of human history is to be understood in the light of the love of God as made known by Christ upon the Cross. There were evil things in the world, no doubt, but they were being remedied. The general tendency was in the right direction. History might be understood as the arena wherein Love progressively established itself against hatred, malice and ill-will. But surely that is not to be said about the world we know so sadly well; surely it is not to be believed that this world is interpreted by the love of God made known in Christ.

It might be sufficient to reply by pointing to the world familiar to the writer of the Apocalypse. He certainly lived through, and may have actually written his book in, that terrible year of the four Emperors, three of whom fought their way to the throne through rivers of blood. But it is more relevant to ask what was in the book when the seals were opened.

" And I saw when the Lamb opened one of the seven seals, and I heard one of the four living creatures saying as with a voice of thunder, Come." What comes? Well, it is what we call aggressive militarism.

" And I saw, and behold, a white horse, and he that sat thereon had a bow; and there was given unto him a crown : and he came forth conquering, and to conquer."

" And when he opened the second seal, I heard the second living creature saying, Come." What comes? Battle. " And another horse came forth, a red horse : and to him that sat thereon it was given to take peace from the earth, and that they should slay one another : and there was given unto him a great sword."

" And when he opened the third seal, I heard the third living creature saying, Come." What comes? Famine. " And I saw, and behold, a black horse; and he that sat thereon had a balance in his hand. And I heard as it were a voice in the midst of the four living creatures saying, A measure of wheat for a penny, and three measures of barley for a penny; and the oil and the wine hurt thou not." A " penny," as we know from the parable of the labourers in the vine-yard was a labourer's full wage for a day; and this " measure " was what was calculated, for purposes of holding out in a siege, as just enough to keep body and soul together. Let a man give all he can earn, and he may just live—maximum prices at their fiercest and worst.

" And when he opened the fourth seal, I heard the voice of the fourth living creature saying, Come." What comes? Death and the grave. " And I saw, and behold, a pale horse : and he that sat upon him, his name was Death; and Hades followed with him. And there was given unto them authority over the fourth part of the earth, to kill with sword, and with famine, and with death, and by the wild beasts of the earth."

Yes; it is our world, sure enough, that provides the contents of that book which was held by the Heavenly King, with all its horrors and terrors.

The four voices of Nature have spoken and the scene shifts. Beneath the altar in heaven, that is in the place of the eternal sacrifice, are seen the souls of those who " had been slain for the word of God and for the testimony which they held." They are waiting. What for? They are waiting till their successors—till we—shall offer our part of the great sacrifice (vi, 9–11).

" And I saw when he opened the sixth seal, and there was a great earthquake" and all the customary concomitants of apocalyptic catastrophe (vi, 12–17) and then follows the vision of the " great multitude which no man could number standing before the throne and before the Lamb, arrayed in white robes and palms in their hands " (vii, 9–17). " And when he opened the seventh seal " (viii, 1)— we expect a description of the blessed life to which these triumphant ones are admitted as the goal of their endurance; but no; " when he opened the seventh seal, there followed a silence in heaven about the space of half an hour," for

> That eternal blazon must not be
> To ears of flesh and blood.

As the Book proceeds there arises over against the figure of the Lamb which stands for Love using sacrifice as its instrument, the figure of the Wild Beast (xiii, 1), which stands for Pride using force as its instrument. And these two principles, represented by the Lamb and the Wild Beast, work out in two civilizations. Pride, using force as its instrument, works out into Babylon the Great, which comes tumbling down; and as often as men build it up it comes tumbling down again (xvii, xviii). And Love, of which the instrument is sacrifice, works out into " the holy city, new Jerusalem," which comes when it comes, and in whatsoever degree it comes, from one source only—" out of heaven from God " (xxi, 2).

Thus the Book of Revelation supplies a clue to the interpretation of History and a criterion of progress. The inner meaning of History is the conflict between the Lamb and the Wild Beast—Love and Pride. This alone gives real significance to politics and diplomacies and wars. Progress consists in the increase of Love and Good-will at the expense of Pride and Violence. We are inclined to think that every new invention is a contribution to Progress; and, of course, it can be so. But will any one dare to say in this year, 1923, that mankind is either better or happier because men have learnt to fly? Some day we may hope that aviation will appear as a contribution to progress; but that day is not yet. Whether or not such an invention marks a stage in progress depends on the use which we make of it. Only the increase of Love is real progress.

The crucial moment in the Vision which we have considered is that when the seer looks for the Lion and finds the Lamb. For the Lamb is stronger than the Lion; He is more truly the figure of might. The Lion represents force. How does force produce its effects? Only in two ways : one is accident, as when a boulder rolls down a mountain side and obliterates a traveller passing below; the other is in giving effect to human purpose under human direction. If then there is any power which can control the wills of men, that power will also control the force which men utilize.

Is there any such power? Yes; one, and only one. It is love expressing itself in sacrifice. The tyrant can so use the force at his disposal as to control my conduct; but he cannot control my will. If I serve him, it is against my will. When God made men with free hearts and wills, He committed Himself to the way of the Cross as the only way by which He could be omnipotent; unless He so loved the world and showed His love, there would be something that escaped His control; He would not be All-Ruler.

When you give a present to a friend, you are perfectly free; your own will chooses to give the present and what present to give. Yet your whole action is determined by the pleasure of the friend for whom the present is intended. And the giving of a present is a form of sacrifice, for the principle of sacrifice is that for love's sake we choose to do or suffer what, apart from love, we should not choose to do or suffer. It need not be painful. Indeed when the sacrifice is accepted with gratitude and the love which prompts it is returned, it is the most delightful thing in life.

But in this selfish world the sacrifice of love must be painful; and it is the very pain of it which makes it fruitful. No one is indifferent when he discovers that some one loves him enough to suffer willingly on his behalf. He may not be so moved as to change his conduct or his character all at once, but he is not unmoved.

Here is a way by which God may control the free hearts and wills that He has made without destroying their freedom. Here is the one way by which He can direct them through their freedom. It cannot be guaranteed that all will respond; but if He is to be Almighty it must be in this way.

There is no promise in this Book or anywhere else in Scripture that a day will come when all men—on this earth or elsewhere—will open their hearts to the love of God and let it direct their purposes. If we hope that, it is because we shrink from the thought that God may fail in His purpose for any human soul. But if the outcome is and must remain uncertain so far as our knowledge goes, the issue at stake is clear. Two powers are at grips in human History : Love and Pride. For each several soul, for every nation, for mankind itself, welfare consists in the supremacy of love and progress in advance towards that goal. Set in the midst of History as the focus and source of the power that can carry us forward is the Cross.

The meaning of History is the triumph of the Lamb that was slain.

(A lecture at Blackpool, August 1923)

The Resources and Influence of English Literature

I ESTEEM IT a great honour that I should have been asked to give this lecture, the first of what will no doubt later on be a very important series. If I were to do it, it was necessary that the title theme of my lecture should be very general, for I am not a special student of any corner or department of literature, and it was perhaps appropriate that the first lecture of the series should deal with literature in some general survey; so it is this that I want to undertake so far as I am able, in the hope that I may illustrate the illimitable resources of literature, and thus do a little towards encouraging any who have not yet turned to it for the joy and the steadiness of mind that it can bring, to believe that there is, in that wide range that it covers, something for everyone and therefore something for them. But, of course, the range is immense, from limericks to tragedy, with everything that falls between.

I would like to say something at first about the ways in which I think most people discover the resources of literature. There is need, I think, for most of us to be sympathetically introduced to some field of literature in which we then find ourselves, even from the outset, at home. There are not many who have the combination of opportunity and faculty to discover that for themselves, unless someone who knows literature itself in something of its width and scope and the temperament of the individual concerned directs the individual to the most appropriate starting-place. That is the trouble, of course, about the handling of literature in schools, for inevitably you are dealing with a whole group of young people at once, when it would be more desirable to deal with each of them individually, and it is probable that what is the right introduction for the majority of those will be the wrong one for a minority; and it is very hard to correct that. No doubt the primary requisite is that whoever effects the introduction, presumably a teacher, should be, himself or herself, an enthusiast. No one can impart an enthusiasm that he has not got, and to have to teach literature which you do not yourself appreciate, must be an intolerable burden to pupil and teacher alike; and therefore I should like, though I suppose it is impossible, that the teacher should always choose what literature he will use as his means of introducing young people to appreciation of literature generally. That makes trouble with the examiners. One of the fundamental facts about education which is constantly ignored, is that the examiners are precisely as idle as the examinees, and that they therefore tend to conduct the examination in the way which saves them trouble, or at any rate to avoid conducting it in a way which would increase their trouble. It is, of course, far more difficult for an examiner to conduct his investigation into the value of the teaching given in any school if the teachers are going to choose the books concerned. It might involve his reading them himself for the first time. But so long as we work through mediums that are prescribed from above, whether universities or any other authority, we are hampering the spontaneity of teaching, and that in the field of literature is disastrous.

What is needed first of all is the teacher's enthusiasm, and then I think that he or she must later take a chance whether or not the particular pupils will be able to respond, though, of course, among the objects of the teacher's enthusiasm those will be selected for which there is the best hope that a response may be forthcoming. If I might illustrate from a reference to my own devotion to Robert Browning, which the Chairman has mentioned, it was my habit, when Headmaster of Repton, to assemble the Upper Sixth of the classical side and the history specialists every week for an hour with me in my own study, instead of in their schoolroom, taking care that there were enough armchairs for them to sit in luxurious comfort, to present to each of them the one-volume edition of Browning, and then to read Browning's poems with them, first reading the poem through, and then talking about it as long as I found anything to say, and then reading through it again; and the only variation in this was that once a year we read *Hamlet*, distributing the parts among ourselves, with myself in the rôle of the Prince of Denmark. Well, I cannot say what the effect was on anything like the majority of those who were subjected to this treatment, but they certainly rather enjoyed it. You see we gilded the pill a little bit by taking it not in a classroom, but in a room of a private house and in the comfort of armchairs; and I do know of several boys now who still read Browning, and two or more who tell me they often recollect what they then read in Browning, as a result of those hours spent together.

Then in the second place, I think that at any rate older pupils above the primary school age may profit by learning from a teacher who avows the limitations of his appreciation, because there are some who will have attempted to enjoy a writer of great repute and find themselves unable to do so, and then suppose that they have no aptitude for literature or it may be for poetry, whereas if the teacher is able to say that he knows—to take my own case—that John Milton is undoubtedly a great poet, but is quite unable personally to derive pleasure from a perusal of his works, it is possible for one or another who has a distaste for Milton, possibly caused by the use of his epics for the purpose of impositions, nevertheless to believe he may enjoy some other poet. I believe that this open avowal of limitations can be quite useful in calling attention to the enthusiasm that the teacher possesses, whereas those other pupils who are able to derive real pleasure from Milton will immediately be conscious of a superiority to their teacher than which nothing is more delightful, than which nothing is a more potent instrument in creating enjoyment of a branch of study.

Of course, there must be allowances made for age and for interests and tastes that correspond with age. I suppose it ought ideally to be the mental age rather than the chronological age of the student, which means that a large part of our population remains permanently at about thirteen. But there is, of course, a stage in appreciation where what appeals most is exceedingly marked and vigorous rhythm. That quality in the human soul which leads primitive man to be content sitting for hours under a tree beating a tom-tom rhythmically exists somewhere deep in the subconsciousness of all of us, and there are some whose appreciation is strongest at that point. There are poems specially qualified to appeal to such, and their taste for poetry may be best developed by allowing it in the first instance to develop itself by exercise upon that kind of material.

Then we want to encourage browsing among books. There are some booksellers, great benefactors of mankind, who allow the public to come into their shops and walk about picking up books and reading bits, and putting them down again, without anyone watching or looking over their shoulder and saying, " That one is seven and sixpence." That is worth a very great deal; I am sure that those booksellers who adopt this practice gain, commercially, more than they lose, while they are certainly conferring a great benefit upon those who frequent their establishments. I remember very well an advertisement that appeared in the *Oxford Magazine* when I was an undergraduate—it did not refer to myself—asking the gentleman who had removed the first volume of *Mommsen's History of Rome*, to send his name and address, so that the others could be forwarded, because these were not sold separately. I have never known whether the advertisers were successful, but, by permitting people to sample this, that and the other type of literature, they were enabling many people again to discover where their capacity for appreciation lay, and then, following the line of their interest, to discover what it might be that literature has in store for them.

N

That leads us to the second consideration in the introduction to literature, namely, the need for facilities. If the public is to be aware of the great treasure house of literature and all that it has in store for every member of the public, then, of course, it is necessary that books should be accessible, and in this we have made great developments of late through the increase of public libraries, and the splendid service rendered by their librarians, to which I am sure that this Council would wish at all times to pay grateful tribute. I hope we may go a little beyond that, and encourage the accumulation of private libraries, however small, and one suggestion which has been made, and which I most heartily endorse, is that we should urge the provision in all new houses of built-in bookshelves, so that those who do buy books will not be faced with what may be for them the really vexatious alternatives of either buying bookshelves, which it may be difficult to afford, or of leaving the books lying about untidily. This is a place where the architects and builders could further the cause that we have at heart, if only they would take it up.

Then, of course, we need, if people are in that way to accumulate libraries, especially the poorer folk, to develop a skill in the choice and to recognize what I have already hinted at, that sympathy between reader and author is indispensable to real appreciation. It is, I suppose, for that reason, that people's capacity for appreciation of great literature varies so much. I know that there have been writers on aesthetics, who have maintained that style is something that should be judged and appreciated quite independently of the meaning of the thing expressed; but I am one of those who agree with the late Sir Walter Raleigh, the great professor of English literature at Oxford, when he said that prior to the question whether the thing is well said, is the question whether it is well that it should be said at all; and that is a point upon which there will inevitably be difference of judgment depending upon taste, but also upon convictions, political, philosophical and religious. So we must recognize the great variety of appreciation which we are likely to find; for even if we deprecate the fact, it is a fact, and unless we allow for it, our service for the public will suffer very badly.

And so I go on to illustrate if I can, in some degree, the richness of the treasure which is offered to us in literature, and I shall confine myself to literature of our own land, one of the greatest at least, and perhaps the greatest, in recorded history. And I begin with what I spoke of as presumably about the simplest form of verbal combination that can be called literature at all, the limerick. What are the merits of a limerick? by what standards do we criticize a limerick? Well, as far as I can see, there are two qualities, either of which will make a really successful limerick. One is extreme simplicity, the falling of the words into rhyme and rhythm without any kind of rearrangement, as for example:

> There was a young man of Madrid,
> Who fancied that he was the Cid;
> When they asked him why,
> He could only reply
> That he didn't know why, but he did.

The beauty of that depends upon its complete and absolute simplicity. There is a slightly simpler one, perhaps, though I am never sure that it is quite fair:

> There was an old man of Calcutta,
> Who had a most terrible stutter;
> " G-g-give me," he said,
> " Some b-b-b-bread
> And b-b-b-b-b-b-butter."

That was a particular favourite of the late Bishop Gore, who on the other hand vigorously protested against one which I specially admired, which illustrates the use of complicated rhythm:

> There once was a gourmet of Crediton
> Who ate pâté de foie gras; he spread it on
> A chocolate biscuit
> And said, " I'll just risk it."
> His tomb gives the date that he said it on.

The main merit here is dexterity, dexterity practically divorced from meaning; it is the kind of pleasure we have in witnessing any great skill of a kind we probably do not possess, although it is directed to the fulfilment of no particular purpose, but merely achieves its own object with perfect neatness, and so gives us the satisfaction that neatness is able to afford—a limited but quite real satisfaction.

Now, I should rank with that, and only just above it, the detective novel, because here again I believe dexterity is the main element in our pleasure. Of course, the essence of a detective story is that it is a kind of game in which the pleasure consists in being beaten; if you spot the criminal before the end, it rather spoils your pleasure. But there are certain rules to be observed; the author must play fair; that is to say, there must be placed before you all the evidence which is sufficient to indicate the criminal, who must have been on the stage pretty well all the time. There are stories, of course, in which you are completely baffled, because the crime turns out to be committed by somebody you never heard of, and then you feel the author has cheated, for anyone could bewilder anyone else that way. All the factors must be there and all the characters must be there, and yet the case must be presented in such a way that you are just beaten, although you had the chance to win, and the pleasure is greater when you win. If it is merely a detective story, the whole interest is in the detection, and that is the real quality of it; and again it is a matter of dexterity, not this time with words, but with plot. But when you combine that with the quality of the thriller, you go on to something more. Of course you can have the thriller which is not a detective story at all, just as you can have a detective story which is not a thriller, but you can also combine them; but as soon as you introduce the elements of the thriller, you have brought in sympathy which is aroused in all of us by courage, and although I do not claim for the thriller that it is a very exalted type of literature, I do claim for it that it is already beginning to show quite definite moral qualities which need not be present in the limerick in any degree at all; and writers of thrillers show that they observe these, because either they make ordinary conventional virtue triumphant in the end, or else they present people who are technically enemies of society, but who conduct their assaults upon it under the impulse of generosity, with a view to the better distribution of wealth; and the kind of sympathy all of us feel for Robin Hood has been very freely exploited in these last days by the writers of thrillers; and their reference is to moral standards, however rudimentary, while in the romantic novel it is quite clear that you are on ground which is common to the romanticist and moralist. Here the readers have a variety of tastes, such that those who have one group of preferences are almost wholly unable to understand what is the charm of the books which fail to make appeal to them. I am one of those who, when reading a novel, wish for two things if possible. I wish for events; I want things to happen; and also I want the people to be agreeable company. Now that, of course, puts me out of court with the enormous bulk of modern literature which steadily refuses to bring forward the character of any person with whom you could endure to spend half an hour in real life. A writer may present a searching psychological study of such persons, and no doubt there is a value in this, a value which seems to me to be fundamentally as pathological as it is literary; but that is merely because I am made that way. I wrote to Mr. Priestley, whom I had not yet met, when he produced *The Good Companions*, to thank him for writing a book which kept me in the company of such delightful people for a long time. He warned me that he might be writing other books in which the characters might not be all delightful, and I must say that I have not enjoyed any of them half as much as that one. This is personal. What I am pleading for is that you must make great allowances for this personal preference; with the ordinary romantic novel there are some of us who are, as it were, seeking a society other than our own, in which we have no responsibility, where we can enjoy intercourse with people who for the imagination are truly alive, but towards whom we have no responsibility at all, and that is very restful. That kind of mental rest is no small social service, especially to tired and jaded people.

But here I must interpolate a little bit, for you will see I have so far been speaking of literature as the occasion of entertainment; and of course there are many for whom it must always be what it is at its best, an opportunity of interpretation. The greatest literature is manifestly aiming at the presentation of a picture of human life in such ways that we may understand it more fully, not with a utilitarian aim, but because there is a joy in the understanding itself. If it has utility beyond that, so much the better, but so far as the creation and the enjoyment are artistic, that further utility is simply an added excellence, but is not part of the sheer excellence of the work of art. But whichever it is, whether entertainment or interpretation, still this question of sympathy comes in. If I am to be entertained I must enjoy the outlook of the author and the company of the people to whom he introduces me; but if I am to receive through the work of art the interpretation of the universe, it must at least not clash with the principles upon which I am prepared to interpret it. It may be based on principles other than my own and so it may enrich my interpretation of experience; but if the principles clash, I shall be involved in a critical and hostile attitude of mind towards it which will be the ruin of artistic appreciation. Let me give an illustration. I am disposed to say that among the worst books ever committed to paper is Hardy's great masterpiece, *Tess of the D'Urbervilles*, because to me it gives the impression that although Tess may no doubt be rightly described on the title page as a pure woman, the net result of the novel is to produce the impression that it does not matter whether she was or not; and that is much more disastrous than if she had been, quite frankly, an impure woman. The creation of that sense of purposelessness and futility in life I regard as the greatest disservice any man can render to his fellows, whether through literature or anything else. Having such a conviction I am quite incapable of yielding myself to the undoubted artistic power that is displayed by Hardy in that great artistic achievement; I remain quite incapable of appreciating it; so let me say once more, don't leave out this varying capacity for sympathy in your estimate of the kind of literature which different people are capable of appreciating, and recognize that it does leave you with a complete impossibility of arriving at final and absolute judgments.

Having come to this theme of interpretation, we pass on from the romantic novel, as we ordinarily think of it, to the great novel, not, of course, that you can have a hard and fast line between any of these categories; but there are some we recognize as plainly light and mainly entertaining, and some we recognize as leading us into the experience of the depths and heights that are contained in human nature; and here I will make one exception to my rule of confining myself to English literature. To me it seems that the novels of Dostoievski derive almost the whole of their power and value from the fact that they are interpretations of life in its heights and its depths, and that if you were not attending to them at all from that point of view you would inevitably be so bewildered by their comparative formlessness and the absence of any particular proportion between the different parts that you would find hardly any intelligible structure in them at all. Structure all comes, so it seems to me, from the beliefs, the convictions which inspired Dostoievski and guided him in the characters which he presents and the proportions he gives to the different episodes. I do indeed regard them as among the greatest masterpieces with which I am acquainted, and I think that they show an interpretation of the real meaning both of human life and of the Christian religion in its dealing with human life, of which I know no equal in fiction or other literature; but I believe that their greatness comes precisely from the fact that their whole structure is determined by the message which the author is concerned to give and, of course, there are always those for whom that is an alien element that ought to be kept apart from the field of literary criticism. If it is kept apart here, I think the result will be to degrade into a low class one whom those who have read him are generally ready to place among the master writers of all time.

I pass from fiction in all its forms to a department of literature which is bound to be an interpretation of life; it is on the whole my own favourite class of books for ordinary reading; history and biography. The essence of history is, I think, that it introduces inevitably a union of science, philosophy and art. Good history must be scientific; for the facts must be accurately observed—records, inscriptions and the like. It cannot be only scientific, because the historian cannot present all the facts that he collects. The historical record of a period cannot be complete; if it were it would take as long to read as the events took to happen. That would mean that the history of a hundred years would take a hundred years to read,

which is absurd; so there must be selection, and the selection must
be governed by some principle.

The only possible principle is to be found in the question, what
constitutes the importance of past events? Then you are at once
embarked consciously or unconsciously upon the philosophical interpretation of human experience in its process through the ages. If
that is an unconscious process, your selection will be a little hap-
hazard, and it is likely that there will be no intelligible principle
which can help the reader to see what is presented in a single
panorama. Of course if you adopt conscious principles you may
adopt those which the reader thinks are certainly wrong. Now, myself, I like historians to be strong partisans. I like to read, for
example, the history of our Civil War written by a strong Royalist,
and by a strong Republican, first one and then the other, and then
make up my own mind. I don't want him to pretend to be impartial,
because I know he is not; and if he pretends to be impartial he will
be deceiving himself and me. And history which is thus both scientific and philosophical also makes use of art; because there must be
art in order that what is presented may be alive, may kindle the
imagination, and through the imagination achieve the stature of
reality.

With history goes biography, and though biography does not
make so great intellectual demands as history, I think in many ways
it is the most satisfactory of historical forms, because now there is no
doubt about the principle which governs the selection of material.
The selection of events is that which helps us to see the life of the
hero as a whole. It should not be such as leads us to like him or to
dislike him or despise him, but to see him as a whole, and so to
understand the various parts of his life in relation to one another,
with enough historical context to see how he fits into it or grows
out of it. I happen to have a particular love for political biography
which illustrates the interplay of private character and public events,
which is at its height in political biography. I rejoice in such stories
as that which Trevelyan gives us in one of the volumes on Garibaldi,
about the way in which it was settled that Garibaldi should be
allowed to cross the Straits from Sicily into Italy. Let me recall it.
Cavour, who was anxious not to offend the respectable statesmen
of Europe, was constantly claiming that the cause of Italian unity
was no revolution and that he had no truck with revolutionaries;
in particular he seemed to be very remote from Garibaldi and dis-
interested in that hero's progress. One day at the Tuileries the
Empress Eugenie remarked to the Italian Ambassador, "You can
tell your master that the English and we have decided not to allow

Garibaldi to cross the Straits." The Ambassador telegraphed to Cavour. Cavour sent for Sir Odo Russell. Sir Odo Russell telegraphed to Sir James La Caita, then a Neapolitan exile in England, who was at that moment engaged in the pedestrian task of examining for the Civil Service and was suffering from a heavy cold. Sir James went to call upon Lord Russell, the Prime Minister. He was told he could not see him. " Does that mean he is out, or engaged? " " Engaged most particularly with the French Ambassador," was the reply. Good heavens! thought Sir James, there is not a moment to lose. " I must see Lady Russell." He was informed that she was upstairs, ill in bed. He took out a visiting-card and wrote on the back, " If you have any respect for your father's memory, see me at once." She sent a message that he might come up. He told her his story. She rang a bell and sent a messenger to the Prime Minister below, telling him at whatever cost he must come up immediately. He, thinking that his wife was *in extremis*, made what excuse he could, and came upstairs. She told Sir James to repeat his story, which he did, and fell into a fit of coughing. Lord Russell said, " You take that cough home to bed and don't be so sure I shall sign the Treaty." The next day the French Ambassador read in the newspaper a statement by the British Prime Minister that " inasmuch as if Garibaldi arrived in Italy he could still effect nothing unless the inhabitants supported him, to hinder him would be to interfere in the internal affairs of Italy, which was against the policy of Her Majesty's Government." I think that sort of thing is really great fun; that sort of thing does occur every now and then in political biography.

I have said nothing about poetry, and though I may say a word, I think it ought to be a talk by itself. I do think we want to help those who are entering on an appreciation of literature, to understand why poetry is usually, though not always, in verse. Let us keep in mind the great saying of Coleridge: " The opposite of prose is not poetry but verse; and the opposite of poetry is not prose but science." Prose and verse are a contrasted pair of terms dealing with the rhythm in which the words are put together. Poetry and science are contrasted terms dealing with the habit of mind in which the object in question is being regarded. But why should poetry usually be in verse? I think it is for this reason, that the whole purpose of art is to help us to understand the object presented as if from within, so that we may enter into real sympathy with it, and may so far as may be share its actual mode of being and understand it; whereas science deals with it from without and considers its relation to its setting in its context and analyses it into its own component parts.

When you speak of understanding people, you always mean that you find yourself in natural sympathy with them, and are not referring to psychological analysis. When you say, "I cannot understand acting like that," you mean "If I had been in that position I could not have done it"; you do not share the motives which led to the action. It is that kind of intimate appreciation which art is always concerned to create, and it does this by concentrating our attention upon the object in such a way that it will not wander. That is why pictures are put into frames. It helps you to avoid looking at anything except the picture. You surround the picture with something not incongruous but entirely alien, and any tendency of the attention to wander is abruptly checked as it reaches the frame. Any object of contemplation is more beautiful when seen framed, as, for example, between trees, than if merely as an open landscape—again I think for the same reason, that we more easily centre attention upon it. And I think that the reason why poets resort to rhythm and rhyme is that in that way they hold the attention fast upon the object; and the rhythms and rhymes will be more elaborate as a rule when the subject is not qualified of itself to hold the attention very fast. I think that is true, though it would be too long a matter to try to prove it in detail; but just consider such a poem as Shelley's *Cloud*; I will see if I can remember the last three stanzas:

> That orbed maiden with white fire laden,
>   Whom mortals call the Moon,
> Glides glimmering o'er my fleece-like floor,
>   By the midnight breezes strewn;
> And wherever the beat of her unseen feet,
>   Which only the angels hear,
> May have broken the woof of my tent's thin roof,
>   The stars peep behind her and peer;
> And I laugh to see them whirl and flee,
>   Like a swarm of golden bees,
> When I widen the rent in my wind-built tent,
>   Till the calm rivers, lakes and seas,
> Like strips of the sky fallen through me on high,
>   Are each paved with the moon and these.
>
> I bind the Sun's throne with a burning zone,
>   And the Moon's with a girdle of pearl;
> The volcanoes are dim, and the stars reel and swim
>   When the whirlwinds my banner unfurl,
> From cape to cape, with a bridge-like shape
>   Over a torrent sea,
> Sunbeam-proof, I hang like a roof;
>   The mountains its columns be.

The triumphal arch through which I march
  With hurricane, fire and snow,
When the Powers of the air are chained to my chair,
  Is the million-coloured bow;
The Sphere-fire above its soft colours wove,
  While the moist Earth was laughing below.

I am the daughter of Earth and Water,
  And the nursling of the Sky;
I pass through the pores of the ocean and shores;
  I change, but I cannot die.
For after the rain when with never a stain
  The pavilion of Heaven is bare,
And the winds and sunbeams with their convex gleams
  Build up the blue dome of air,
I silently laugh at my own cenotaph—
  And out of the caverns of rain,
Like a child from the womb, like a ghost from the tomb,
  I arise and unbuild it again.

Well now, there you have a theme which, unless it were for that intense rhythm, would not, I think, grip the imagination. But let us pass to something quite different, if I may take the other extreme at once, and consider a passage where the introduction of rhyme or complication of rhythm would be inopportune. Consider Macbeth's speech when he hears of Lady Macbeth's death:

She should have died hereafter;
There would have been a time for such a word—
Tomorrow, and tomorrow, and tomorrow,
Creeps in this petty pace from day to day,
To the last syllable of recorded time;
And all our yesterdays have lighted fools
The way to dusty death. Out, out, brief candle!
Life's but a walking shadow; a poor player,
That struts and frets his hour upon the stage,
And then is heard no more: it is a tale
Told by an idiot, full of sound and fury,
Signifying nothing.

If you begin to complicate that metre at all (it is, of course, a metrical masterpiece), if you begin to complicate, to make it involved, or if you were to try to introduce rhyme into it, you would make confusion by its irrelevance. I suggest this as the kind of way, or one kind of way, in which we may help people to see the aesthetic value of rhyme and rhythm, as they constitute the real beauty of poetry.

   It is in poetry most of all that we must expect diversity of tastes and appreciation; and I am going here, having the opportunity, to avow one more conviction which I do not think would be likely to appear in *The Times Literary Supplement*. I have read, not very much, but a certain amount of the work of the younger poets and the modern poets generally. A great many of them are mainly expressing the mode of blankness which goes with absence of any power to interpret life, and there are some others who have an interpretation of life. I am in most sympathy with those whose interpretation is Christian, but I do not think that is the decisive feature. It does seem to me that the pure poetic form is better in the case of those who really have something to say, than in the case of those who are expressing distress because they have nothing to say.

Well, this great body of literature exists, as I have said, mainly for the enrichment of our lives on its own plane and in its own right, and we ought not to ask what justification it has got or for what purpose it is useful; and yet, of course, it serves a great many purposes beyond itself. It has undoubtedly in the past done much to stimulate social reform. The novels of Dickens had a very great effect in that direction. Some of the hideous blemishes in civilization which he described, some of the absurdities which he satirized, were abolished largely as the result of the stirring of the imagination and feelings which was due to him. There has been for many people a store of inspiration to patriotism and courage in the great literature of our history, as expressed in the ballads and poems that follow on the ballads; and when you come to the higher range of beauty in literature, you are always on the edge of religion, and so I should close with one word concerning that department of literature of which I spoke at the outset as the highest of them all. It may be indeed that there is a Divine Comedy, and perhaps Dante did find and express it in his great poem; but apart from that it is in tragedy in this sad mortal state of ours that the greatest heights have been reached; and here certainly we are dealing with a rich interpretation of life; for if the poet is successful, or the dramatist is successful, he carries us through sympathy into real participation of his own experience, so that we are different, if only by a small amount, for ever after; and when a man has once faced the terror of life in *Macbeth*, or its horror in *Othello*, or its vast grey gloom in *Hamlet*, or its black darkness shot through flames of anguish in *King Lear*, and has seen all this not as something repellent but redeemed by beauty and so made sublime, he must be able to face the terrible aspect of life with new courage, that is largely born of that experience.

(The first Annual Lecture of the
National Book Council, May 21, 1943)

Social Witness and Evangelism

NOT LONG AGO a friend confronted me with this challenge: " If a visitor from Mars had come to Europe in about 1935 and had visited Russia and Germany, he would have had no doubt what was the aim in those countries of the Communist and the National Socialist parties; if he had then come to England, would he have been able to form any similar conception of the aim of the Christians in it? " Of course, one's first tendency is to say that the two cases have no real similarity; political parties must have definite aims or be doomed to futility; a religion is too deeply penetrating and too widely pervasive in its essence and influence to be compassed by a formula. It is a thing of the spirit; to define it is to materialize and degrade it; and so forth. Yet, while there is truth in this which we neglect at our peril, I think our visitor from Mars, if he had found his way into the Church of the Catacombs, or the centres of the early Franciscan movement, or the early days of the conversion of Uganda, would feel that he had been face to face with a very definite and concrete force, conscious of itself and its aim, even if its character and purpose could be but vaguely indicated in words.

There would be both truth and justice in the reply to our challenge that the object of the community of Christians is to make Christians —to make Christians of some sort out of those who are not Christians at all, and to make better Christians out of those who are already some sort of Christians. Yet this is insufficient; for that is an aim which, in the contemporary world, is entirely impracticable. The very air is full of every kind of propaganda; men's minds are obscured and their time is preoccupied with claims other than religious. They see the use and value of many other competitors for their attention; they do not see the use or value of Christianity. They are not, as a rule, hostile to it; they regard it as a perfectly legitimate and harmless hobby—a refined occupation for the leisure of the mystical; they even have some respect for its moral judgments, though they often dissent from them. But they feel no need of its help, no obligation to heed its warnings. To a very great extent the nation has drifted away from any distinctively Christian beliefs.

This is not to say that it has become irreligious. There is a very widespread Theism—a belief in a righteous God who in a general

198

sense rules the world, though He is not regarded as demanding of the individual any more exacting requirement than what may enable him to say, " I have not done any harm to any one." Goodness is thus thought of primarily in a negative way, and the judgments of God are thought of as falling, if anywhere, on outrageous sinners or on nations which follow a policy that involves misery for multitudes. The idea of sin, as distinct from acts of conscious ill-will, is not often present in men's minds; and the whole notion of redemption is so alien from them as to be unintelligible.

There is a deeper stratum of real though latent faith which is tapped by great national occasions or by some personal or family events, especially bereavement. But here too what we find is a Stoical Theism tinged with Christian emotion. It is very real and very precious. We do both Church and Nation a grave disservice if we disparage it. But it is far short of thorough-going Christian discipleship.

We have to recognize also that there is, or at any rate there was before the war, a great part of our population which had scarcely any interest in general ideas or activities expressed in or supported by such ideas. The typical " bungalow city " on the fringe of our great towns was inhabited by people who had largely lost all sense of purpose in life; they earned their livelihood in occupations that did not interest them; their aim was chiefly to earn what they could spend upon their leisure; and that leisure they occupied with amusement. Such people are the victims of a faulty social and educational system; but to many they seemed fortunate because they had the appearance of prosperity; and the type was increasing rather than diminishing. The war has ended that type of existence. But when the war is over, the forces which generated it will be again at work, and will produce the same results unless effective measures to counteract these can be initiated.

In more thoughtful circles, this purposeless attitude to life was encouraged by an unscientific use of the natural sciences in education —and that in two ways. The student in the laboratory, as he makes his experiments, must have no aim in view except to carry out each experiment correctly and observe its results accurately. He is watching something which goes on its own way and no hopes or feelings of his, no judgments of good and bad, must be allowed to influence his observations or his inferences. Therefore he is not being trained to offer a responsible reaction to the world he studies. He is acquiring an admirable intellectual integrity, but he may acquire it at the cost of ethical vacuity. I have called this an unscientific use of the sciences, because the truly scientific attitude towards them recognizes the

limitation of the methods of the laboratory as being applicable only
to what can be weighed or measured. It is true that at one time some
scientists were disposed to say that only these methods would lead
to real knowledge and under their influence science itself was pressed
more and more in the direction of pure mathematics. That is a
respectable tendency, discoverable in Plato. But with the development of biology that tendency has been reduced. If by scientific
method we mean accurate observation, valid inference and verifica-
tion by experience it is necessary for us all. A full education must,
however, supplement these studies with others, such as history or
literature, where it is not possible to achieve absolute precision or
certainty, but where the personal response of the student is challenged at every turn. But this consideration has been neglected over
a large part of the secondary education which has been developed
since the last war, and we have to deal with a generation for which
the predominant intellectual influence is moulded by that educational
defect. The result is a divorce between intellect and emotion, with
consequent strains and tensions both in the body politic and in the
psychological constitution of those in whom that divorce has been
effected.

This attitude of detachment, encouraged in the more educated
by the lack of balance and adjustment in our education, is reinforced
by the complexity of political life. The ordinary citizen is bewildered
by the number of questions with regard to which decisions are
needed, and the way in which they are interlocked with one another.
So he is disposed to abandon the effort to reach any conclusion or
to take any responsible action. He notices that when men touch the
complicated structure of social or international life, they often produce results exactly opposite to those at which they were aiming. He
feels that it is all beyond him; he decides to look after his own affairs
and leave politics to experts or fools. But in reaching that decision
he is taking the very important political action of repudiating
democracy; he is also shirking, or at least relieving himself of, a
burden of responsibility. Thus from another side he is pressed
towards an irresponsible and purposeless existence.

But there are other factors in the situation to be noted. The
traditional character of our people contains some qualities certainly
akin to, and almost certainly due to, the moral teaching and influence
of Christ. There is a deep and constant stream of kindliness, and an
attitude to life which is outraged by the lack of kindliness. There is
strong feeling for family and home—all who have had touch with
the men and women in the Forces know this. And there is a widespread reverence for our Lord, even when there is no intimate know-

ledge of the Gospel story and no acquaintance with or acceptance of
any theological interpretation of His Work or Person.

I have attempted in the foregoing paragraphs to sketch in outline
the country which Christians must aim at conquering; the material
out of which they are to attempt to make the future Christians. In
whatever degree my sketch is accurate, it indicates the special quality
of the Christian task today and the special difficulties attending
upon it.

Some take so serious a view of the situation that they advocate
a concentration of all attention on the central citadel of religious
faith. They ask for a definite statement of Christian doctrine—
" Catholic " or " Protestant," according to their varying convictions
—and while they desire full co-operation with all who can share
their aim, they desire also a sharp definition of Church membership
corresponding to the sharp definition of doctrine. Vagueness of outline is their special enemy, because it seems to them incompatible
with effectiveness either of witness or of action. There is much in
the temper of our time which responds to this. Men do wish to be
clear about what is offered to them for belief or asked of them in
practice; then they can accept or repudiate, conform or dissent; but
they know where they are.

On the other hand, there are also some who shrink from this
degree of definition on two grounds. First, they see and regret its
divisive tendency, which they think leads to a loss of effectiveness
by its hindrance to united witness—a loss which in their judgment
is greater than the gain in effectiveness to be expected from sharp
definition. Secondly, and more profoundly, they think the way of
sharp definition involves a lack of sensitiveness to the gradations of
spiritual apprehension and consequent injustice to those who cannot accurately or fairly be classified under one heading or another.
The formula " either—or " is seldom appropriate to personal apprehensions and relationships; the crude dichotomy of the dilemma can
seldom do justice to the complex delicacy of spiritual realities.

Perhaps it is a sufficient indication of my own attitude to this
matter to say that from the standpoint of effectiveness both seem to
me to be urging a vital consideration. We need definiteness and we
need unity. If we could all agree upon the definitions, this would
create no difficulty; but we cannot. Consequently, each combining
group should try to be clear and explicit with regard to its own
distinctive principles, while making the boundary line thus drawn
as inclusive as is possible without compromise of the principles themselves; and that all should co-operate on a basis as definite as their
various distinctive principles thus set forth will permit—the most

obvious field for such co-operation being the proclamation of the Christian principles of moral and social life.

Here once more the question of co-operation and compromise arises; for many accept in fact the Christian principles of moral and social life without accepting Christianity itself. Should Christians co-operate with these? If they decline they lose power in advocating action which they believe to be right; if they co-operate, they may conceal the grounds of their conviction and create a false impression with regard to the relative importance of faith and political achievement; for it may appear that faith in God is valued chiefly as a source of energy for accomplishing what can be conceived and arrived at without it. Once again the true solution is to be found, not in a choice as between two exclusive alternatives, but in a wise combination. The Christian will co-operate in action with all who agree with him about what should next be done. But he will take care that his own judgment is formed on Christian principles, and is as little as possible affected by sectional or partisan attachments; and he will seek opportunities of stating his proposals on the basis of Christian faith and Christian principles, when he can make it clear that his advocacy of the proposals is not—so far as the two things fall apart —the securing of specific material reforms, but the expression of loyalty to Christ and the exemplification of the power of His Gospel.

For I am convinced that in this period of history social witness is an indispensable instrument of Evangelism. We cannot obtain a hearing for our primary message if with regard to the evils of which men are chiefly conscious we have to say that for these it contains no remedy. We must find where men are, and then, taking them by the hand, lead them to the true source of power and peace. But we can do little as long as we call to them across an intervening gulf; and we can do nothing if we direct our appeal to some region of interest where they are not to be found at all.

It would indeed be a fatal error to suggest that the only reason why the Church should proclaim the divine law for society is that it supplies for our age an indispensable preliminary to effective Evangelism. On the contrary, it is a primary obligation even though no Evangelism should follow. The Church is called to bear witness to the truth concerning God and Man as this is communicated to it by the Word of God—that Word which speaks through nature, through history, through conscience, and supremely through Scripture as focused in the record of Jesus Christ who is that Word made flesh. God in Creation fashioned physical nature with its own laws, which cannot be broken; He also fashioned human nature with its

own laws, but with power of choice to obey or to break those laws;
but man does not by breach of the law escape its control, for he has
to suffer the inevitable consequence of his choice, which is God's
judgment upon it. The Church as witness to the Word of God must
proclaim the divine law for man and the divine judgment. It may
be that this is what the world now chiefly needs from it. That witness, like the message of the prophets, involves direct intervention in
the political sphere—not indeed in the region of ways and means,
but in that of principles, including the denunciation of particular
expedients which offend against right principles. This is a plain
duty on its own ground, but one to which the Church may the more
eagerly devote itself because it is today the indispensable preliminary
to Evangelism.

Now it is an undoubted feature of the age in which we live that
men feel their individual lives to be overshadowed and controlled by
impersonal forces. The Industrial Revolution in its various stages of
development has done much to depersonalize human life. With
mass-production applied not only to material goods, but to recreation,
entertainment, and education, the arena of obvious individual
responsibility is vastly restricted. That is an evil; it is not to be
acquiesced in, but rather to be corrected; first of all, however, it must
be recognized as a fact. Its consequence is that the call to individual
conversion is not likely to be widely effective unless it is prefaced by
evidence of social concern and ability to effect social changes. Our
social witness, apart from its own intrinsic value as a contribution
to social welfare, is an indispensable introduction to effective evangelism on a wide scale or as directed to those who stand quite apart
from the Church.

Of course this must not be interpreted as a suggestion that it is a
substitute for evangelism. On the contrary, a Christian approach to
questions of social justice will lead us back to a renewed belief in the
need for individual conversion and dedication. The essential Gospel
does not change. From generation to generation, it is the proclamation of the Holy Love of God disclosed in His redeeming acts. Belief
in that Gospel sends us forth to remedy conditions which degrade
the children of God or make it harder for them to believe in Him
or to obey Him; and as we strive to effect the reforms for which,
from age to age, the changing circumstances call, we find that the
chief condition of success is the reform of men and women, the
effective calling of them to faith in God and obedience to Him.
And as we see this ourselves, we must make it known to others; part
of our social witness itself must be the perpetual warning that, whatever the social and economic system, human selfishness will find

o

ways of exploiting it unless it be extirpated by the power of the Gospel; and this cannot be carried out wholesale; it is done now for this soul, now for that; it is the essence of individual conversion. The Gospel itself impels us to the task of social witness; our social witness leads us and all who hear us back to the gospel.

To set our social witness in this context has the added advantage of helping us to determine, not only its content in general, but also the point or points on which we should concentrate our attention if we are to make any distinctive Christian contribution to social progress or to the saving of our society from the collapse towards which some observers believe it to be hastening. This is a matter of fundamental importance. It too easily happens that Christians, being stirred in conscience to a new sense of social responsibility, look round for the most hopeful remedies or reconstructions proposed by other parties or persons, and seek to throw the weight of Christian witness into the scales on behalf of these. Thus, for example, I have no doubt that those Christians who strongly supported the League of Nations after the last war were on the whole on the right side; it was a great and noble effort in the right direction. But in its very nature it was no more than a political device, the success of which must depend on the spirit—in this case, the spirit of dedication—in those who worked it; for it was always evident that it would not work unless each nation joining it was ready to face the horrors of war in support of international order when no interest of its own, other than the preservation of that order, was involved; and the very form of the League contained indications of that persistent self-will in the nations which, if uncorrected, was bound to wreck it. We ought to have mingled more of purely Christian warning and criticism than we did with our commendation of the scheme in general. For our concern is with the spirit in the first place, and with the political device chiefly as an expression and channel of the spirit.

The Christian approaches the particular problem of his own generation in the light of certain unchanging truths, as he believes them to be, concerning God and Man. These may be summarized briefly as follows: (1) Man is fundamentally a child of God, who created him to be the conscious recipient of the divine love and endowed him with the capacity, but did not impose upon him the necessity, to respond to it; each man has therefore a status and dignity which is logically prior to and in all ways independent of his relationship to any earthly authority or association—family, nation, and state included. (2) Men do not in fact respond to the love of God with answering love in more than a very partial degree; they set up their own standards of value and pursue their own interests, irrespective of God's purpose or the good of mankind at large. This leads them into strife and in order that they may have liberty either to follow their own interests effectively or to develop their capacity for love, there is need of a Law which can exercise an effective restraint upon the exercise of selfishness. (3) This Law can never cure the evil, for it appeals to self-interest in the very process of regulating it. Thus it may even intensify the spiritual evil while it checks the more disastrous outward effects of it. The best it can effect, if left unaided, is a balance of competing selfishnesses, where each prevents others from calamitous expression. (4) There is a radical cure—the gospel of the Love of God, by which men can be won from their original self-centredness to respond freely to the Love of God by the dedication of their lives. But this cost God the Agony and Bloody Sweat, the Cross and Passion; and it becomes effective in men and women only by radical conversion. Therefore the Christian will not expect to see a terrestrial Utopia established by what is called social reform alone; he will make his first concern the conversion of all whom he can influence to full Christian discipleship; but he will also set himself to do what he can to make the inevitably defective system expressed in and upheld by Law as far as may be one which eases rather than hinders the task of conversion.

The social witness of the Church is thus at one and the same time a preparation for the full gospel and a consequence of it. It is a preparation for it because the words which must be used derive their meaning in the minds of the hearers from experience of home and community. If a child has grown up in a home tyrannized over by a brutal and drunken father, the doctrine of the Fatherhood of God may be horrible and repellent to him, and the opening words of the Lord's Prayer have no appeal. If there is no experience of common life where each feels that he is both needed and welcome and also that he carries some responsibility for the welfare of the whole, it is far harder to attach real meaning to the fellowship of the Church or the Communion of Saints. By fashioning, so far as we can, the conditions which foster the community life in the home and in the wider society which the child enters on leaving school, we are at the same time creating the conditions which facilitate both interest in and acceptance of the Gospel itself.

And this same social witness is a consequence of the Gospel for those who already believe it, because that Gospel, accepted in their hearts, impels them to do all they can to remedy injustice, to alleviate distress, to create fellowship, and to promote the development of fully matured persons in fellowship. The Christian knows that this end cannot be attained without the preaching and the acceptance of the Gospel itself; but he seeks so far as possible to have the social order as his ally and not his antagonist as he preaches it.

For he must recognize that the social and economic structure is the most potent of all educational forces moulding the characters of those who grow up within it. In the formation of character three main forces co-operate or interfere with one another—the family, the school, and the community as a whole. In our dislocated system we ought to add as a fourth the Church, though ideally this acts as an educational influence chiefly through all the other three. Of these four the community itself is the most powerful. Where family, school, and Church are all effectively at work together, they may do much to mould a character sharply at variance with the outlook and standards of the community so far as this impinges upon that character, and where relations within the family are entirely happy, a family of strong tradition can set upon its growing members a mark which nothing will obliterate. It is hardly possible for the Church to gain sufficient access to the child or adolescent to effect very much unless it has the family and the school, but especially the family, as channels of its influence. Today, with families detached from the Church and a community no longer consciously Christian or aspiring to be so, we often expect the school to do by itself what it is in fact quite powerless to do. This is a mistaken response to a true instinct; for, as we shall see, it shows appreciation of the vital point in the whole situation, but frustrates its own aim by excessive simplification. We cannot thus isolate the school, or any other *ad hoc* device for dealing with youth; but it is true that youth provides the key to our spiritual political campaign.

The Christian principles from which we start require that we should approach the whole social problem and every part of it from the standpoint of the true interest of men and women as persons. Thus, for example, we shall agree that it is desirable to increase economic output to the maximum, because this increases the resources for fully personal life and the number for whom such a life becomes possible. If then it appears that the methods adopted to increase output are such as to stunt or distort the personality of those engaged in its production, or to set up false human relationships between them, the supreme end is being frustrated by the means chosen for its attainment. Maximum output is not a true end of human enterprise; the end is fullness of personality in community; nothing economic is a true end. Consequently all economic methods and structures must be subject to criticism on non-economic as well as on economic grounds. On economic grounds they must be tested by the question whether they are fully efficient or, in common speech, do they work? And this question must be asked of any improvement of them proposed on humanitarian grounds. But the other—the non-economic—question must be kept in view: does this economic method or structure either help or hinder the development of persons in community.

Now when we approach the existing political, social, and economic order with that question in mind we are bound to reach the conclusion that some elements in it truly promote that end, that some hinder it, and that much might be done to make it an order more able to help and less able to hinder. But if our concern as Christians is bound to be with the development of persons in community—the divine purpose in Creation, we shall concentrate our attention on the influences making for true fellowship on the one side or for gangsterism or sheer self-seeking on the other. As primary conditions for the attainment of our end, we shall be concerned with housing and nutrition. We shall insist that provision must be made whereby every child is born into a family housed with the decency and dignity needed for a real home and should be provided with the food, fresh air and light necessary for healthy bodily development. The State, and therefore all of us acting through the State, can do much to ensure these two provisions. The State cannot do much to secure that in the home provided there shall be a full and happy family life. That is more directly the responsibility of the Church through its influence on the parents; and no amount of trouble with that object can be too great. The Church is in fact already active in this field on a very large scale, though there are many homes to which it cannot gain access in such a way as to make its influence very potent.

Beyond the provision of suitable housing and the food, light and air required for healthy growth, at terms within the means of the parents, the Christian will press for full educational opportunity for all till maturity is reached, which is never earlier than the sixteenth birthday, and will do what he can to secure that the education provided is inspired by faith in God and finds its focus in worship.

In these fields the Christian will be pressing the State to go further and faster along roads on which it has already started. We now come to the almost unoccupied field of adolescence—the boys and girls in their later 'teens. It is true that the State had just before the war initiated its scheme for " The Service of Youth "; it is also true that the new organizations set on foot during the war in preparation for service with the Navy, Army, and Air Force have entered the field and are not likely to vacate it. None the less, we have here an arena for activity which is almost untouched, the neglect of which till now has been deplorable and the continued neglect of which would probably lead to disaster.

The principle to be applied was stated by Mr. H. A. L. Fisher in introducing the great Education Bill of 1918: " Every citizen until the age of eighteen should be regarded as primarily a subject of education, not primarily a factor in industry." I have an interest in that formulation, because I offered it to Mr. Fisher myself when I went on behalf of the Workers' Educational Association to see him at the Board. He did not express any welcome to it at the time; but he included it in his own speech in the House of Commons, to our great satisfaction. Twenty-five years—a quarter of a century—have passed since then, and very little has been done.

This neglect is both morally wicked and socially perilous. It is morally wicked because it is acquiescing in the exposure of unformed characters to temptations which they have no adequate strength to resist. And it is socially perilous because a disaffected youth is the seed plot of most dangerous movements. In all parts of the world we may find proof of this. And those who study the evils of our own social life with a view to finding the remedies are brought back from every department of their study to this as the crucial point where issues are decided for good or for ill.

The school-leaving age is still fourteen.[1] At a time when the sons of wealthy parents go to public schools as that singularly feckless and irresponsible kind of animal known as a " fag," the sons and daughters of poorer parents are thrown out into the rough and tumble of the labour-market to find what jobs they can. They are members of no community; they do not belong to anything or anybody. That is the great evil. The cessation of book learning is a loss to many, though there are some who gain little from that after sixteen. The loss of oral instruction and the influence of teachers is probably greater. But the supreme evil is the absence of any community to which the children belong. Voluntary organizations, of which the vast majority were directly or indirectly agencies of the Church, did much to supply the need for the 20 per cent. of the adolescent population whom they affected before the war. The Government's service of Youth promised well, but had not had time to develop its potentialities when the outbreak of war checked further progress. Now the pre-Service corps of various kinds are helping to fill the gap.

For those whose approach to social questions is directed by concern for " the development of persons in community " this is the

[1] This was written in 1943, of course.

point today of primary anxiety and must be the arena of concentrated action. The early influence of home, school, and Church is largely negatived by the experience of the years between fourteen and twenty. We have the experience of other countries to guide us and to warn us. If the young folk are allowed to feel that the community has little regard or concern for them, especially if by tolerating unemployment it suggests that it has no place or use for them, they become a fertile seed plot for revolutionary ideas which usually have little enough about them of faith in God or charity towards men. A modern nation which neglects its youth deserves all that it may get. But our concern is not so much with the dangers to our traditional civilization as with the characters of the young people themselves. God made them for fellowship with Himself and therein with one another. It is our responsibility to see that they have every opportunity of growing into that twofold fellowship.

The first necessity is to raise the school-leaving age to sixteen. No doubt that cannot be done at once; both buildings and teachers must be provided and equipped. Incidentally, there is urgent need for the reduction of the size of classes—once more in the interest of developing personality—and it may be that this should take precedence of the rise from fifteen to sixteen in the school-leaving age; the rise to fifteen should be made universal at the earliest practical moment. From sixteen to eighteen there is need for a variety of training wide enough to include apprenticeship and such participation in industrial production as has, or can be so directed as to have, educational value. The educational and industrial authorities will have to co-operate in new ways for this purpose.

Around the secondary school should grow up all manner of associations and guilds which will retain their members till eighteen or twenty and every boy or girl in the school should be attached to one or other of these. Thus leaving school will not mean passing out of the life of a real community into almost complete lack of attachment to any one or anything.

On the intellectual side, this extension of education will be a sound economy; for the real result of what is spent on education up to the age of fourteen is only gathered at or after the age of sixteen, and then only if the study has been continued. A subject may be well taught and genuinely learnt up to the age of fourteen yet it will be totally forgotten by the age of twenty unless it is either studied or practised in the intervening years. Many men as we find them in the Forces knew a fair amount about English history at fourteen, but now know only the stories of the nursery school, like Alfred and the cakes. This rather than any defect in the religious teaching given in elementary schools is the explanation of the ignorance of the Christian religion among men and women of the Forces about which so much is said. Of course, it may be urged that the school should have implanted an interest in religion, or any other subject taught, such as will lead to continuance of study or practice or both after school-days are over; but unless the school is supported by family tradition and the usual custom of young folk lately released from school, it cannot be expected to achieve this for pupils of fourteen or even of sixteen, though at the later age there is a little more hope. We have been expecting of schools something altogether beyond their capacity.

We need to establish such a social order that home, society, school, and industry are all in fact co-operating in the task of fashioning persons in community; especially is there need to consider the educational influence of industry. It may be that great value will be found in works-schools; but the vital matter is that as far as possible the work itself should be interesting and that its social value should be brought home to those who do it. Great strides have been taken lately in the development of industrial welfare. But it is possible for this to be carried very far without any regard to those affected as persons. Sometimes we are told of admirable plans for welfare, with the remark appended that since these were adopted output has increased by 15 per cent. That creates the feeling that the worker is a specially intricate piece of machinery which runs best with a special lubricating oil called "welfare." But there are also accounts of improved efficiency resulting from measures designed to show the social significance of the work and so make the worker feel that he and his work are wanted. That is the supremely important point —especially with young folk—to make them feel that society has a use for them and a need of them, and at all costs to avoid the opposite feeling that they have been born into a world which goes its way ignoring them.

It is not part of my purpose now to discuss methods of handling this problem of care of adolescents, beyond saying that it seems to offer in a supreme degree opportunity for that combination of statutory regulation with voluntary enterprise and service which has been so marked a feature of our social organization generally. We need action by the State both for securing universality and for the supply of the necessary resources; we need voluntary enterprise and service because of the greater elasticity which they can bring into play, and because they provide more expectation of and opportunity for the spirit of dedication. In the end the work is personal. All education proceeds by the intercourse of the less mature with the more mature mind, whether in personal meeting or through the medium of books, and it is wholesome in proportion as the more mature mind is perfect in quality. That is why the only perfect education is one which finds its focus in communion with Christ.

I would summarize the contention of this Lecture as follows: (1) Among the manifold activities by which the one purpose of God is fulfilled through His Church, some attain special importance at particular times and places. (2) To the Church in our land to-day the most urgent call is to renewed Evangelism. (3) The heart of this is the same in every age and region—the proclamation of God's redeeming acts and the call to men to answer His love with theirs. (4) But the context in which this is presented varies from age to age and from place to place, and in our country to-day its context should be the sickness of our society and the power of Christ to heal that no less than the sickness of individual souls. (5) In its approach to the social problem, the Church should fasten on what is most closely akin to its own message. God created men for fellowship with Himself and therein with one another; and earthly society should be as close as possible a realization of that fellowship. Our task is to mould society into such a fellowship and train citizens as members of it. (6) So our aim is defined as the development of persons in community; and we shall test all actual situations and all proposed changes by their tendency to help or to hinder that aim. (7) To this end, we shall urge the necessity of adequate housing; of wholesome food, light and air; of education to full maturity. (8) But, in view of the neglect hitherto of the age group fourteen to twenty, the vital importance of this period of life in the formation of character and the disastrous consequence of damaging experience at this age both to the persons affected and to society as a whole, the Church should concentrate its main energy of thought and action upon this point.

In most of the aims thus set forth, and conspicuously in connexion with the point on which attention and energy are specially concentrated, the Church will work with all who share its immediate aims; but it will never conceal its own ultimate aim—the fashioning of persons regarded as children of God in community, not only with one another, but with God made known in Christ. It will insist that only through fellowship with Him can men reach true fellowship with one another. The evangelistic purpose will never be out of mind and will often come into the forefront as the really governing consideration. Yet the social witness and effort will not be undertaken or valued solely as preparation for this, but rather as obligatory in themselves; for to develop persons in community is the divine purpose and to carry this as far as we can is true obedience to God and service to Him. It is work which we ought to do for its own sake, and it opens the way to the work which is more distinctively, but not more genuinely the Church's task.

I fear it is true that the imaginary visitor from Mars with whom we started would at present find it hard to say what Christians in this country are aiming at. I urge that we should so organize and concentrate our energies that in the course of a few years he would say: "These people judge every subject first by personal qualities and personal relationships; they are devoting themselves to the development of free and fully matured persons in living community with one another; and they do this because they are dominated by faith in God, who made men and women for free fellowship with Himself and therein with one another."

In parts of this programme the Christian will work with non-Christians who share his convictions with regard to the next step to be taken. But he will also know that within the area of that co-operation the goal cannot be reached. For our fellowship with God is made possible only by His own atoning work which He has wrought in Christ; and our full fellowship with one another is possible only through our fellowship with Him. So the gospel of the Cross, which sends us forth to do all we can for social justice and human fellowship, still stands when our utmost effort is expended, calling to new achievements. We seek and call others to seek God's kingdom and His justice in every sphere of life and in all its manifestations; but we find that justice in its perfection and truly enter that Kingdom only when as penitent sinners we kneel before the Cross. There alone is the focus of our fellowship; to our need of the Cross the very failure of our merely social enterprise will lead us back.

[APPENDIX A, on the Training of Adolescents, has been omitted as no longer quite relevant to the circumstances of today.]

APPENDIX B

Evangelism in the Modern World

I have tried in the text of the Lecture to give some analysis of the distinctive features of the modern world so far as it is detached or alienated from Christianity. Here I should wish to add a few suggestions with regard to the approach to the task of evangelism which this seems to indicate. I have attempted this before in an address on the subject of " Evangelism To-day," which is printed in a little book called *The Hope of a New World* (Student Christian Movement Press); but some of the points which I then made I want now to amplify.

The essential task of the evangelist does not vary; it is to proclaim the unchanging gospel. But there may be need to win for this a hearing from those who are ill disposed to listen, because they start with the conviction that it has nothing which concerns them. Their minds move, as we saw, in a circle of ideas alien from the whole Biblical view of the world, and if we offer the great Biblical truths, especially if we do this in Biblical phrases, they will have no notion what we are talking about. It is not only a matter of language, though that is very important. Those of us who have read even a little theology are under a constant temptation to use words and phrases which are unfamiliar, unmeaning, and even unsuggestive to the ordinary devout layman. That, however, can be avoided by the taking of a little trouble. The serious difficulty is the absence from the minds of those whom we would address of the ideas we wish to utilize, and the presence there of other ideas which are incompatible with these. The words " sin " and " redemption " both stand for ideas which the modern mind finds it very hard to assimilate. To some extent evangelism must be a process of re-education. But this is not quite so serious as might appear. For so far as this modern mind is unable to apprehend the gospel, it is also unable to apprehend human relationships; and in the experience, though not in the conscious thinking, of our hearers there is present what we need to find as the " eye " into which the " hook " of the gospel can fit.

The frame of mind about which I am speaking has two main features, both due to the undue prominence of the physical sciences in our recent thinking and education. One is the tendency to suppose that only what can be measured or weighed is really knowable or indeed apprehensible by the mind at all; the other is the spectator attitude.

No one really lives by the belief that only the measurable is real. In all our human dealings we are confronted by the immeasurable and the imponderable. Men do not choose their friends or their wives by the methods appropriate to the laboratory. One of the evil results of this habit of thought is that it tends to create a divorce between intellect and emotion, to the grievous detriment of both. It is usually possible to persuade such a man that in fact the intellectual apparatus by which he is accustomed to account for the world is ill-suited to account for a large part of it. If we wish to stimulate our own imagination on this subject or find telling illustrations for the confounding of the materialist or determinist, we can do no better than read Professor Macneile Dixon's fascinating Gifford lectures on *The Human Situation*, specially Lecture VIII. Our first step may very well be to persuade our hearers to think as human beings about their own human relationships. Then they may be ready for the moment when the evangelist confronts them with the Living God. But for the consideration of that moment we must wait a little while.

The other feature of the scientifically trained mind is its spectator attitude to life. Professor J. L. Storrs told me, after a visit to Germany early in the period of Hitler's ascendancy, that he had little hope, because the intellectuals, who should have been leaders in resistance to the return of barbarism, adopted towards it the attitude of spectators and made such remarks as "I am afraid things must get worse before they get better." These men hated what they observed; but they did no more than observe what they hated; they did not attack it. Hitler represents an insurgence of the emotional element in Nature against a detached and ineffectual intellectualism which could offer no resistance when attacked.

This spectator attitude is proper and, indeed, necessary in a laboratory; there emotional reactions will seriously distort the apprehension of truth. It is quite inappropriate in human relationships and in religion. Our education is in a fair way to hand over human relationships to passion divorced from thought, and to make religion a mere matter of personal opinion or feeling or both, but not the total self-committal of a man to God which alone is true religion.

But the blame must not all be laid on our educational methods or even on the ascendancy over our minds which science has won by its amazing achievements. True, it has not begun to explain anything whatever; and its best representatives are quite aware of this; but it has given us a mastery over unexplained natural forces which has led to the growth of great cities, mass production, and altogether a vast enrichment of our material life with a sense of man's ability to control the world to his own benefit if only he has the will.

The evangelist will seize upon that "if only." For it seems that man has not the will. And if not, how is he to get it? Perhaps the trouble is that each man and nation decides what is for the benefit of the world from their own standpoint. Anyhow, we seem to turn into a curse all the things which should be for our benefit. (At this point a perusal of *Down Peacocks' Feathers*, by the Rev. D. R. Davies, is recommended.)

Man, aided by his science, has sought to be independent. In fact he has achieved a hitherto unparalleled degree of "frustration." Neither this word nor the thing it stands for figure in earlier literature so prominently as in the novels and social treatises of the last generation. Frustrations and inhibitions crop up everywhere. But here is something to lay hold of. For the best extant description of frustration is to be found in the latter part of Romans vii. And if you read that, substituting the word "complex" for the word "sin," you have a very modern account of a very prevalent modern complaint. We have to remember that sin is something much more than conscious wrongdoing; it is the cause of wrongdoing, conscious or unconscious. Of course, there is no guilt in unconscious sin; but sin has a far wider connotation than guilt, and part of our difficulty is due to our having given too little prominence to this important fact.

What is the source of this sense of frustration in its modern form? Largely it is the absence of any sense of purpose in life. For many people the war has removed it, by giving people an object to live for and to die for. But the war effort is manifestly insufficient as a source of purpose for life, partly because it will abruptly come to an end, and partly because it does not cover the whole of life. The last consideration accounts for the curious combination in our time of splendid self-devotion, endurance, and fellowship in service with a serious collapse in honesty and in sexual morals. People do not see the connexion between these and the war effort. Their purpose in life inspires them to self-devotion and endurance; it does not sustain them in honesty and chastity. Nothing is adequate as a purpose to govern life except the purpose of God.

But if we are to bring people to face this, we must deliver them from the spectator attitude to life. This is due partly to faulty education, but partly also to the complexity of modern life. How shall the individual citizen affect this vast machine in which he is caught up? How shall he understand the intricacies of political, social, and economic life enough to have the confidence to act in relation to them? He feels trapped. So he looks on, losing any sense of responsibility, and therefore bereft of any aim in life except to earn enough to amuse himself in his spare time.

At this point, as we saw in the lecture, the social witness of the Church can help. For it points to principles by which judgments can be formed concerning the existing situation and concerning suggested remedies. On those judgments actions can be based. The Church can by its own social teaching enable men to see round and through the tangle of contemporary economic forces and so help them to feel that they are escaped from the trap.

But it must be mainly through their personal relationships that deliverance is to be sought—those relationships in which every one is conscious of responsibility for action; such are a man's concern for his wife and children, the question whether or not to marry now on an inadequate income or wait in hope of a larger one—and the like. Scarcely any one will talk materialistic determinism in front of problems like these. There is the direct impact of personal claims and personal challenges. And we have got to bring people to see that the gospel presents such a challenge and such a claim. So long as people discuss God in the third person—whether He exists and of what nature He is—they are in a frame of mind for which apprehension of the truth about Him is impossible. God must be to us neither It nor He, but Thou. The question is not, Shall I think this or that about God? but: Shall I obey and worship, or not, the God who confronts me in a relationship as personal and direct as that which a man has to his father or his wife? Knowledge *about* God is valuable in its place; but knowledge *of* God alone has saving power.

All that has been said hitherto is concerned only with the removal of obstacles and the winning of a hearing for the gospel itself. And now all depends on the evangelist. For the knowledge *of* God which presents the personal challenge and personal claim can be imparted only by one who has it. We preach chiefly by what we are, not by what we think or feel; and this is as true of the witness given from the pulpit as of the witness given in the factory or the shop. The commission to the Evangelist as to the pastor depends on his ability to give an affirmative answer, with whatever consciousness of failures, to the question of the Lord Jesus, " Lovest thou Me? "

Let us put together the key phrases in a great passage where St. Paul speaks of the ministry of evangelism. It is in the Second Epistle to the Corinthians:

(1) "We have this ministry " (iv, 1). There is the fact. Why God called us we do not know; but He did, and here we are. Let us not doubt the reality of our vocation, however unfit for it we were and are.

(2) "As we obtained mercy, we faint not " (iv, 1). The source of our confidence is not our characters, our ability, our eloquence, or anything which is really ours; the source of our confidence is that, though we have failed Him so badly, God still trusts us. Penitence is the source of spiritual power. Only two voices can call effectively to the Cross. One is the voice of the sinless Redeemer, with which we cannot speak; the other is that of the sinner who knows himself a sinner and knows himself forgiven.

(3) " For we preach not ourselves, but Christ Jesus as Lord, and ourselves as your servants for Jesus' sake " (iv, 5). If we preached ourselves, we should need to have qualities to exhibit. But our part is to stand on one side and point to Him. And as we do this we take our share in the accomplishment of the purpose with which God made the world.

(4) " Seeing it is God, that said, Light shall shine out of darkness, who shined in our hearts, to give the light of the knowledge of the glory of God in the face of Jesus Christ " (iv, 6). Creation and Redemption are parts of one divine activity. It is God, who at first said, " Let there be light," who enlightened the world when " the Word was made flesh." And the meaning of human life and history, with all its wars and diplomacies and politics and loves and hates is just the onward march of that divine purpose to " sum up all things in Christ " and establish that reign of Love which is the Kingdom of God.

(5) " Wherefore if any man is in Christ, there is a new creation " (v, 17). He is re-born and re-made. And the principle of the new order into which he is re-born is reconciliation and perfect fellowship.

(6) " But all things are of God, who reconciled us to Himself through Christ, and gave unto us the ministry of reconciliation; to wit, that God was in Christ reconciling the world unto Himself, not reckoning unto them their trespasses, and having committed unto us the word of reconciliation. We are ambassadors therefore on behalf of Christ, as though God were intreating by us; we beseech you on behalf of Christ, be ye reconciled to God " (v, 18–20). There is our message. The ambassador has no message of his own, no policy; he has to transmit and commend the message and policy of the government he represents. So we too have no message of our own; we are to be the transmitters of God's message, which does not change.

How are we to do this, especially when we remember that what we are is more eloquent than what we say?

(7) " We all, with unveiled face reflecting as a mirror the glory of the Lord, are transformed into the same image from glory to glory, even as from the Lord the Spirit " (iii, 18). The light we are to shed on the path that we and our hearers must tread is not our own; we turn our faces to that light, " the Light of the World," " the Light of the knowledge of the glory of God in the face of Jesus Christ," that we may reflect its rays into our comrades' hearts. But

a faulty mirror gives a distorted reflection. What is the cure for this? I am told that flaws in a physical mirror may be corrected if the mirror is exposed to the sun. Certainly that is true of the spiritual mirror. It is the exposure of our souls constantly to the source of the true Light that enables us to reflect that light and to reflect it with ever-increasing fidelity.

"He that abideth in Me and I in him, the same beareth much fruit."

(The Beckly Social Service Lecture, 1943)

The Church in the Bible

LET ME BEGIN by reciprocating what has already been said about the pleasure that it is certainly to me, and also I believe to the Free Church Moderator, that we so frequently take the boards together. It is, I think, increasingly for the welfare of the Christian life of this country that all those who confess the name of Christ should unite in their profession to the utmost possible extent, because there is no doubt that our witness is weakened by the appearance of division, and the world outside has very little conception of the vast amount of unity that we really do enjoy and the great proportion of our teaching upon which we all agree. One of the features of the Bible Society throughout its history has been that it has drawn together all those who base their faith upon the Scriptures. I think that the reason why I accepted the invitation to come and speak here today was much more that I am unwilling to refuse an invitation from this Society than that I had anything of particular value to say to those who came to listen. I think it probable that all I have to say is in your minds already, and the most I can hope for is that some of you may be glad to have it recalled. I do not think that I shall say anything that is new to you.

The attitude of thinking people towards the Bible has undergone great changes in the recent period, and, as so often happens with a series of such changes, the process ends by bringing us back to a standpoint much more like that from which the process started than to an intervening one. Not without modification but with real enrichment, we have in the main come back to the traditional Christian conception of the Bible as fundamentally the record of God's dealing with men and His revelation of Himself to them through His dealings with them. There has been a period during which it has been treated by a section of Christendom much rather as a record of man's changing (whether advancing or not) conception of God, and it would be very wrong to deny the benefit this approach to the Bible has brought in the way of additional illumination, though in the nature of side-lights rather than the intensification of central light; but that process seems to me to have completed itself. The more we have attempted to read the Bible as if it were fundamentally the record of man's discovery of God, the more it has proclaimed itself to be the record of God's self-revelation to man. Of course, the two things cannot be totally apart. Revelation which is not received is barren and futile, and it is only so far as men have been able to appreciate what God has been disclosing that the revelation has become effective or there has even been a possibility of recording it. But it does make a vast difference whether we start from the standpoint of the student of human discovery or the standpoint of the student of divine revelation. The more men attempt to treat the Bible as a record of human discovery, the more they become aware that in so treating it they are deserting its own testimony concerning itself. You can never exhaust its meaning along that line. You can enrich your apprehension of God's nature and purpose, but that is all, and you come back to the divine declaration.

How, then, has the revelation been given? What has been its medium? It has been through the dealings of God with His people all down the ages. Dr. Goudge was fond of saying that there are in the Bible only two primary doctrines—the doctrine of God and the doctrine of the Church—and I believe this is true. It is the record of God and the people of God—of God's dealings with His people and the response, or the failure in response, on the part of the people; but all the way through it is, so to speak, the intercourse of God with His people. In other words, the hero of the Bible on earth is a community. You go back to the earliest periods at which it may be claimed that we are in the Bible dealing with anything like history as we ordinarily understand the word, and you still have a community conscious of a commission from God. If the scholars are right who think that the name of Abraham stands for a tribal migration, rather than an individual (to my mind a rather fantastic notion), then it only sharpens my point, for Abraham himself is in that case a community. It is with the call of Abraham that the distinction of " the people of God " appears. He is called out from among his own people, not knowing where he goes, under a sense of divine impulse, and becomes the father of the people of God. The promises to which St. Paul many centuries later will look back are given in the first instance to Abraham, and if we are to speak of anyone on the human plane as the founder of the Church it must always be of Abraham that we speak.

We Christian people greatly damage our own capacity to understand the Bible by ignoring the continuity of the people of God from the Old to the New Testament, a continuity on which the New Testament itself so strongly insists. We have been so conscious of something whose importance cannot be exaggerated—of the new start that was made in Christ—that we have ignored the continuity that none the less exists between this and the old Covenant. If it is true that all the way down there is this uninterrupted life of the community, though passing at one moment through a crisis which reduced the community to a single Figure, then it is also true that the prophets and the evangelists and the psalmists and the wise men of the Old Testament all speak to the community as its own members. The voice of prophecy comes to the Church from within the Church; the proclamation of the Gospel is from within the Church to the Church; it is not given to it from without, it is received by it from within. The people of God is constituted as His by His own act, by His act in the calling of Abraham, by His act in the saving from death and afterwards the instruction and inspiration of Moses, by His act in the guidance of the people through their history and the sending to them of His prophets, by His act in delivering Jerusalem from Sennacherib and surrendering it to Nebuchadnezzar (both accepted by the prophets as part of the divine purpose), by His act in the restoration from the Exile, and supremely by His act in the Incarnation of the Son of God in Jesus Christ and the coming of the Holy Spirit. The foundation is the acts of God, and if by the Gospel we mean the acts of God as distinct from the record of the acts, then of course it is true that the Church rests upon the Gospel, but if by the Gospel we mean the record of the acts we must remember that the record is composed within the Church which the divine act had created, and is addressed to the Church by inspired members of it.

We are presented, then, with the picture of this commissioned community, a body of persons believing that as a body they are entrusted with a truth about God which they have to uphold before the world and by which they at least, whatever may be true for others, are to guide and judge their lives. The New Testament insists upon the identity of the people of God both in the Old Testament and the New. The Church in the New Testament is the body of those who are the heirs of the promised Kingdom and in whom its powers are already at work. It is the creation of God, the creation of a people for His own possession; it is the Israel of God after the spirit, and, as I have already said, we have got to give, I will not say equal weight, but corresponding weight at all times to the two aspects, namely, that the Christian Church is continuous with the chosen people of the old Covenant and that in Christ it is re-founded and launched upon a new career.

Perhaps it is worth while to indicate a few of the New Testament evidences of this continuity. The position of Abraham, Isaac and Jacob in the Kingdom, as Christ Himself proclaimed it, is one piece of evidence. If you are to sit down in the Kingdom, it is with

Abraham, Isaac and Jacob that you sit down. I have already quoted the references of St. Paul to the Church as the Israel of God. In the great passage in the first Epistle of St. Peter where a whole string of titles is appended to the Christian community and intended for Christians alone, every one of them is a description of Israel in the Old Testament. It is " an elect race " (that comes from Deuteronomy and Isaiah), " a royal priesthood " (Exodus), " a holy nation " (Deuteronomy and Isaiah), " a people for God's own possession " (Exodus, Deuteronomy, Isaiah and Malachi) "' that have now obtained mercy " (Hosea). In the Book of Revelation the twelve Apostles of the Lamb correspond to the twelve patriarchs. The twelve Apostles receive according to St. Matthew a promise that they shall sit on twelve thrones judging the twelve tribes of Israel. The very choice of twelve was an indication that in our Lord's mind His Church was a continuation of the Old Church, and I suppose that we may take it for granted that the four and twenty Elders represent the patriarchs and the Apostles together—the people of God before its redemption in Christ and after. Undoubtedly the figure of the Vine involves amongst other things the identification of the Christian community with Israel, for it is a figure constantly in the Old Testament, and, as I believe, the words " I am the true Vine " were spoken in the Temple Court with the great golden vine in full view, representing what Israel was called to be. The emphasis is on the word " true," as the Greek suggests. " It is in Me that all this is fulfilled; but not only am I the true Vine; you, My disciples, are the branches."

It is with that that we start in our effort to search out what it is that is presented to us in the Bible concerning the Church or the people of God, and at first, as we all know, it is a nation that begins with Abraham and to which the successive generations belong by physical descent, though that is never of primary significance. That is, so to speak, the condition of its continuity, but not the essence of its quality. Its quality is always its response to the call of God, first in Abraham himself and then in his successors, the response which later finds its expression in the Covenant.

We are told again and again of the special distinction that is made of Israel by the fact that the relationship of this people with God was a Covenant relationship, a moral and spiritual relationship and not that physical connexion which united the gods of the other nations with the people who served them. In their case the greatness of the god was bound up with the greatness of his people, but in the Old Testament God is at all times presented as complete and perfect in His majesty and righteousness. His people are called upon to serve Him, but the relationship is a moral relationship, and if they are faithless He can cast them off. Jehovah and Israel are not bound together as Chemosh and Moab are bound. Part at least of the significance of the whole series of prophets is that they had arisen within this people, recalling the people to the nature of the commission which they hold. I know it has been said that every reformer, however novel the proposals he is making, always tries to commend them by insisting that they are really part of the inherited tradition. (I suppose that is anyhow a good way for radicals to try to allay conservative apprehensions!) But it is certainly true that the prophets of Israel are always pointing back to what was demanded of Israel in the formative period. They are never conscious of coming on the field with something strictly new; their task is to resist new temptations which come from the development of various kinds of culture and civilization and which tend to lure people away from the faith and obedience which had seemed to be more perfect in the simple days of wandering in the wilderness. It always seems to me that there was an opportunity for any dialectician present to suggest that their faith had not been so simple nor their obedience so complete, and it might have been pleaded that there was not the amount of retrogression with which the prophets charged the people. The essence of the matter is that they did not feel they were entrusted with new revelations; what they felt was a call to bring people back to what God had always asked of them, not that He asked something new; He had always asked righteousness and they had always known what righteousness was and had always recognized the righteousness to which the prophets recalled them in generation after generation.

Then, as we know, it becomes apparent that only some of the people will rise to the height of their calling. The nation as a whole seems to be so permanently obstinate that there is no hope of their fulfilling the commission entrusted to them, and the hope begins to be centred upon the remnant instead of the whole people. With the Exile comes the great sifting. Until the date of the Exile the prophetic faith that the God of Israel was the God of all the earth who could be served only with righteousness had been the faith of a minority, which from time to time gained ascendancy, when it was accepted by the reigning monarch, but on the whole it remained the faith of the minority, and every king's attempt to interpret it in the direction of working it out in the life of the people is followed by a reaction, as Hezekiah for example is followed by Manasseh and Josiah by Jehoiakim and Zedekiah. Then the people go into Exile, and broadly speaking, though I cannot claim this is expressly true, it would seem that those who had not accepted the prophetic faith more easily settled down and made their homes among the heathen where they were living. What is certainly true is that all those who returned were possessed by that prophetic faith, and from that time onwards the faith of Israel as it is represented in Palestine is the old prophetic faith which was quite expressly proclaimed by Amos, that God, the God of Israel, is the God of all the earth and only by righteousness can He be served. From that moment onwards Israel, which had always contained the Church within the nation, is both nation and Church in one.

But even at the moment of the Return, the great prophet of the Exile, the unknown author of the second part of Isaiah and of the songs of the Servant of Jehovah, begins to see that even those who return are not going to rise to the height of their calling. To begin with the Servant of the Lord is the whole nation so far as it has returned; then it comes to be only a part of the nation; then there is doubt and division among the interpreters, but to my mind the note is quite decisive, and in Chapter 53 of Isaiah it has become a single figure, on Whom the Lord lays the iniquity of us all.

Turn back and approach this from the side of human apprehension and you have the development of Amos proclaiming God's sole sovereignty on the very ground of His righteousness, Hosea announcing the tidings of His love, Isaiah proclaiming His purpose as the guiding principle in the government of political and private life, Jeremiah penetrating the secret of suffering, Ezekiel first quite clearly envisaging the awful and eternal responsibility of the individual before the Eternal God, and that same great prophet of the Exile gazing as from afar upon the mystery of the Divine Agony and Redemption. With him the chosen people, the Israel of God which has been proclaimed to be His servant in the world, has become contracted to a single figure. And so it came to pass. When our Lord went out from Jerusalem bearing His Cross, He was alone; the disciples had forsaken Him and He alone was fulfilling the commission which belonged to His people. By the way in which He bore the consequences of His faithfulness and in which the seal was set upon that faithfulness by God Almighty in the Resurrection, He became the means of drawing unto Himself, Who is the holy people of God, people of every nation and language, so that the people of God is now not a physical nation, Israel, but all those who by the outpouring of the Holy Spirit released by the revelation of the Divine Love in Him are drawn into that intimate fellowship with Him, which enables St. Paul to speak of them as positively limbs of His Body. It is the people of God transformed and transfigured, but still the same people of God, in which we have our place to fill, so that we claim as part of our inheritance the whole teaching of the prophets and do not take our start from the evangelists.

All the way down God has worked through this community of people, not only in isolated individual instances but in a social group, because the nature of man is fundamentally a social thing and if man is to be redeemed it must be a social redemption. Within that group arise those whose sensitiveness to the divine impulse is keener than that of their fellows, and they become its prophets and they become the evangelists and pastors and teachers of the whole Church. But just as in Israel the prophets are themselves Israelites calling upon their fellow Israelites to be true to the divine commission, so in the New Testament, those who wrote the Gospels are themselves members of the Church calling upon their fellow Churchmen to be worthy of their calling wherewith they are called.

The essential instrument of God is the community of persons, and the Book is the instrument of the community. The Gospel is always the Gospel " according to " somebody; it is never the naked Gospel. So St. Mark begins, " The beginning of the Gospel of Jesus Christ the Son of God . . . ," but it is the Gospel as St. Mark bears witness to it, as he had received it, as it had passed through his mind and soul for him to communicate to us. I believe it is certainly of divine intention, and it is of quite evident blessing to us, that we cannot point to a particular saying and say, " There undoubtedly are the sounds which our Lord uttered on earth." Each has passed through a human mind. It is to be the influence of His Spirit upon the spirits of men—not some external authority which gives precise directions and lays fetters upon the movement of mind and spirit. So within the Church men had their apprehension of the great Divine Act and set it forth, and while the Synoptic Gospels are rightly so-called because they present on the whole a common view, yet there are diversities of tone and emphasis among them. The Fourth Gospel, which I personally believe to be the surest historical guide of the four, is none the less in the same way the apprehension of that disciple who was in some sense the most intimate of all with his Lord and wrote out of the experience of that intimacy, so that it is not merely the memory of uttered sounds but the record of an achieved experience.

Everywhere, therefore, the testimony is from faith through faith to faith. But nowhere is it the pedestrian communication which would have been achieved if we can imagine the disciples moving about with photographic or phonographic apparatus. It is a living thing which comes to us, the Living Word of God on which the reformers loved to dwell and which they so carefully distinguished from the printed page—never merely to be identified with it but always something more.

Then this community is spoken of as the Body and Bride of Christ, the Body which is to be His instrument as our bodies are the instruments of our spirits, fulfilling His purpose in the world and growing to the fullness of its stature as new nations and peoples are brought into it, adding a new capacity to what our Lord can actually do for men in this world. There is part of the meaning of St. Paul in preaching the Church as "the fullness of Him Who all in all is being fulfilled." It is being built up into fullness by His power. As new races are brought in, each with its own divinely given talent to be devoted to the divine service, each will render a testimony to God and show forth His glory in a way that was impossible until that time came. So St. Paul sees the "one man in Christ Jesus," in whom there was neither Jew nor Gentile, bond nor free, male nor female, growing to fullness of stature, till we all come to that one man in Christ Jesus, full grown, the measure of the completeness of the stature of the Christ.

Side by side with this is the picture of the Church as the Bride of Christ, she who is to be His satisfaction and delight. "He shall see of the travail of His soul and be satisfied." How He sees it is through the manifestation of His holiness and love in His members as they show Him forth to the world—always His by right but not yet in fact—until all men become the members of His Body so that He can use them.

Here we have the great hope for the future fellowship of the world, the hope that is based upon the unity that men have in Christ as distinct from any unity that they construct. We must never think of the Church as primarily an international body; that suggests bringing together the people from different nations and trying to weld them into one. In the New Testament it is nothing like that. There, the Church is one in Christ, not because people come together and constitute a unity, but because there is a unity given already in Christ into which they are incorporated. It is always that way—never the other—and it makes a profound difference in all our approach. Let us consider the situation when this war ends. If it should be necessary to bring together the Christians of this country and of Germany on the basis of their different nationalities in order that they might find a way of re-establishing friendship, how desperately hard, if not impossible, that task would be. But, of course, we have not anything of that sort to do. All we have to do is to come together as those who are one with a unity that has never been broken, because it is not in us but in Christ. That is the God-given focus of the unification of mankind, the working out of which is entrusted to us. It carries us further than the theme of " The Church in the Bible," but let us recognize that the Bible is quite clear as regards the indication it gives us for the foundation of our Christian unity, something which we find extant and to which we yield ourselves. The whole Church exists in Jesus Christ and was complete on the Resurrection morning. We are joined to it, but we never constitute it. In that Church as it is presented to us in the Bible there is, as it seems to me, quite clearly from the beginning a distinction of ministry and laity, neither exalted above the other but both having a special function. The Ministry is not something which is first of all devised by the Church when it comes together to consider how to carry on its mission, but something found to be extant when the physical presence of the Lord had been withdrawn at the Ascension and consciousness of new power came with the outpouring of the Holy Spirit. What is found is the community of Christians with the apostolate as the focus of government and leadership.

That is the kind of principle to which we may go back and find a basis on which we may approach a consideration of the reunion in outward form of the Church which is always one in Christ so far as it is true to Him. And in this Church the powers of the coming Kingdom are already at work. One of the great divisions which has arisen among Christian people is concerned with the relation of the Church to the Kingdom. St. Augustine—most unfortunately, I think, but most naturally in the circumstances—identified the promised Kingdom with the Church as an historical organization. That did not exhaust his thought on the subject, but he did make that identification. On the other side there have been periods when very large numbers of Christians have thought of the Church rather as a convenience which is being utilized in preparation for a Kingdom which is something entirely belonging to the world beyond and the final coming of our Lord. I cannot believe that either of these corresponds to what is presented to us in the New Testament, for there is surely no doubt at all in the New Testament that the Kingdom is already established; it has come in Christ. If there were no other evidence I should not want to press the saying of our Lord before the High Priest; but I think that as so much else in the New Testament points the same way, it is quite fair to press what He declares when asked if He is the Christ. " Henceforth (not ' hereafter ' but ' from this time onward ') there shall be the Son of Man seated on the right hand of Power." Daniel's prophecy is now fulfilled. Merely to have recognized that the High Priest used the expression and to have repeated Daniel's prophecy would scarcely

have been " blasphemy "; but He quite clearly referred it to Himself
as He was before them. The Kingdom is at work in the world but
is not consummated, and the Church as it is set before us in the
Book of the Acts and referred to in the Epistles of St. Paul is certainly not something in which the Kingdom of God is as yet
consummated. The powers are already at work; it is the " earnest "
of the Kingdom; it has the " first-fruits " of the Kingdom, but it is
not more than the first-fruits, because these powers are at work side
by side with so much that is drawn from the world around and
from the lower nature of its members. The powers of the Kingdom
are available to its members if only they will open their lives to the
power of Christ and allow Him to dominate their thoughts and
hearts and wills.

That is an outline sketch of the Church in the Bible as I have
come to see it. I have not the least doubt that there is a vast amount
more to be said on that great theme, probably of greater importance;
but I believe that these thoughts are in themselves true thoughts,
and that they have for us some very obvious implications in face of
the problems which confront all Christian people in the world today.

(A Lecture at the Bible House, London, E.C.4.
October 8, 1943)

Thomism and Modern Needs

NOT LONG AGO I was honoured by an invitation to address the Aquinas Society which I gladly accepted, choosing as my subject the title of this article. Since then it has been suggested that I should publish as an article the substance of that address, and I readily do so. It would be impossible to reproduce the address itself, because it was delivered from notes which were no more than headings, and these I destroyed as soon as the address was delivered. That, however, is of no consequence. What is important is not to recover what was said on a particular occasion, but to promote consideration of the teaching of St. Thomas in its bearing on the needs of our time.

I must make clear at the outset the fact that I am not in any serious sense a student of St. Thomas—as, for example, my father was. I have read a considerable portion of his writings with close attention, but without that perpetual comparison of one passage with another which is alone entitled to be called " study " in relation to any great writer. I speak, therefore, from a general impression which may be due to interpreters and critics of St. Thomas as much as, or more than, to himself. If so, those who are real students of his work can easily confute me, but may none the less be glad to have their attention called to points at which the current presentations of his doctrine have produced on one mind at least an impression calling for correction.

We most conveniently start from our modern needs; and among the greatest of these is our need for a map of the country through which the pilgrimage of our life on earth must lie. When I was growing up there was a general sense of security—illusory, no doubt, but none the less influential on that account. Certain principles were universally accepted, so far as outward profession went. The theological doctrines of Christianity were widely challenged, but not as yet its ethical teaching. The great Victorian Agnostics not only believed that the Christian way of life would still claim the homage of those who discarded Christian dogma; they desired that it should, and took it for granted that all well-disposed persons shared their desire. There was an accepted body of convention with regard to the way in which we should try to live. And society found a place for us—a very inadequate place for many, but broadly speaking some place for all.

229

Moreover the evident abuses of social life were being remedied. Progress might be slow, but it was certain. At such a moment there is little need for a map; the whole countryside is sign-posted, so to speak, and it is fairly easy to find one's way about.

For those who have grown up since 1914, and especially since 1919, all this is changed. There is no security; for very many society seems to have no assured place at all; the conventions of the nineteenth century are no longer accepted; the weight of authority is with science, not with religion; the lure of fashion is with self-sufficiency, not with traditional morals; and the Christian way of life is openly challenged by Marxist Communism, by Nazism, and by irresponsible hedonism accepted as a principle.

The war, it is true, has delivered us for the moment and the citizens of the belligerent nations have found in service of their countries a cause for which they are ready both to live and to die; such a cause at once gives unity to life. But this cause does not cover the whole of life, so that while our morale is very high in relation to all that perceptibly affects the war-effort, it is decidedly low in other respects. And the war will end one day; the cause that now gives unity and meaning to so many lives will no longer be exerting its influence. Then multitudes will feel bewildered and lost; they will not know where they are, whither they are going, nor even whither they wish to go. They will desperately need a map of the country.

No one disputes that the most complete map ever drawn is that of St. Thomas Aquinas. Some hold that his map is vitiated by the acceptance of some cartographical illusions; others hold that his map needs correction in some important respects, but that our most hopeful line of advance is to start with his work, making such corrections as we think it needs. To which of these two groups we belong is likely to depend on our admitting or repudiating the possibility of natural theology and the value of analogical argument from created nature, including human nature, to the nature of the Creator. It is not sufficiently understood in England that on the European Continent this more than anything else is the point at issue between Catholicism and Protestantism. The Continental Reformers had so interpreted the Fall of Man as to leave in fallen human nature no capacity for recognizing divine truth; all faculties were vitiated; and between fallen nature and the divine incorruption no analogy was possible. This finds its logical expression in the doctrine of Karl Barth that any man's response to divine revelation is as much a miracle as the occurrence of the revelation itself. God's impact on the world, for this view, is vertical only; there is no horizontal guidance of man through the processes of nature, including his own, or through the movement of history.

In my own mind there is no doubt on which side of that division we should stand. The Bible, which is interpreted by the Reformers and their disciples (rightly, as I think) as the record of a vertical thrust of the Word of God into the horizontal process of history is none the less itself the prophetic record and interpretation of that process regarded as the arena where a divine purpose is being fulfilled and divine judgments are manifest in the operation of casual laws. Again I see no alternative to the acceptance of the method of analogy. The use of the word " Father " in relation to God is itself inevitably analogical. And these inevitable analogies are safe only if the principle of analogy is recognized and accepted so that the use of it may be regulated.

The principle of Natural Law or the Natural Order is of special importance and value in relation to sociology. Many of the troubles of the modern world come from the confusion of means and ends. St. Thomas vindicates the saying of St. Augustine that *omnis humana perversitas est uti fruendis et frui utendis* by pointing out that *lex aeterna primo et principaliter ordinat hominem and finem* (Sum. Theol. Pt. I. Q. II, A71). It is in the light of this principle that St. Thomas reaches his defence and limitation of the rights of property, a most wholesome doctrine much needed in our day, avoiding as it does the unsocial outlook of the individualist and the socialist's check upon initiative (see Sum. Theol. Pt. II. Q. II., A66). In his conception of property and in the principles which underlie the doctrine of the Just Price and the Prohibition of Usury, I am convinced that St. Thomas offers exactly what the modern world needs. Of course, adjustments to new conditions are required, and the first of the points at which I desire some modification of Thomist doctrines arises from this need for adjustment.

I come now to the points in which it seems to me that supplement or modification is required. It is very likely that I hold this view because my study of St. Thomas is inadequate. So far as that is so, I submit that the fault is partly in his recent interpreters; and if one result of this article is to lead real students to show that St. Thomas meets our needs but has been commonly misrepresented, it will have served a useful purpose.

(1) The first point is not likely to be seriously questioned. In the thirteenth century the framework of European society was fairly stable. There was a ladder of advancement for a really able boy or young man through the education and offices controlled by the Church. But, broadly speaking, the grades of society were fixed and

had their several rights, obligations and responsibilities. The serf or villain had few liberties, but he had security; and at the other end of the scale, public opinion exacted varied forms of service from the Lord of the Manor or feudal magnate. The modern horror of irresponsible wealth—of economic power divorced from social service—was almost unknown.

The social teaching of St. Thomas—as for example the criterion of the Just Price—has this situation in view. The application of his principles to our fluid society, where there is irresponsible wealth at one end and liberty (in law at least) without much security at the other—a society based on contract rather than on status—requires great adjustments.

(2) The new and less stable order of society is due in part to the new concern for individual personality. This was the great feature of Renascence and Reformation thought. It often received faulty expression; the Cartesian *Cogito ergo sum*, whereby the individual self-consciousness was made the pivot not only of epistemology but of metaphysic, and the self-seeking aggressiveness of men and nations characteristic of the " modern " epoch are the perversions of something true and important. The earlier philosophy of ancient Greece and Rome, and the medieval philosophy were deficient in appreciation of Personality as a mode of Being. To me it often seems as if St. Thomas is speaking of the human genus without due recognition of the fact that one characteristic of this genus, differentiating it from all others, is the high degree of individuality discoverable in the specimens—a degree so high as to make the particularity of each as fully constitutive of his essence as the generic quality. This, if true, is a principle of supreme importance for applied ethics. From the new emphasis on this has come the change from the society of status to that of contract; from this also spring the next three needs for adjustment in the Thomist tradition to which we now proceed.

(3) One consequence of the static quality of the medieval social framework was the elimination from ethics of all consideration of either the direction or the methods of social progress. What was required was an ethical interpretation of the existing order and ethical guidance for conduct within that order. There was no criticism of the order itself in the light either of its own underlying principles or of some accepted ideal. In our day one main theme of ethical debate is the justifiability of the social and economic order which we find existing. The individual is conscious of a responsibility for upholding it, mending it or ending it. This results from that experience of constant change—commonly but (as a rule) unjustifiably called progress—which has become familiar during the last century and a half.

We tend to forget how recent this experience is. The changes of social structure are due to the application of power—water, steam, electricity—to economic production and the vast increase in ease and rapidity of communication. In our own country this has led to urbanization on a vast scale, and the transference of effective social power from the landowner to the capitalist. There are signs that the era of rapid change may be closing and that the next two centuries may be a period of renewed stability; but that expectation may be falsified at any moment by a new scientific discovery, such as the way to release and utilize atomic energy.

If change is to continue we need help to guide its course wisely; if stabilization is to be expected, we need to secure that what is stabilized is as sound ethically as we can make it; and that involves consciously directed change before stabilization takes place. Here is a main need of our time for which Thomism gives little help, though of course it remains true that its fundamental principles can still supply the foundation on which to build. There is a danger that devotion to St. Thomas without readiness to supplement his teaching may make us blind to one chief duty of our generation, and make us the allies of the forces of inertia.

To say this is not to criticize St. Thomas, for what we are seeking is the answer to a question proposed to us by our experience but without any relation to his. We need to develop a type of responsible citizenship for which his world made no opportunity.

(4) The new emergence of individuality and consequently of responsible citizenship has led the modern world, so far as it is deeply religious, to a profounder understanding of sin. It is, I think, characteristic of the Reformation, as contrasted with the medieval tradition and that of the Counter-Reformation, that it gave a new emphasis to Sin as distinct from sins. Perhaps perspectives have been damaged by the fact that so much of Moral Theology has been written under the impulse of a desire to meet the needs of Confessors and Spiritual Directors for guidance in their difficult and delicate task. The matter of confession is conscious sin recognized as such; and this is bound to be for the most part particular rather than general. The penitent confesses sinfulness in general and passes at once to the particular sins which he is conscious that he has committed. So the Moral Theologian, in his proper desire to help, is liable to be content with a perfunctory definition of sin and proceed at once to its particular manifestations. Thus he concentrates attention on objective acts of sin from which the penitent by confession dissociates himself, and thereby diverts attention from the essential sin which is the perversion of will issuing in those acts. This easily

tends in practice to an unconscious Pelagianism—which I still regard as "the only heresy that is intrinsically damnable." For the suggestion is easily given that if we can find the right spiritual and psychological technique for remedying what we have seen to be wrong, we can put ourselves right with God.

There is no trace of this in St. Thomas himself—quite the contrary—and so far as there is need for modification of his teaching here it is rather in its manner than in its content. But at this point the quasi-mathematical method of exposition is inevitably misleading. Its merit is a clarity achieved by the elimination of rhetoric or any emotional element. It is thus unable to express that tragedy of human nature to which Luther made men once more alive. Certainly we need to recover the sense or feeling—not only the intellectual conviction—of utter impotence to respond to the divine will, and of complete dependence for all power to serve God upon the divine grace. Whatever may be true of St. Thomas himself, the Thomist tradition as commonly presented does not adequately convey the awful pervasiveness and penetrating potency of sin in all departments of human life, including in its sphere of poisonous influence even our worship and our generosity.

(5) With the insufficient appreciation of individuality in the traditional Thomist scheme there goes an insistence on the priority of knowledge as distinct from love—or, to speak with the greater accuracy of technical terms, there is insufficient appreciation of "affective knowledge." Of course it is true that I cannot love anyone of whose existence I am ignorant; but when in fact I meet him, my affective reactions towards him govern the extent and quality of any knowledge or understanding of him that I shall reach; and for fullness of knowledge love is the indispensable condition. St. Thomas knew all about this in his own experience; he did not, as I think, give it expression in his systematic writings. I suspect that it was a consciousness of this which led him at the end to say that all his theological writings were "straw"; the real faith of the man appears in the Eucharistic hymns.

This theme of "affective knowledge" is admittedly most difficult to handle, and is for that reason commonly avoided. But the result of this is to distort perspectives in many ways. I think, for example, that I can trace exactly this distortion in the attitude towards "aridity" which finds expression in the Spiritual Letters of Dom Chapman, and the grounds which he gives for preferring St. John of the Cross of St. Theresa. But there is no space here to work out what is almost as obscure and involved as it is important. My point is that the inadequate appreciation of individuality in Thomism leads to an insufficient emphasis upon actual personal relations—what some moderns call " meeting "—alike in morals and in religion.

(6) Connected, as I think, with the foregoing is the too conceptual interpretation of Revelation. Thomism proceeds upon the widely accepted view that Revelation is given in propositions. I should contend that the primary medium of Revelation is events. This Revelation can only become fruitful through the apprehension and interpretation of the events by minds enlightened by the Holy Spirit to that end; and their interpretation must be expressed in propositions. These propositions may fitly be described as " truths of Revelation "; but they are not " revealed truths." The action of the Holy Spirit does not override or cancel the personal and individual qualities of the prophet, but uses these. There may therefore always be other, though of course not incompatible, truths to be learnt from the event which is the primary Revelation. And in all Revelation what is revealed is not a truth concerning God but God Himself in action. Thus in the supreme instance the essential Revelation is the Birth, Life, Death, Resurrection and Ascension of Jesus Christ—which are accordingly recorded in the Creeds. But while many saw His acts and heard His words, it is only of a few that St. John writes " we beheld His glory "; the Revelation became effective through minds attuned to receive it as what it really was. Yet the event is primary, not the interpretation; and penitent sinners can kneel together at the Cross in perfect unity of gratitude and adoration, though they may differ very widely in their interpretations of the Atonement which was there wrought. This point is of considerable importance in connexion with the relation of theology to personal religion and the basis of religious communion.

I offer, then, these six points as those where I think Thomism requires modification or supplementation if it is to meet modern needs: (1) recognition that the social order is no longer static; (2) a fuller appreciation of individual personality; (3) a new emphasis on responsible citizenship; (4) a greater emphasis on Sin as distinct from sins; (5) a fuller recognition of the place and value of " affective knowledge "; (6) an apprehension of Revelation as given primarily in Events. Some of these are far-reaching, but would be less disturbing to the Thomist scheme as a whole than was the whole method of St. Thomas to the outlook represented by St. Bernard, which he superseded. It may be that those are right who tell us, as Professor A. E. Taylor has told me, that our age has more to learn from St. Bonaventura than from St. Thomas. I should like to believe that because I am by temperament a Platonist rather than an

Q

Aristotelian. But no one is equal to St. Thomas as a map-maker of the spiritual and moral world. If our need is, as I think, first and foremost for such a map, we do well to go back to him, making such modifications as our own survey may dictate.

(*Blackfriars*, a monthly review edited by the English Dominicans, March 1944)

A Christmas Broadcast

ALL KINDS OF PEOPLE, whatever their religious beliefs or disbeliefs, have adopted Christmas as the festival of family and friendship. It is a great thing to have such a festival generally recognized, whether its religious basis is accepted or not. It helps to keep together friend-ships which may be drifting into forgetfulness, and it strengthens the bonds of affection alike between friends and among kinsfolk. Christmas is itself a very real influence for the maintenance of good-will amongst men.

But it has only come to have that character because of what Christian people have regarded as its true significance for all the centuries since men first observed it. What Christians commemorate today is not merely the Birth of a Child who grew up to be a remark-able man; it is the turning point of human history and the appear-ance within it of the Eternal God revealing Himself in a human life. " The Word was made flesh, and we beheld His glory."

As the generations pass, men's knowledge increases and their habits of thought change. The framework in which they set that central figure varies almost indefinitely from age to age; but the Figure itself remains, and always again makes good the claim to the central place in the thought and the loyalty of men. There have been times when men thought of God chiefly as a mighty Sovereign ruling over the world from a far-off heaven; there have been times when they have thought of Him chiefly as a Universal Spirit moving and working in every part of His creation. Naturally their way of approaching the Christmas message has also varied; and often these variations have seemed to shake the foundations of belief, when in reality they were only changing its emphasis. There is no cure for the anxiety which springs from modern perplexities so good as a little knowledge of the history of thought. There have been so many perplexities, each a product of modern thought in its own day; and the central faith of the Gospel has survived them all.

Let us try to see this central faith of the Gospel in the framework supplied by the knowledge and thought of our own time. If the triumphs of Natural Science have any meaning at all, as distinct from the obvious conveniences with which they have supplied us, it is that all the Universe is knit together in an intelligible system. Whatever happens at any time or place is linked up with everything else by the chain of cause and effect. Reality is one. So far as it can be said to have a character, this is made known in some degree in everything that happens if only we can see what happens in its context. But we can never see the whole context, because that is the whole extent of space and time. So we find ourselves baffled in our attempt to construct for ourselves a notion of the character of this great Reality in which we live and move and have our being, because one set of facts leads to one conclusion and another set of facts to a quite different conclusion. There is much in Nature which leads us to suppose that it is the work of an Artist of exquisitely tender sensitiveness; there is much also to suggest that it is the work of a being who enjoys the spectacle of suffering, or else that it is a soulless mechanism grinding out its products without any concern whether they include suffering or not. But it is hard to believe that it is mere mechanism, because then it is impossible to account for the very existence of such intelligence as we have ourselves. And to suppose that the Creator is a demon is to suppose that a Being who had all the possibilities before Him chose evil by deliberate preference; and that introduces irrationality at the heart of the Universe which science insists on our regarding as rational.

The Gospel begins at the other end. It does not invite us to gather all our knowledge together and find in it what meaning we can. It points to a historic Figure and declares that if we will accept Him as the revelation of the meaning of the world and of life, we shall find that for all perplexities their solution begins to appear, and, though the solution is never complete in this world, it is enough to give those who follow this way of thought and life an ever increasing confidence that their faith is true. We clamour to know the character of Ultimate Reality; the Gospel points us to Jesus Christ. " Lord, show us the Father and it sufficeth us. ' He that hath seen Me hath seen the Father.' "

> I say, the acknowledgment of God in Christ
> Accepted by thy reason, solves for thee
> All questions in the world and out of it,
> And has so far advanced thee to be wise.

It is this which gives to Christmas its significance. And here I want to insist that the value of this belief depends primarily upon its truth. If it is a beautiful fiction, its power is gone. The claim of the Christian Gospel is not chiefly that it is uplifting, or that it is comforting, or that it meets our needs, or that it cures our spiritual diseases. Its claim is first and foremost that it is true. If it is true, all those other benefits follow; but if it is not true, they do not follow.

Moreover this truth is to be grasped in all its glorious and over-whelming paradox. That paradox is at its height on Christmas Day. When we think of God in Christ upon the Cross, we are thinking of Him as revealed in One whose love never failed before the worst attacks and insults of malice and contempt. When we think of God in Christ risen from the dead, we are thinking of Him as revealed in One who overcame the last enemy of man. On Good Friday or Easter Day the characteristic of Christ to which our minds are turned is one which we readily conceive to be an attribute of Divine Majesty. But today we are called to worship the Baby in the manger. Here is the most awe-inspiring mystery of all:

> That the great Angell-blincking light should shrinke
> His blaze, to shine in a poore shepherd's eye;
> That the unmeasur'd God so low should sinke
> As Pris'ner in a few poore Rags to lye;
> That from His Mother's Brest he milke should drinke
> Who feeds with Nectar Heav'n's faire family;
> That a vile Manger His low Bed should prove,
> Who in a Throne of stars Thunders above.

> That He whom the Sun serves, should faintly peepe
> Through clouds of Infant flesh; that He the olde
> Eternall Worde should be a Childe, and weepe;
> That He who made the fire should feare the cold;
> That Heav'n's high Majesty His Court should keepe
> In a clay cottage, by each blast control'd;
> That Glories self should serve our Griefs and feares,
> And free Eternity submit to yeares.

I cannot even begin now to work out what this means for us except in one respect. It certainly means that all which makes child-hood delightful to itself and to others is part of the divinity of God. As in the mighty theatre of Nature " it is the glorious God that maketh the thunder," so in the intimacies of home life it is the ten-derly loving God who reaches towards us with the tiny hands of the baby who depends on his elders for all things. In all that stirs the affection of our hearts no less than in what lends authority to the challenge of conscience, God is calling to us. As we think of the Baby in the manger to whom this day the worship of a world is offered, let us remember that His Childhood, with all other periods of His Life, tells us something of the eternal truth of God. We have learnt from His Ministry that God loves as men love—only more intensely and more constantly; we have learnt from His Death that in God as in men there is suffering—only more terrible and combined with a completer self-forgetfulness. Let us learn from His Infancy that God desires love and mirth as children desire them, so that in our merry-making also we may be near to God. We have often made of our religion a stern thing which stands at the gateway of pleasure and says No. We forget that Christ compared John the Baptist to the children playing at funerals, who mourned that others might lament, but compared Himself to children playing at weddings, who piped that others might dance. We forget that our Christmas parties are, or at least may be, as truly as our worship in Church, a form of Divine Service. If we have made our religion sombre by thinking of the tragedy of Christ's Death, or glorious by thinking of the triumph of His Resurrection, let us make it intimate and merry by thinking of His Childhood.

So let us feast and be merry, not because tomorrow we die but because today Jesus Christ is born; and if that is the reason for our merriment, it will be such as to bring no sorrow in its train. If we Christian folk believed our own Gospel wholeheartedly and lived in any degree worthily of it, we should be full of an infectious gaiety. Our faith is feeble, and our lives do not correspond with it. There must be in our religion other factors besides joy and mirth. But today when heaven and earth unite; when angels couple together God's glory and man's peace; when Love comes down—Love all lovely, all divine—to make its home on earth; today let us be merry in the presence of God. And when today is over let us carry that divine merriment into our sombre and busy lives, and let all our mirth be such as Love Divine inspires.

So it will be with us if we can join the Shepherds and the Kings in their worship at the manger cradle. For to worship is to humble one's self before Him to whom worship is given and open one's heart to receive Him. If we can humble ourselves before the innocence of helpless childhood and open our hearts to receive its simplicity, its trustfulness, its happiness, its love, then for us too Christmas will have been the birthday of Love Divine in the hearts to which we invite and welcome Him. Once more then, as when the day began, so now as it draws to a close—Come let us adore Him, Christ the Lord.

Varia

May I here be allowed to suggest for your consideration some reflections upon that special problem of the ethics of punishment which
is brought up by the present [1930] public discussion of the death
penalty? I believe Jeremy Bentham was perfectly right when he laid
it down that the main influence of the State should be exercised
always on the side of the limitation of penalties, as any form of
excessive punishment defeated its own aim in that it encouraged a
callousness in people by the very violence of the suffering inflicted,
and thus did more harm by lowering the public impression of the
accepted standard of treatment of citizens than it did good by its
deterrence. I suggest that the defence of the death penalty has
always been based in the main on its deterrent power and I believe
that the example of the State taking life, even when it only does so
in return for a life already taken, does more to lower the value of
human life in the minds of its citizens than the deterrent influence
of this penalty can do to protect the lives of the citizens. In this way
I believe that the main influence of the retention of the death penalty
is rather to increase than to diminish the number of murders.

Secondly, a very great amount of harm is done by the working
up of popular sympathy for a criminal awaiting execution, so that
a very large amount of sympathy that ought to be enlisted in the
upholding of the majesty of the law is, in fact, arrayed against the
law. For these two reasons, which seem to me the most important,
it seems to me quite plain that it would be for the benefit of society
that the death penalty should be abolished, and I wish to suggest
that it is on such grounds that the Christian must argue the question.
Believing as he does in the life after death, he must not oppose
capital punishment on the ground that he is doing to this person
something final which puts him out of existence, or that he is inflicting on him the greatest possible injury known to us. The death
penalty must be opposed on the ground that it renders impossible
the effective maintenance of the standard which the law demands
of the Christian; and in this way to those who in the past have upheld and enforced this penalty because they believe that it engen-

dered a reverence for human life, we can claim that we are not destroying but fulfilling their law.

I have tried to speak dispassionately and rather coldly about a subject which naturally excites, and should excite, our deepest sympathies. I have done so because I was specially asked to deal with this subject and it is one which I do not think can be profitably considered except in a somewhat cold and analytical fashion.

(*The Ethics of Punishment*,
The John Howard Memorial Sermon, 1930)

THE ABDICATION

There is some danger that regret for the loss of brilliant qualities and sympathy for the Monarch, who in the critical days was confronted with a most painful choice, may divert our attention from the fact that the occasion for this choice ought never to have arisen. The harm was not done in December, nor even in October when he announced to the Prime Minister his intention of marriage, but much earlier. It has happened to many a man before now to find himself beginning to fall in love with another man's wife. That is the moment of critical decision; and the right decision is that they should cease to meet, before passion is so developed as to create an agonizing conflict between love and duty. That decision has often been taken by men of honour. And when the power of personal attraction is reinforced by the glamour of a throne the moral obligation is the more urgent for that reason.

. . . Let us remember that any kind of love which can be in conflict with duty is not the love of which the Gospel speaks. The love which has its roots in mutual attraction and in passion can be united with that love which is the very nature of God and the best of Christian graces; and this takes place in a multitude of marriages; but the qualities are two, not one; and the great sayings of the New Testament about Love or Charity—the Greek word for both is *Agapé*—must not be used of the passion which arises in a man and woman who have for one another a mutual attraction—the Greek word for which is Erós. It is nowhere said, for example, that Erós covers a multitude of sins.

(*York Diocesan Leaflet*, January 1937)

What Christians Stand For in the Secular World

THE DISTINCTION BETWEEN the tasks of Church and of society, of churchmen and citizens, is seldom clearly drawn; and the result is confusion and impotence. Either Christians try to act as churchmen in the world, only to find that the world refuses to be ordered on the principles proper to the Church; or else they look out for the secular policy most congenial to their Christian outlook, only to find that their Christianity is a dispensable adjunct of no practical importance.

Church and State are different, though they may comprise the same people; and each has its own appropriate sphere and method. Churchman and citizen are words with a different connotation even when they denote the same person; and that person, the individual Christian, has to exercise both of these different functions. As long as he acts quite unreflectively he is likely to maintain the distinction and the appropriate balance fairly well, though he is also likely as a citizen to be excessively swayed by currents of purely secular thought and feeling. Moreover, it is almost impossible in these days to retain that naïve spontaneity. Reflection or its fruits are thrust upon us, and when once that process has started it must be carried through. It is half-baked reflection which is most perilous.

In the nineteenth century men still assumed a Law of God as universally supreme. In this country, at any rate, it was widely believed that God, whose nature was revealed in the Gospel and proclaimed by the Church, was also the orderer of the world and of life; in only a few quarters was the alienation of the actual order from any subjection to the God and Father of Jesus Christ perceived or stated. The Church was, therefore, free to concentrate its main energies on its distinctive task of proclaiming the Gospel of redemption, without any sense of incongruity with the ordering of life in the world outside. Theologians could undertake the task of showing that Christianity enables us to " make sense " of the world with the meaning " show that it is sense." And those of us who were trained under those influences went on talking like that; I was still talking like that when Hitler became Chancellor of the German Reich.

All that seems remote today. We must still claim that Christianity enables us to " make sense " of the world, not meaning that we can show that it is sense, but with the more literal and radical meaning

of making into sense what, till it is transformed, is largely nonsense
—a disordered chaos waiting to be reduced to order as the Spirit of
God gives it shape. Our problem is to envisage the task of the Church
in a largely alien world. Some would have us go back to the example
of the primitive Church or of the contemporary Church entering on
an evangelistic enterprise in a heathen country; this means the
abandonment of all effort to influence the ordering of life in the
secular world and concentration of all effort upon what is, no doubt,
the primary task of the Church, the preaching of the Gospel and
the maintenance among converts of a manner of life conformed to
the Gospel. They advocate a spiritual return to the catacombs in the
hope that the Church may there build up its strength till, having
the shield of faith intact and the sword of the Spirit sharp, it may
come forth to a new conquest of a world which has meanwhile
returned to a new dark age.

But this is a shirking of responsibility. The Church must never
of its own free will withdraw from the conflict. If it is driven to the
catacombs it will accept its destiny and set itself there to maintain
and to deepen its faith. But it cannot abandon its task of guiding
society so far as society consents to be guided. It has a special
illumination which it is called to bring to bear on the whole range
of human relationships, and if, for lack of this, civilization founders,
the Church will have failed in its duty to men and to its Lord.

But if so, it must be active in two distinct ways. It must at all costs
maintain its own spiritual life, the fellowship which this life creates,
and the proclamation of the Gospel in all its fullness, wherein this
life expresses itself. Here it must insist on all those truths from which
its distinctive quality is derived—that God is Creator and man with
the world His creature; that man has usurped the place of God in
an endeavour to order his own life after his own will; that in the
Birth, Life, Death, Resurrection and Ascension of Jesus Christ God
has Himself taken action for the redemption of mankind; that in
the Holy Spirit given by the Father through the Son to those who
respond to the Gospel, power is offered for a life of obedience to God
which is otherwise impossible for men; that those who are thus
empowered by the Spirit are a fellowship of the Lord fitly called
the Church; that in that Church are appointed means whereby men
may receive and perpetually renew their union with their Lord and
with one another in Him, and so increase in the Holy Spirit. All
this must be maintained and proclaimed. And unless the Church is
firm in its witness to its own faith, it will have no standing-ground
from which to address the world.

But standing firm upon its own ground, it can and must address the world. By what convictions constantly in mind will Christians called to such a task direct their actions?

BASIC DECISIONS

There is in fact more widespread agreement than is generally supposed with regard to these basic convictions. I do not mean that they are universally accepted among Christians; there are currents of Christian thought in all denominations which are directly opposed to some of them; and many devout Christians have as yet not turned their attention in this direction at all. But among Christians who have seriously and thoughtfully faced the historical situation with which we are dealing there is, as I have proved by testing, an observable convergence which may be presented in five affirmations; but as these are acts of faith, resting on a deliberate choice and involving a specific determination of the will, I speak of them rather as Decisions.

1. *For God who has spoken*
   A vague theism is futile. The cutting edge of faith is due to its definiteness. The kind of deity established (if any is at all) by the various " proofs "—ontological, cosmological and the like—is completely insufficient; it is usually little else than the rationality of the world presupposed in all argument about the world. The Christian has made a decision for God who has spoken—in nature, in history, in prophets, in Christ.

It follows that the value of man and the meaning of history is to be found in the nature and character of God, who has thus made Himself known. The value of a man is not what he is in and for himself—humanism; not what he is for society—fascism and communism; but what he is worth to God. This is the principle of Christian equality; the supreme importance of every man is that he is the brother for whom Christ died. This is compatible with many forms of social differentiation and subdivision. It is not compatible with any scheme which subjects a man's personality to another man or to any group of men such as the government or administrators of the State.

The purpose of God is the governing reality of history. Progress is approximation to conformity with it and fulfilment of it; deviation from it is retrogression. The nature of God is a righteousness which is perfect in love; His purpose, therefore, is the establishment of justice in all relationships of life—personal, social, economic, cultural, political, international. Many " humanists " share that aim, and Christians may well co-operate with them in practical policies from time to time. But a "decision for God" involves a sharp separation in thought, and, therefore, in the long run in practice, from many dominant tendencies of our time which seek the whole fulfilment of man's life in his earthly existence.

God has given to man freedom to decide for Him or against Him. This freedom is fundamental, for without it there could be only automatic obedience, not the obedience of freely offered loyalty. God always respects this freedom to the uttermost; therefore, freedom is fundamental to Christian civilization.

But though man is free to rebel against God, and can indeed do marvels through science and human wisdom in controlling his own destiny, yet he cannot escape the sovereignty of God. To deviate from the course of God's purpose is to incur disaster sooner or later—and sooner rather than later in so far as the deviation is great. The disaster ensues by "natural laws" as scientists use that phrase—that is by the causal processes inherent in the natural order. But these laws are part of God's creation, and the disasters which they bring are His judgments.

Yet because man has so great a power to shape his own destiny he is responsible for using this. Belief in God is used by many Christians as a means of escape from the hard challenge of life; they seek to evade the responsibility of decision by throwing it upon God, who has Himself laid it upon them. Faith in God should be not a substitute for scientific study, but a stimulus to it, for our intellectual faculties are God's gift to us. Consequently a decision for "God who has spoken" involves commitment to the heroic, intellectual and practical task of giving to spiritual faith a living content over against the immensely effective this-worldliness of Marxism and secular humanism, while absorbing the elements of truth which these movements have often perceived more clearly and emphasized more strongly than Christians in recent times have done.

2. For Neighbour

As the first great commandment is that we love God with all our being, so the second is that we love our neighbour as ourselves. Here we are not concerned with that duty, but with the fact that underlies it whether we do our duty or not—not with what ought to be, but with what *is*. This is that we stand before God—that is, in ultimate reality—as bound to one another in a complete equality in His family. Personality is inherently social; only in social groupings can it mature, or indeed fully exist. These groupings must be small enough to enable each individual to feel (not only to think) that he can influence the quality and activity of the group, so that he is responsible for it, and also that it needs his contribution, so that he is responsible to it. He must feel that he belongs to it and that it belongs to him.

It is characteristic of much democratic thought that it seeks to eliminate or to depreciate all associations intermediate between the individual and the State. These, as the foci of local or other departmental loyalties, are nurseries of tradition and, therefore, obnoxious in the eyes of some prophets of progress. But it is in and through them that the individual exercises responsible choice or, in other words, is effectively free. The State is too large; the individual feels impotent and unimportant over against it. In his local, or functional, or cultural association he may count for something in the State, so that through his association he may influence the State itself, as alone he can scarcely do.

Thus the limitless individualism of revolutionary thought, which aims at setting the individual on his own feet that he may, with his fellows, direct the State, defeats its own object and becomes the fount of totalitarianism. If we are to save freedom we must proceed, as Maritain urges, from democracy of the individual to democracy of the person, and recollect that personality achieves itself in the lesser groupings within the State—in the family, the school, the guild, the trade union, the village, the city, the county. These are no enemies of the State, and that State will in fact be stable which deliberately fosters these lesser objects of loyalty as contributors to its own wealth of tradition and inheritance.

Christianity has always favoured these lesser units. The Catholic Church itself is composed of dioceses, in each of which the structure of the Church is complete, representing the family of God gathered about the Bishop as its Father in God. And the civilization which the Church most deeply influenced was characterized by an almost bewildering efflorescence of local and functional guilds of every sort.

The revolutionary and mechanistic type of thought finds its classical and fontal expression in Descartes' disastrous deliverance, *Cogito, ergo sum.* Thus the individual self-consciousness became central. Each man looks out on a world which he sees essentially as related to himself. (This is the very quality of original sin, and it seems a pity to take it as the constitutive principle of our philosophy.) He sets himself to explore this world that he may understand and increasingly control it. In the world he finds a great variety of " things." He studies these in his sciences of physics, chemistry, and biology, according to their observable characteristics. Among the " things " are some which require a further complication of his

method of study, giving rise to psychology. But though he is now
allowing for instincts, emotions, sentiments, purposes and similar
factors, his attitude is the same as toward " things " which lacked
these qualities. He organizes these psychological " things " in ways
calculated to extract from them the result he desires. He may, for
example, as an industrial manager, introduce welfare work because
he can in that way increase output. He might even, in an ultimate
blasphemy, supply his troops with chaplains with no other object
except to keep up military morale.

Now, in all this he is treating persons as things. His relation to
them is an " I—it " relation, not an " I—Thou " relation. This latter
he only reaches so far as he loves or hates, and only in this relation
does he treat persons as they really are. He may do very much what
the enlightened man of purely " scientific " outlook does: he provides for the welfare of employees, if he is an employer, and is, of
course, glad that it pays; but that is not his motive: his motive is
that they are human beings like himself. So he supplies what he
would wish to have, and hopes and works for the time when they
will not depend on him for what their welfare requires, but will be
in a position to supply it to themselves. For he will prefer fellowship
to domination.

It is in love and hate—the truly " personal " relationships—that
we confront our neighbour as he is, a man like ourselves. Even hate
has an insight denied to the egoist who coldly manipulates human
beings as his pawns, and men resent it less. Most of us would rather
be bullied than mechanically organized. But hate too is blind, partly
from its own nature, partly because men hide from an enemy, as
they do from a cynic, what is deepest and tenderest in their nature.
Only love—the purpose of sheer goodwill intensified by sympathetic
feeling—gives real insight and understanding.

We cannot command that love. Those who live with God become
increasingly filled with it. But none of us can so rely on feeling it as
safely to plan his life on the supposition of its emergence when
required; and when we consider secular society as a whole we know
that we cannot count on it in volume adequate to the need. Indeed,
in the relationships of politics, commerce and industry it cannot find
expression and can scarcely arise. To this we shall return. What we
have to notice at present is that the primary relation between persons
—by which in every generation multitudes of men and women have,
consciously or unconsciously, guided their lives—has been relegated
to a subordinate place by men's headlong eagerness to explore the
secrets and exploit the resources of this wonderful universe. In the
concentration on wealth we have tended to overlook the more funda-

mental and more difficult problems of the adjustment of our personal relations to one another.

It is a question whether it was primarily a false understanding of reality that gave free rein to men's egoisms and ambitions; or whether their inherent selfishness inclined them to misread the true nature of things. To whichever cause we assign the greater weight, men's self-centred aims and a false philosophy have co-operated to bring about a profound misunderstanding of the meaning of human life and to create the state of things which we see today.

Science, which has been perhaps the chief influence in giving its distinctive cast and colour to the modern consciousness, is essentially an expression of the individualistic approach. As scientist, the individual stands over against the world, measuring, weighing, experimenting, judging, deciding. The gains which have resulted from this approach and activity are incalculable. We can today only regret the timidity which led Christians in the past to oppose the advances of science. No enlightened Christian today would question the right of science to investigate everything that it is capable of investigating. It is certain that the problems of our complex society cannot be mastered without a continuous expansion of scientific knowledge, more particularly in the field of the social sciences.

It is none the less vital for the health of society that we should realize that, while man is meant to have dominion—and we cannot, therefore, be too thankful for the gift of science as an instrument, and are under an obligation to make the fullest use of it—the scientific attitude is only one approach to reality and not the most fundamental and important. As scientist the individual is monarch; he sits in the seat of judgment and asks what questions he will. But the situation is fundamentally changed when he encounters another person who, like himself, is monarch in relation to the world of things. In the encounter with another person or group he is no longer free to ask what questions he will and to order things according to his choice. Questions may be *addressed* to him from a source over which he has no control, and he has to *answer*. He is no longer sole judge, but is subject himself to judgment.

This profound difference between these two approaches to reality, which are uninterchangeable, is often hidden from us, because it is always possible to bring the relations between persons into the framework of the self-centred view. After the collision has taken place we can reflect upon it and fit it into our picture of the world. At any moment we can step out of the arena of conflict and take our place on the spectator's bench. So ingrained has the habit become that, without being aware of it, we continually have recourse to this form of escape. There is an immense deal that we can learn about persons with the aid of science; but so long as we study them medically, psychologically, sociologically, we never *meet* them. And it is precisely in meeting that real life consists.

It will need a strong and sustained effort to emancipate ourselves from the one-sidedness of the individualistic attitude and to penetrate to the full meaning of the truth that the fundamental reality of life is the interplay, conflict and continuous adjustment of a multitude of different finite points of view, both of individuals and of groups.

Acknowledgment of this truth would create a wholly different spiritual and intellectual climate from that which has prevailed in recent centuries. Men would still strive, no doubt, to gratify their desires and seek their own aggrandisement; they would not desist from the attempt to domineer over others. But these tendencies would be kept within bounds by a public opinion more aware than at present that in pursuing these courses men are doing violence both to their own nature and to the true nature of things. It would be recognized that men can live at peace with one another only if each individual and each group renounces the claim to have the final and decisive word. Society would have restored to it the sanity which comes from an understanding of human finitude.

A decision for sociality as the basic truth of human existence would create an outlook and temper so different from that which has been dominant in the modern era now drawing to its close as to create a new epoch in human history.

Between the decision for God and the decision for neighbour there is a most intimate connection. In the New Testament these are always intertwined. We should in all remembrance of God remember also our neighbour, and in all thought of our neighbour think also of God. Our highest act of worship is not a mystic " flight of the alone to the Alone," but a fellowship meal, a Holy Communion. We come before God as " Our Father " to whom all His other children have the same right of access; the truth about God is, among other things, His universal Fatherhood. So too the truth about our neighbour is not only what he is to us nor what he is in himself, but above all what he is to God. His relationship to God is the ultimate fact about him, and if we are to think rightly about him or act rightly towards him, we must have that relationship full in view. We must cease to think and feel either in the vertical dimension wherein we are related to God, or in the horizontal dimension wherein we are related to our neighbours, and substitute the triangular relationship, God—Self—Neighbour, Neighbour—God—Self.

3. For Man as Rooted in Nature

The most important thing about man is his relation to God and to other men. But his life has also been set in a natural order, which is God's creation. A fundamental duty which man owes to God is reverence for the world as God has made it. Failure to understand and acknowledge this is a principal cause of the present ineffectiveness of the Christian witness in relation to the temporal order. It is one of the chief points at which a fundamental change of outlook is demanded from Christians. Our false outlook is most of all apparent in the exploitation of the physical world. As animals we are part of nature, dependent on it and inter-dependent with it. We must reverence its economy and co-operate with its processes. If we have dominion over it, that is as predominant partners, not as superior beings who are entitled merely to extract from it what gratifies our desires.

There are two major points at which failure to recognize that man's life is rooted in nature and natural associations leads to mistaken and vain attempts to solve the problem of society. The first grave error characteristic of our time is a too exclusive occupation with politics to the neglect of other equally important spheres of human life and activity. It is assumed that the ills from which society is suffering can be cured, if only we have the will and the right aims. It is forgotten that man is not a being ruled wholly by his reason and conscious aims. His life is inextricably intertwined with nature and with the natural associations of family and livelihood, tradition and culture. When the connection with these sources from which the individual life derives nourishment and strength is broken, the whole life of society becomes enfeebled.

Recognition of the vital importance of centres of human life and activity that underlie and precede the sphere of politics must not be made an excuse for evading the political decisions which have to be made in the near future. It is not a way of escape from political responsibility. Far-reaching decisions in the political sphere may be the only means of creating the conditions in which the non-political spheres can regain vitality and health; but the recovery of health in those spheres is in its turn an indispensable preliminary to political sanity and vigour.

The present plight of our society arises in large part from the break-down of these natural forms of association and of a cultural pattern formed to a great extent under Christian influences. New dogmas and assumptions about the nature of reality have taken the place of the old. New rituals of various kinds are giving shape to men's emotional life. The consequence is that while their aims still

R

remain to a large extent Christian, their souls are moulded by alien influences. The real crisis of our time is thus not primarily a moral, but a cultural crisis. In so far as this is true, the remedy is not to be found in what the Church is at present principally doing—insisting on ideals—or in efforts to intensify the will to pursue them. The cure has to be sought in the quite different direction of seeking to re-establish a unity between men's ultimate beliefs and habits and their conscious aims.

Christians must free their minds from illusions and become aware of the impotence of moral advice and instruction when it is divorced from the social structures which by their perpetual suggestion form the soul. It must be remembered that when exhortation and suggestion are at variance, suggestion always wins. Christians must take their part in recreating a sound social and cultural life and thereby healing the modern divided consciousness, in which head and heart have become divorced and men's conscious purposes are no longer in harmony with the forces which give direction and tone to their emotional life.

But, secondly, if Christians are to have a substantial influence on the temporal order, it is not only necessary that they should have a clearer and deeper understanding of the positive, character-forming function of the non-political forms of human association, but their whole approach to social and political questions needs to be much more realistic than it has commonly been in the past. The Christian social witness must be radically dissociated from the idealism which assumes men to be so free spiritually that aims alone are decisive. There is need of a much clearer recognition of the part played in human behaviour by subconscious egoisms, interests, deceptions and determinisms imposed by man's place in nature and history, by his cultural patterns and by his sinfulness.

It has to be recognized that society is made up of competing centres of power, and that the separate existence of contending vitalities, and not only human sinfulness, makes the elimination of power impossible. What has to be aimed at is such a distribution and balance of power that a measure of justice may be achieved even among those who are actuated in the main by egoistic and sinful impulses. It is a modest aim, but observance of political life leaves no doubt that this must be its primary concern.

If Christians are to act with effect in the temporal order, it is necessary, as was said at the beginning, to distinguish more clearly than is commonly done between the two distinct spheres of society and Church, or the different realms of Law and Gospel. We also need a clearer and deeper understanding of the difference between justice, human love and Christian charity. The last transcends both justice and human fellowship while it has contacts with each. Associations cannot love one another; a trade union cannot love an employers' federation, nor can one national State love another. The members of one may love the members of the other so far as opportunities of intercourse allow. That will help in negotiations; but it will not solve the problem of the relations between the two groups. Consequently, the relevance of Christianity in these spheres is quite different from what many Christians suppose it to be. Christian charity manifests itself in the temporal order as a supranatural discernment of, and adhesion to, *justice* in relation to the equilibrium of power. It is precisely fellowship or human love, with which too often Christian charity is mistakenly equated, that is *not* seriously relevant in that sphere. When the two are identified, it is just those who are most honest and realistic in their thinking and practice that are apt to be repelled from Christianity.

There is scarcely any more urgent task before the Church than that this whole complex of problems should be thought out afresh, and it is obviously a task which can be successfully undertaken only in the closest relation with the experience of those who are exposed to the daily pressures of the economic and political struggle. The third decision involves a commitment to a new realm in Christian thought and action; the citizen and the churchman should remain distinct though the same individual should be both.

4. For History

It is a question of vital importance whether history makes any fundamental difference to our understanding of reality. The Greek view was that it does not, and through the great thinkers of antiquity the Hellenic view still exercises a powerful influence over the modern mind.

In the Christian view, on the other hand, it is in history that the ultimate meaning of human existence is both revealed and actualized. If history is to have a meaning, there must be some central point at which that meaning is decisively disclosed. The Jews found the meaning of their history in the call of Abraham, the deliverance from Egypt, and the covenant with God following upon it. For Mohammedans the meaning of history has its centre in Mohammed's flight from Mecca. For Marxists the culminating meaning is found in the emergence of the proletariat. The Nazis vainly pinned their hopes to the coming of Hitler. For Christians the decisive meaning of history is given in Christ.

Christianity is thus essentially a continuing action in history

determining the course of human development. The Christian understanding of history has much closer affinities with the Marxist view,
in which all assertions about the nature of man are inseparably
bound up with the dynamics of his historical existence, and with
other dynamic views of history, which understand the world in terms
of conflict, decision and fate, and regard history as belonging to the
essence of existence, than with the interpretations of Christianity in
terms of idealistic thought which were lately prevalent.

A decision for history confronts us with two urgent practical
tasks. The first is to disabuse the minds of people of the notion,
which is widespread, and infects to a large extent current Christian
preaching, that Christianity is in essence a system of morals, so that
they have lost all understanding of the truth, so prominent in the
New Testament, that to be a Christian is to share in a new movement of life, and to co-operate with new regenerating forces that have
entered into history.

The second task is to restore hope to the world through a true
understanding of the relation of the Kingdom of God to history, as
a transcendent reality that is continually seeking, and partially
achieving, embodiment in the activities and conflicts of the temporal
order. Without this faith men can only seek escape from life in
modes of thought which, pushed to their logical conclusion, deprive
politics, and even the ethical struggle, of real significance, or suc-
cumb to a complete secularization of life in which all principles
disintegrate in pure relativity, and opportunism is the only wisdom.

5. *For the Gospel and the Church*
This understanding brings us face to face with the decision
whether or not we acknowledge Christ as the centre of history. He
is for Christians the source and vindication of those perceptions of
the true nature of reality which we have already considered. In the
tasks of society Christians can and must co-operate with all those,
Christians or non-Christians, who are pursuing aims that are in
accord with the divinely intended purpose of man's temporal life.
But Christians are constrained to believe that in the power of the
Gospel of redemption and in the fellowship of the Church lies the
chief hope of the restoration of the temporal order to health and
sanity.

What none but utopians can hope for the secular world should
be matter of actual experience in the Church. For the Church is the
sphere where the redemptive act of God lifts men into the most
intimate relation with Himself and through that with one another.
When this is actually experienced the stream of redemptive power

flows out from the Church through the lives of its members into the society which they influence. But only a Church firm in the faith set forth in outline earlier in this essay can give to its members the inspiration which they need for meeting the gigantic responsibilities of this age. Spiritual resources far beyond anything now in evidence will be needed. It may be that the greatness of the challenge will bring home to Christians how impotent they are in themselves, and so lead to that renewal which will consist in re-discovery of the sufficiency of God and manifestation of His power.

(A Supplement in the *Christian News Letter*, February 1944)

Christianity as an Interpretation of History

AT A MOMENT when, as very seldom, history is being made, not only
year by year but almost hour by hour, if only we can turn our minds
that way it may be all the more profitable for us to raise the question:
" What is the meaning of this history in the end? " Apart from the
gratification of our wishes or someone else's wishes, is there something that gives to it the significance that is the same for all men
and in the discovery and working out of which we should find the
secret of wellbeing and of peace?

Let us not suppose that merely by understanding the secret we
should also have learned the art of living by it. That is a further
question, and so the whole problem of the present day and the
human will, and even of the human conscience, will have to be
considered. But if we are to have any understanding of history at all,
we need to discover some principle, or group of principles, which
we may trace out in its workings, and in obedience to which we
may shape our own contribution to history.

Now what is it that gives meaning to any process? We are inclined
at first to say that the only thing that will give meaning is approximation to a goal, that there must be some fixed end to be realized,
and that only if we come nearer to it can we say that there is real
progress, while any failure to draw nearer is either stagnation or
retrogression.

It has not once, but several times, been laid down by philosophers
that if history is to have a meaning it must be finite in itself: the
idea of an infinite progress is unmeaning. But is that necessarily
true? Let us grant that one of the things that gives meaning to any
process is approximation to a goal, and that if we take history to be
a process limited in time, beginning with a definite act of creation
and ending with a definite consummation, this no doubt will be one
way of discovering a significance in it.

It is not the only way, and it is very important, I think, to realize
that there are two ways. I believe that Christ helps us to find a
meaning along both ways, but more certainly along the second than
along the first.

There would be real meaning in an infinite progress if it meant
the wider and wider illustration of a principle which set no limits

to its own application. If, for example, we think that the good of life consists in the steady development of that relationship between persons which under the influence of Christianity we call *love*, there is no reason why this should not be developed to a strictly infinite extent through an increasing multiplication of the number of persons between whom the relationship is established: and while in one sense you would have reached perfection if it should ever occur that there was complete love established between all of the persons who exist while they are very few, yet there would be more of the perfecting if the same relationship were established between a vastly greater number.

I am not arguing that that is the course of history, nor am I arguing that the development of that kind of relationship is possible between an indefinite number of persons, but it is quite clear that you would have there—supposing it to be possible—a course, a process, which had quite definite meaning and which could be called an infinite progress without any kind of contradiction.

In the same way, there may occur within history some central event which supplies a standard of judgment for all that has gone before and after, which by its mere occurrence, being the kind of event it is, supplies a standard for all the process in all its parts, and then every part can be interpreted by its relationship to that single event.

This, at least, Christianity does claim to offer us in the life, the death and the resurrection of Jesus Christ. This, at least, it sets before us as a standard of reference, by which we are to interpret the course of history up to that event. Past history has its importance just so far as it is preparing for the coming of the Christ, and similarly all history from that day onwards, if the truth of the Incarnation be accepted, is to be judged by a backward reference to that event. Is subsequent history a working out of the principles of that life? Is it an exemplification of the rhythms of that life, death and resurrection, or is it something that is leading men further away from what is there set forth as the absolute standard of value, so that there must be recovery before even equilibrium is reached, let alone progress again set on foot? In all of these ways that I have dealt with, it is possible to give a real meaning to history.

Let us consider for a moment what are the alternative theories of history that are offered from other quarters.

The ancient Greek philosophers, so far as they developed the theory of that subject at all, arrived at a belief that all things at last return to the same condition from which they have started, having gone the complete round, upon which they must then set out again, just as the planets moving about the sun come back to the same place and then begin their course once more.

That is not a suggestion that gives any real meaning to history. All that it will enable you to do, and it was in this way that the Greeks used it, is to relate the process of history to an assumed time-less reality, something which is eternal not in the sense of containing all temporal process within itself, but in the sense of excluding both time and change completely. They felt that if the time process merely revolves in this way in an endless cycle, it could be the per-petual manifestation of that eternal reality. The idea has taken possession of some of our poets from time to time, and they have nearly always taken it for granted that the beginning of the cycle, at any rate, is good; and that we may well sing—" The world's great age begins anew," in tones of triumph.

Why it should be supposed that the beginning is particularly good, except that the end is so bad, I see no reason for presuming.

Then there is the theory of continuous progress. In dealing with that, it is necessary to determine what is progress, and most of those who have upheld it as something that is inherently characteristic of the movement of history have been very slow to offer us a definition of Progress. If it merely means something different every day, there is no reason to regard that as progress. In fact, for progress we need a direction or a standard, a fixed standard by reference to which we may judge whether we are nearer to it or further from it.

Unless something very like a Christian background of the world is accepted, why should we believe in this continuous progress in face of what Science has to tell us about the apparent running down of the forces or energy that constitute the universe?

The Darwinian picture, biological evolution, has laid hold of men's imagination, and for some reason the second law of thermo-dynamics has not; but the second is the more fundamental of the two, and if we have nothing but what Science can tell us about the world, we are left with a picture of a great mass of energy steadily dissipating itself until at last there will be an undifferentiated mass of cold and lifeless material. That certainly cannot be called Progress.

We return, then, to the presuppositions, as we may call them, of the Christian scheme, and pass on to one other question concerning Progress, which happens to be of outstanding importance in our time.

What in the whole of any conception of progress is the place of the human individual, the person? That is the great political ques-tion of our age; that in the last resort is the question at issue in the war, because the totalitarian conception of life is one which reduces the individual to a mere episode in the life of his race or his state, for which therefore he exists, his whole value being found in his serviceableness to the race or the State. From that flows a quite definite type of ethics, the type of ethics of which the typical expression is that justice is the treatment of each individual in the way that most conduces to the interests of the State, a flat denial of what we have learned to mean by the word Justice, but a definition officially issued in Germany some years ago.

And indeed, if the individual has no status other than that which I have described, it is hard to see how any claim can be made good to what used to be known as " the rights of man." We may like to believe in them. We may think life is more interesting and agreeable if based on such a belief, and then we may contend earnestly for that belief, for that type of life. But we cannot, as far as I can judge, find any means of making this position good against the contrary view; and the pressures of life in the direction of a rigid collectivization are so strong that I do not for a moment believe that our belief in the inherent value of the human person can be maintained except on the basis of the conviction that he is himself the focus of that principle which gives to history its meaning.

If the world is the creation of God, if God is fitly called Father, if mankind consists of His children whom He has created for eternal life in fellowship with Himself, then, of course, the whole position is reversed. Then the individual has a dignity and a status greater than that of his state or his race, which, except so far as they are the sum total of himself and his colleagues, become the one a machine and the other an accumulation of persons whose value is in themselves; not indeed the value which they have *for* themselves, for that is the way to egocentricism and to rivalries, conflicts of all kinds, and wars; but the value which they have in themselves for God; and if our valuation of human life rests on the belief that God loves His children, and that Christ died for us all and for each, then we can simply speak about the value that is in each individual without becoming involved in endless rivalries and conflicts, for the very ground on which the value is asserted is one which at the same time prohibits us from using that as a basis of an argument in defence of any selfish policy.

Then let us turn to the biblical presentation of history. All the way through such a conception as I have just outlined is not so much in the background as in the forefront of it. God is the Creator: He is the Father: men are His children. His purpose is the meaning of history. History is the arena wherein that Divine purpose is being fulfilled and the Divine judgments are made manifest. Here let me pause for a moment to say a word about this thought of the Divine judgments in history, because it is the source of so much profound and, as it seems to me, most unnecessary misunderstanding.

I find many people who think that if you speak of any event in history as a Divine judgment, you mean that it is something arbitrarily introduced by God from without—an expression of His wrath against some kind of conduct on the part of men; as though He lost patience, and said: " I will put up with it no longer." No doubt there are passages in the Old Testament which, taken by themselves, would give ground for such a conception: the way in which, for example, God is depicted as sending the Flood upon the earth. But if we will only follow the lead that our Lord so constantly gave us, of looking for the activity of God not chiefly in what is exceptional and otherwise inexplicable, but precisely in the ordinary, the reliable, the predictable, then we shall be set free from this danger. We shall no longer trace the hand of God only when we can give no other explanation, but we shall say of every explanation that science offers to us, that it is showing us the way in which God is carrying out His work.

A judge who, sitting in a law court, pronounces an arbitrary judgment, is abusing his office. The function of the judge is to effect the complete connexion between the general law and the individual case brought before him, and there must be nothing arbitrary about it. A particular judgment is the bringing about of precisely that connexion. The law says that men who steal shall go to prison. A particular individual is charged with theft, and the business of the court is, first to determine whether he indeed committed it—that is the verdict—and then to ensure that the decree of the law takes effect upon him—that is the sentence. It is the bringing together of the general law and the individual case. But it is only necessary to have an elaborate apparatus for this because of the limitations of human power and knowledge. A Divine judgment is exactly the same thing. It is the taking effect of a constant law upon those who have brought themselves under its operation.

This law is a law of God who is love; therefore it must be His law that those who embark on selfish courses must bring calamity upon themselves and others, because they are going contrary to the fundamental nature of reality, which is the character of God. They are breaking the law, and when the calamity comes in accordance with the law there is no arbitrary intervention, but it is a Divine act. It is the working out of the Divine purpose, as expressed in the law which attaches calamity to selfish choices. And the judgments of

God are of that kind. When the prophet Zephaniah says, " Morning by morning he bringeth his judgment to light, he faileth not "; what he is exhorting us to do is to trace in the operation of those laws which govern human nature, as there are other laws which govern physical nature, the working out of the Divine purposes. They are the judgment of God because they are the consequence which the law of God brings about as human action conforms to, or breaks, that law.

But if it is true (and this is the first biblical position, surely) that God is the Creator and that therefore His purpose is the explanation of history, then everything turns upon the character of God. Throughout the Old Testament we find more and more a vivid sense of the character of God growing through the illumination of the minds of the prophets, especially upon two points which were seized and in their turn seized the mind of Israel together—the righteousness and the universality of God. I say " universality " here rather than " unity," because though the idea is fundamentally the same, this is the relevant aspect of it. To say that there is only one God is to say that He is God of all the earth.

We all know that in the early stages Israel had learned that for it there was only one God to be truly worshipped, the God who had made Himself known to Abraham, and later more fully to Moses; but Israel also believed that there were real gods of the other nations. In the Book of the Judges there are many utterances which are quite meaningless unless that is the belief of the speakers; and the prohibition of the worship of other gods was not based upon the realization that there is only one God of all the earth, but upon the special relationship between God and His chosen people Israel, with whom He had entered into a special relation by covenant. But with the realization that God is fundamentally righteous there came also the understanding that there is only one moral law for men, and to call God righteous and to claim that He is the God of all the earth must go together. It is always most rash to say that any idea was at any time really proclaimed for the first time. Adumbrations to it are sure to be perceptible at earlier dates. But I suppose that the first prophet to set this quite clearly before the conscience of the people was Amos; and we can imagine the shock it was, after they had listened to those great denunciations of their neighbours, to hear of the punishment that they were bringing upon themselves by their neglect of the Divine law and purposes, the consequence of their own ill deeds. But even that would have been less of a shock than what he says in the 9th chapter in the celebrated words: " Are ye not as children of the Ethiopians unto me, O children of Israel? saith the Lord. Have not

I brought up Israel out of the land of Egypt—and the Philistines from Caphtor, and the Syrians from Kir? "

It was true as they themselves believed that He had guided Israel, but it was also true that He had guided those neighbours whom they had hated and despised.

That conception finds its fullest expression, perhaps, in the closing verses of the 19th chapter of Isaiah, when the prophet, addressing people who are near to being crushed between the mighty armies of Assyria and Egypt says: " In that day shall there be a highway out of Egypt to Assyria, and the Assyrian shall come into Egypt, and the Egyptian into Assyria, and the Egyptians shall worship with the Assyrians. In that day shall Israel be the third with Egypt and with Assyria; a blessing in the midst of the earth; for that the Lord of hosts hath blessed them saying Blessed be Egypt my people and Assyria the work of my hands and Israel mine inheritance." It is as if you were to say, " In that day shall Britain be the third, with Germany and Japan, even a blessing in the midst of the earth: Whom the Lord of hosts shall bless, saying Blessed be Germany my people and Japan the work of my hands and Britain mine inheritance."

Think of the shuddering horror with which a defeated Israelite would hear the words " Blessed be Egypt my people."

So there grows this conception of God as the universal King and therefore of His purpose as being the all-embracing family of His children. Israel was indeed the chosen people. But for what? It is about that that the Book of Jonah was written. They were a chosen people to give their witness to the other nations, even to their oppressors. Israel has gone down as it were into the belly of the whale, into captivity, swallowed up by the great empire of Assyria. Israel must use the opportunity to preach to the people who have taken them captive, and be the means of bringing them to repentance and to the knowledge of the true God.

All the way through, the prophets became more and more aware that their nation as a whole will fail to rise to this call. So they began to accept the exile, seeing in it the means by which God will sift out His people. And so it was. Before the exile those who held the prophetic faith in the universality of one righteous God were a minority. From time to time they held power, but they were a minority.

After the exile those who came back not only contained a majority of those who held this faith, but were a completely unanimous assembly of confessors to it; the rest did not return and the exile did sift the people. They were passed through it as through a sieve, and only those who were of the pure prophetic faith returned to live as the people of God in His chosen place. And as they returned, that remnant, one prophet at least arose among them, saying that they too will be unable to rise to the height of their calling. And as his picture of the perfect servant of the Lord develops to the way in which at last it should be fulfilled—the single individual on whom the Lord lays the transgressions of us all—so we are ready for the great moment in the New Testament; for while here is His purpose —the purpose of working out the law of God through the hearts and lives of His people—it is thwarted all the way through by the self-will that is in them and is the source of nearly all their evil. How is that to be changed? It cannot be changed by teaching, by eloquent appeals.

It will not be changed by their own suffering, for the capacity to respond to suffering is itself a spiritual grace. There is only one thing that can do it—a disclosure of the love of God itself, the love from which this purpose of building up a great society sprang, in such a form as to touch human hearts and awaken human consciences. So the Divine love lived a human life and died a human death, and from that moment onwards we can see two things.

Along the lines that we glanced at in the beginning, the goal is the kingdom of God, the sovereignty of Love—such love as God had shown upon the Cross. But the focus of history is that disclosure itself, so that history will still be full of meaning even though the wilfulness of men prevents us from going forward under the attraction of that love into a fuller and fuller fellowship between man and God and man with man. It will still be judged by its relationship to the Cross, for purpose, for policy, for choice and for ambition, and find its standard of reference there.

How does it look in the light of that?—with the knowledge that what is there set forth is the eternal God into fellowship with whom it is our destiny, unless we frustrate it, to enter, so that elsewhere if not here the perfect fellowship of love shall be built up, through the power and the redeeming love of God in Christ and the power of the Holy Spirit quickened in the hearts of men in answer to it?

So we get the picture in the Book of the Revelation where the Book of Destiny is taken from the hands of the heavenly King and opened by the Lamb that had been slain and all Heaven joins in the cry: " Worthy art thou to take the Book and to open the seal thereof, for thou wast slain." By His death He interprets those mysterious processes of man's living, because by His death He introduces into it power by which it will have two choices given to it, not only the meaning that comes from reference to the standard of perfection in Christ, but also the meaning of coming into closer and closer fellowship with Him.

There was a dispute at one period in the Church, whether Christ would have become incarnate if man had never sinned. The followers of St. Francis, always taking the rather sunnier view, claimed that the Incarnation was in part the flowering of the human creation and would in any case have occurred as the crown of the Divine purpose in man. The Dominicans on the whole took the view that if man had remained without sin there would have been no need for the coming of Christ into the world. He came for the sole purpose of redemption. There can be no settlement of that controversy. We may incline to one side or the other, but let there be no doubt about the actual fact. Man had embarked upon a selfish course. It was, in fact, for his redemption that Christ did come, and it remains the fact that only in the power that is discoverable in the Cross of Christ can man turn history into the thing that God designed it to be and in which he may find his own satisfaction.

One more question. Are we, then, to think of the goal to which history moves as something within it or beyond it? How far are we to accept what would seem to be the natural answer to the prayer " Thy Kingdom come on earth as it is in heaven "? Or how far are we to be resigned to the thought that in this world it cannot come, that the realization of our hopes is beyond history altogether?

What is the answer to this?

First, we must work towards the reign of love on earth. To that we are called, and it is by doing that that we fit ourselves for entry into the reign of love beyond. Whether or not our hopes are to be fulfilled in this world, at least it is by working towards their fulfilment and praying for it that we become qualified for the perfect fellowship in the life eternal. When we have the growing hope of eternal life in the New Testament, there can be no occasion for dismay. This life, after all, is for such a little time for any of us, or any of those who pass through it.

We must work, we must strive and prepare for the coming of the kingdom in this world; but we must recognize that the first form of its appearance will not be the already perfect achievement of love, but the establishment of justice between what are still fundamentally self-centred wills and groups of wills rather than the relationship of pure love. If we can get that far, we shall at least have gone a very long way from where we stand at this moment.

But secondly, in any case, the final consummation cannot be here;

for it must be a fellowship of the servants of God in all generations, and our mortal conditions here make that impossible.

So we work and pray for the coming of the Kingdom on earth, but we are relatively indifferent in our answer to the question to what extent in fact it may be accomplished here. Our duty is to do our utmost: of that there is no doubt. But the Christian hope is not primarily a hope that human society will become the fulfilment of more than Utopian dreams. It is the hope that through the way in which we live and the society wherein we find ourselves, we fit ourselves for fellowship in the great communion of saints, the fellowship of all the servants of God in all the generations, in perpetual communion with Himself.

So we have our starting-point and direction—God as Creator and His purpose. We have our redemption and inspiration, our per-perpetual point of reference and the new source of our energy in Christ's Passion. We have our ultimate hope in God's Kingdom, to be increasingly established here if men will only repent and open their hearts to His spirit, that He may work in them towards that fellowship of love which will be perfectly established in eternity where the will of God is perfectly done.

(The first William Ainslie Memorial Lecture, delivered at St. Martin's-in-the-Field, on " D " Day, June 6, 1944)

moptogress.com

Printed in the United States
43849LVS00002B/71

9 780718 891176